D1165635

BULLDOGS!

WRITING
Brennan Taylor and Brian Engard

EDITING
Amanda Valentine

ADDITIONAL EDITING
Ryan Macklin

COVER ILLUSTRATION
Jaime Posadas

INTERIOR ILLUSTRATIONS
Jaime Posadas and Kurt Komoda

CARTOGRAPHY
Ralf Schemmann

LAYOUT & GRAPHIC DESIGN
Fred Hicks

INDEXING
Krista White

FATE SRD MATERIAL
Fred Hicks, Rob Donoghue,
and Leonard Balsera

PLAYTESTING
Bill Segulin, Krista White,
Markus Siebler, Rich Flynn,
Christopher Grau, Brendan Conway,
Gil Hova, Michael Thompson,
Alison Boehm, Justin Reeves,
Ryan Leary, Jessie Thomas,
Eryn Kiten Heater,
Chino Cougar Devine,
Sean "The Great Seamus" Breitenbach,
Nick Annanziata, Declan Thurmond,
Brian Engard

Open Game License Version 1.0a

The following license text is the property of Wizards of the Coast, Inc. and is Copyright 2000 Wizards of the Coast, Inc ("Wizards"). All Rights Reserved.

1. Definitions: (a)"Contributors" means the copyright and/or trademark owners who have contributed Open Game Content; (b)"Derivative Material" means copyrighted material including derivative works and translations (including into other computer languages), potation, modification, correction, addition, extension, upgrade, improvement, compilation, abridgment or other form in which an existing work may be recast, transformed or adapted; (c) "Distribute" means to reproduce, license, rent, lease, sell, broadcast, publicly display, transmit or otherwise distribute; (d)"Open Game Content" means the game mechanic and includes the methods, procedures, processes and routines to the extent such content does not embody the Product Identity and is an enhancement over the prior art and any additional content clearly identified as Open Game Content by the Contributor, and means any work covered by this License, including translations and derivative works under copyright law, but specifically excludes Product Identity. (e) "Product Identity" means product and product line names, logos and identifying marks including trade dress; artifacts; creatures characters; stories, storylines, plots, thematic elements, dialogue, incidents, language, artwork, symbols, designs, depictions, likenesses, formats, poses, concepts, themes and graphic, photographic and other visual or audio representations; names and descriptions of characters, spells, enchantments, personalities, teams, personas, likenesses and special abilities; places, locations, environments, creatures, equipment, magical or supernatural abilities or effects, logos, symbols, or graphic designs; and any other trademark or registered trademark clearly identified as Product identity by the owner of the Product Identity, and which specifically excludes the Open Game Content; (f) "Trademark" means the logos, names, mark, sign, motto, designs that are used by a Contributor to identify itself or its products or the associated products contributed to the Open Game License by the Contributor (g) "Use", "Used" or "Using" means to use, Distribute, copy, edit, format, modify, translate and otherwise create Derivative Material of Open Game Content. (h) "You" or "Your" means the licensee in terms of this agreement.

2. The License: This License applies to any Open Game Content that contains a notice indicating that the Open Game Content may only be Used under and in terms of this License. You must affix such a notice to any Open Game Content that you Use. No terms may be added to or subtracted from this License except as described by the License itself. No other terms or conditions may be applied to any Open Game Content distributed using this License.

3. Offer and Acceptance: By Using the Open Game Content You indicate Your acceptance of the terms of this License.

4. Grant and Consideration: In consideration for agreeing to use this License, the Contributors grant You a perpetual, worldwide, royalty-free, non-exclusive license with the exact terms of this License to Use, the Open Game Content.

5. Representation of Authority to Contribute: If You are contributing original material as Open Game Content, You represent that Your Contributions are Your original creation and/or You have sufficient rights to grant the rights conveyed by this License.

6. Notice of License Copyright: You must update the COPYRIGHT NOTICE portion of this License to include the exact text of the COPYRIGHT NOTICE of any Open Game Content You are copying, modifying or distributing, and You must add the title, the copyright date, and the copyright holder's name to the COPYRIGHT NOTICE of any original Open Game Content you Distribute.

7. Use of Product Identity: You agree not to Use any Product Identity, including as an indication as to compatibility, except as expressly licensed in another, independent Agreement with the owner of each element of that Product Identity. You agree not to indicate compatibility or co-adaptability with any Trademark or Registered Trademark in conjunction with a work containing Open Game Content except as expressly licensed in another, independent Agreement with the owner of such Trademark or Registered Trademark. The use of

any Product Identity in Open Game Content does not constitute a challenge to the ownership of that Product Identity. The owner of any Product Identity used in Open Game Content shall retain all rights, title and interest in and to that Product Identity.

8. Identification: If you distribute Open Game Content You must clearly indicate which portions of the work that you are distributing are Open Game Content.

9. Updating the License: Wizards or its designated Agents may publish updated versions of this License. You may use any authorized version of this License to copy, modify and distribute any Open Game Content originally distributed under any version of this License.

10 Copy of this License: You MUST include a copy of this License with every copy of the Open Game Content You Distribute.

11. Use of Contributor Credits: You may not market or advertise the Open Game Content using the name of any Contributor unless You have written permission from the Contributor to do so.

12 Inability to Comply: If it is impossible for You to comply with any of the terms of this License with respect to some or all of the Open Game Content due to statute, judicial order, or governmental regulation then You may not Use any Open Game Material so affected.

13 Termination: This License will terminate automatically if You fail to comply with all terms herein and fail to cure such breach within 30 days of becoming aware of the breach. All sublicenses shall survive the termination of this License.

14 Reformation: If any provision of this License is held to be unenforceable, such provision shall be reformed only to the extent necessary to make it enforceable.

15 COPYRIGHT NOTICE

Open Game License v 1.0 Copyright 2000, Wizards of the Coast, Inc.

Fudge 10th Anniversary Edition Copyright 2005, Grey Ghost Press, Inc.; Authors Steffan O'Sullivan and Ann Dupuis, with additional material by Jonathan Benn, Peter Bonney, Deird'Re Brooks, Reimer Behrends, Don Bisdorf, Carl Cravens, Shawn Garbett, Steven Hammond, Ed Heil, Bernard Hsiung, J.M. "Thijs" Krijger, Sedge Lewis, Shawn Lockard, Gordon McCormick, Kent Matthewson, Peter Mikelsons, Robb Neumann, Anthony Roberson, Andy Skinner, William Stoddard, Stephan Szabo, John Ughrin, Alex Weldon, Duke York, Dmitri Zagidulin

Fate (Fantastic Adventures in Tabletop Entertainment) Copyright 2003 by Evil Hat Productions, LLC. Authors Robert Donoghue and Fred Hicks.

Spirit of the Century Copyright 2006 by Evil Hat Productions, LLC. Authors Robert Donoghue, Fred Hicks, and Leonard Balsera

Bulldogs! Copyright © 2011 Brennan Taylor/Galileo Games. All rights reserved. Bulldogs! created by Eric Coble, Chuck Cooley, Robert Cooley, Nathan Crowder, and C. Austin Hogan.

Cover illustration © 2011 Jaime Posadas.

Interior illustrations © 2010, 2011 Jaime Posadas and Kurt Komoda.

Cartography © 2011 Ralf Schemmann

In accordance with the Open Game License Section 8 "Identification" the following designate Open Game Content and Product Identity:

OPEN GAME CONTENT

The contents of this document are declared Open Game Content except for the portions specifically declared as Product Identity. Non-rules related elements of the setting, including capitalized names, organization names, characters, historical events, organizations, and the ten core species, are Open Game Content.

PRODUCT IDENTITY

All artwork, logos, symbols, designs, depictions, illustrations, maps and cartography, likenesses, and other graphics, unless specifically identified as Open Game Content, as well as rules-related elements of the proprietary setting, such as aspects and species abilities associated with setting elements, are to be considered Product Identity and subject to copyright.

Printed in the United States of America.
ISBN 1-887920-05-6
http://galileogames.com/bulldogs-fate

Table of Contents

Introduction

Who could be desperate enough to sign his life away for five long years? Desperate enough to take a job hauling volatile and hazardous cargo to the most dangerous places in the galaxy? Planets where the very air is a corrosive acid. Planets where the locals might cut your throat just so they can turn you into a nice steak. Planets where petty thugs and warlords are engaged in constant running gun battles and you're just as likely to catch a blaster shot in the skull as get a signed delivery manifest.

You are, that's who. Welcome to Bulldogs!

Bulldogs! is sci-fi that kicks ass! Bulldogs! is a high action space adventure. Bulldogs! is about freebooting ruffians flying from planet to planet causing trouble. Bulldogs! is about far future technology—sci-fi movie technology that probably wouldn't work given what we know about the universe today, but who cares? Bulldogs! is about blasters and faster-than-light travel. Bulldogs! is about hopping from planet to planet and running into a vast variety of weird aliens. Bulldogs! is about being shot at and pissing off powerful locals and fleeing just in time. Bulldogs! is about starship dogfights and ambushes by space pirates in rarely traveled star lanes.

Welcome to Bulldogs! You'll be flying in a starship and kicking ass in no time.

Bulldogs! Overview

Here's what you'll find in this book:

Chapter 1: The Galaxy

What is this place? What can you expect to find in the world of Bulldogs!? Get the low down on the distant galaxy where Bulldogs! is set, the main galacto-political situation, and where you stand.

Chapter 2: FATE Basics

This is a general overview of the system Bulldogs! uses, an open-source game engine called FATE. FATE drives the high action, kick ass style of Bulldogs!

Chapter 3: Alien Species

Sci-fi isn't worth much without loads and loads of crazy aliens. At least that's our take on it. We've got ten core species to populate the galaxy, but we also provide the tools for you to build your own.

Chapter 4: Crew Creation

You've got to have a crew to run a space ship. Here's where we lay out how to make up your gang of motley ruffians. The more dangerous, the better.

Chapter 5: Aspects

Aspects are the most important feature of your character in Bulldogs! That's why they get a whole damn chapter. Find out what they are and how to use them to juice your game to giddy heights.

Chapter 6: Doing Things

You sure as hell aren't going to just sit around. Bulldogs! is about action, and this is how you get it. We describe how your character can get what she wants, and how other people will try to get what they want from you.

Chapter 7: Advancement

You won't be a low-down schmuck forever. This is how your character improves. You may start out as a complete bad ass, but you'll only get badder as time goes on.

Chapter 8: Skills

Did we say aspects were the most important thing on your character sheet? Yeah, we did. Skills may come second, but this is what your character does, and why she's the best at it.

Chapter 9: Stunts

Sometimes you need that extra little boost, that something special to tip you over the edge from simply awesome to completely kick ass. Stunts are how you get there, what makes you stand out from the crowd.

Chapter 10: Gear

Guns. Chain swords. Neutron scramblers. This is where you gear up and get ready to face your foes or go down trying. Don't bring a knife to the gunfight.

Chapter 11: Ships

It's not much of a space adventure if you can't get there. Build your ship and get ready for the space battles.

Chapter 12: Running the Game

So far we've concentrated on players of the crew. Here's where we give the Game Master the tools she needs to put the game together and run it.

> Bulldogs! uses the FATE system. If you've played other FATE role-playing games, such as **Spirit of the Century** or the **Dresden Files RPG**, the system in Bulldogs! will be familiar to you. Fair warning: We've made a few changes to create the unique Bulldogs! feel, so take a close look even if you're a FATE veteran.
>
> If you haven't played a FATE game before, don't worry; you'll be able to learn everything you need to know from this book.

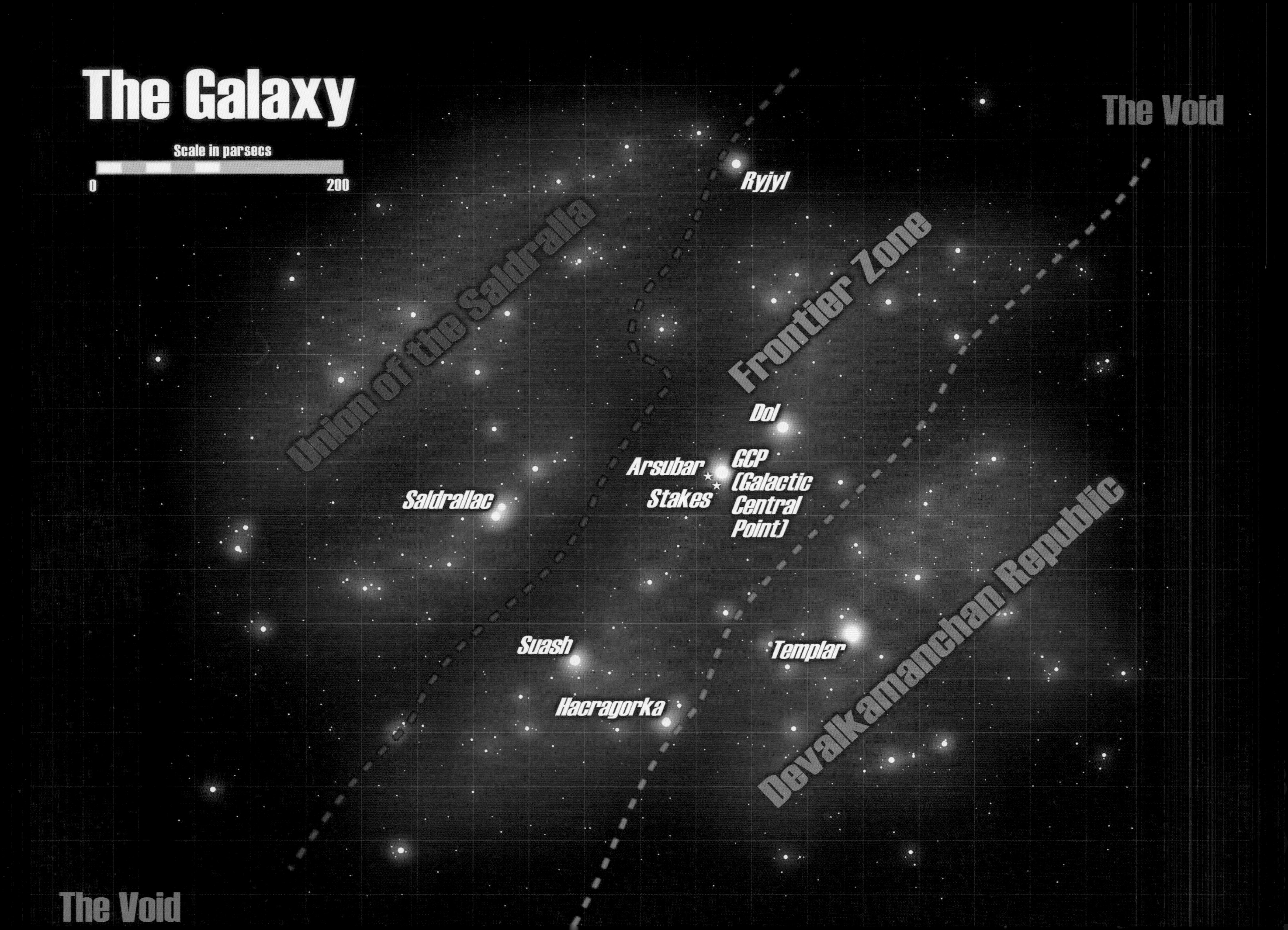

The Galaxy

The Void

The Void

The Void

The Void

Devalkamanchan Republic

Frontier Zone

Union of the Saldralia

Scale in parsecs

0   200

Ryjyl

Dol

Arsubar
Stakes

GCP
(Galactic
Central
Point)

Templar

Saldrallac

Suash

Kacragorka

The Galaxy

Setting Basics

This is the galaxy. A rough, undifferentiated mass of stars. No central hub, just stars scattered somewhat randomly throughout. It's not pretty, but it's easy to travel around and there's no radiation-saturated core where life can't exist. Every system in the galaxy can be reached and explored, although some haven't seen any starfarers for centuries.

Two massive star empires glower at one another from opposite sides of the galaxy. The Thousand Years War they fought is now centuries past, but no one forgets the power these empires can wield. They cracked the stars with their fleets; entire planets and suns were destroyed in their clash. Now, they have a long-standing but uneasy truce, kept from confronting each other by the independent Frontier Zone. Their tentacles still reach out, manipulating the rulers of these independent planets, fighting proxy wars against one another, probing for weakness.

The Frontier Zone is your home. A patchwork of governments and jurisdictions, making it a hotbed for trouble—and adventure! You're just the type to take advantage of the opportunities and dangers of the wild frontier.

A Little Bit of History

Centuries ago, the galaxy was split between two massive star empires. On one side, the Theocracy of Deval and Kamanch, home of the Templari. The Templari held a strong belief in their own superiority, which led to their domination of half of the galaxy; their massive fleets and deadly armies, fueled by religious fervor, subjugated thousands of worlds and enslaved countless other species.

On the other side was the Union of the Saldralla, a pragmatic and ruthless alliance of worlds. The freedom enjoyed by the citizens of the democratic Union was extended to all neighboring worlds whether they liked it or not, by force or political manipulation. In time, they too ruled half the galaxy.

When these two empires clashed, they sparked the Thousand Years War. The war cost trillions of lives, as both empires deployed horrendous weapons that could destroy entire planets and even solar systems. Eventually, the empires ran out of resources and will; it was clear that neither could emerge victorious without suffering a fatal blow from its enemy.

At that point, a historic conclave took place. The empires signed the Treaty of Arsubar, laying out a truce. Each empire retreated to smaller boundaries and created the Frontier Zone, a zone of neutral planets between the two empires, intended to keep the peace.

Now, centuries later, this is where the galaxy sits. Two great star empires, each controlling a bit more than a third of the stars in the galaxy, are separated by a broad band of unaligned planets in the Frontier Zone. Cold war. The empires aren't satisfied, but neither is willing to make the first move. Agents and proxy governments fight among the frontier planets, while the Zone itself is a patchwork of jurisdictions that's led to a prosperous yet wild area that's home to opportunistic traders, freebooters, and pirates. Your home.

The Frontier Zone

This broad band of unaligned worlds cuts a swath through the galaxy's center. The Zone is full of autonomous planets, independent solar systems, and small interstellar governments, alliances, and mini-empires. Going even a short distance is likely to get you into an entirely new jurisdiction. The pirates, smugglers, and other scofflaws who live in the Frontier consider this one of the Zone's better features.

The Alliance of Federated Frontier States is the body nominally in charge of this mess, but in practice it has no authority. Lacking an executive branch or armed forces, there isn't a lot it can do. Every government in the Zone has an equal voice in the AFFS Assembly. This means you're at the mercy of whatever local cabal or warlord runs the system, planet, or space station you happen to be on right now.

It's hard to find people to trust in the Frontier, so spacefarers and those who travel through the Zone a lot rely on reputation and an informal network of contacts. Spacers are a breed apart, and criminal and trade alliance networks are the primary method to find people you can work with on a new planet. Bounty hunters also do good business in the Zone, since governments often extend bounties on crooks who skip out of the system after committing some crime.

Aspects

PATCHWORK OF JURISDICTIONS

Invoke: evading pursuit, "We just left Korrell Consortium space."

Compel: issues with proper legal authorization, "Well, that writ was good two systems over. It's nothing but words on the screen over here."

"ON THIS PLANET, I AM THE LAW."

Invoke: you're in tight with the locals, "Well, my buddy's the administrator of this station, so you might want to rethink that."

Compel: local hopped-up bosses can mess with you, "I don't give a damn who you work for. Write an appeal to the AFFS if you want."

YOUR REP IS ALL YOU'VE GOT OUT HERE

Invoke: your rep is good (or scary), "I heard you were a fair dealer. Let's talk."

Compel: you've left a trail of infamy, "Aren't you the guy who shot up the bar on Galvatorix V? My brother lost an eye in that gunfight."

> You'll see a list of aspects attached to each of the regions and organizations in this section. If you're new to FATE and don't know what aspects are, don't worry! They're explained later (page 53, **Aspects** chapter).
>
> You only need to know two things right now. If you **invoke** an aspect, it helps you. An aspect is **compelled** when it causes complications.

The Galactic Central Point System

The most famous of all the systems in the Frontier Zone, Galactic Central Point got its name because it's close to the geographic center of the galaxy. GCP is home to several important planets and satellites and it serves as the main galactic trade hub. GCP makes a great headquarters if you're working in the Frontier; even if it isn't your main base of operations, you're bound to come through here at some point.

Thanks to one of the quirks of the Treaty of Arsubar, GCP is also headquarters for some of the most powerful companies in the galaxy, the Pangalactic Corporations (PgCs). They can operate legally in both empires and the Frontier, and the PgCs are among the most powerful entities in the galaxy. It doesn't pay to cross one of these massive corporations. Your employer, TransGalaxy, is based on the planet Arsubar in GCP and is one of these PgCs.

Aspects

EVERYTHING COMES THROUGH GCP

Invoke: you're looking for something rare, "A third-generation KC targeting matrix! I didn't think you could find these anywhere."

Compel: there are things you *don't* want to see, "Oh, crap. I was hoping no one would ever see that recording. I guess Iggy's going to be looking for me now."

CENTER OF THE UNIVERSE

Invoke: everyone knows this place, "I'll see you in GCP in two weeks."

Compel: GCP natives think everyone else is a provincial, "What hick planet did you say you came from?"

BUSIEST SYSTEM IN THE GALAXY

Invoke: there are lots of opportunities, "I gotta get these to Stakes by mid-week. No questions asked."

Compel: it's easy to get lost in the shuffle, "You're too late. Another crew picked up the job an hour ago."

The Empires

The two major galactic empires rule every star system outside the Frontier Zone. Although you live in the Zone, your travels will likely take you into both empires eventually.

The Devalkamanchan Republic

The Devalkamanchan Republic is the new name for the old Theocracy of Deval and Kamanch. A popular revolt among the Templari overthrew an older dictatorship just before the Treaty of Arsubar was signed and now all Templari elect the Imperial Parliament. These voting rights don't extend to non-Templari. The Templari rule over all of the other alien species within the Republic, and these other species are no better than slaves.

The Templari are quite religious and militaristic, and they have a great fondness for regulation and order. Their elected government is quite conservative on most religious and military issues. The ruling species firmly believes in their own superiority, which poses problems for less deferential travelers from outside the Empire. And heaven forbid you leave your documentation on board ship. They'll throw you in jail in no time.

Aspects

"Papers, please."
Invoke: you've got a legalistic mind and possibly a hand for forgery, "I've got signed and notarized authorization, here, here, and here. You've got to let me in."
Compel: everything isn't in order, "This stamp is a week out of date. Come with me, please."

Never Mouth Off to a Templar
Invoke: you want to goad a Templar into an extreme reaction, "From your looks, I thought your father was a Ken Reeg."
Compel: you are injudicious and accidentally insult one, "You dare? Die, sub-creature!"

Iron Fist of the Empire
Invoke: you're threatened by lawless elements, "Pirates? Don't you realize we're in Devalkamanchan space?"
Compel: you're engaging in illegal or subversive activities, "This is Captain Jak'l of the 6th Nova Legion. Surrender at once."

The Union of the Saldralla

Also called the Saldrallan Empire, the Union stands because it stands as one. All residents in good standing within the Union can vote, and species of every sort sit on the Great Assembly of the Union. The Assembly appoints all the other government officials including the emperor, called the Grand Saldralla. The Grand Saldralla isn't even necessarily a member of the Saldrallan species.

Although all this sounds great, the Union isn't only pragmatic, it's also ruthless. The governing philosophy of the Union is to give a pleasant and peaceful life to its citizens. To make sure its citizens have this pleasant and peaceful life, the government always does whatever it takes to ensure that threats, both external and internal, are quickly and permanently suppressed. Outside threats are destroyed or co-opted into the Union, and internal threats tend to just disappear without any fanfare.

Aspects

Peace at any Cost
Invoke: it's hard for people to start stuff with you in the Union, "You'd better put that away or the authorities are going to have questions."
Compel: they bring the hammer down when you start something, "It may be just a bar brawl to you, but serious injuries resulted. You'll see the judge in the morning."

The Union Stands as One
Invoke: communication and organization are top-notch, "I got your message and decided to meet you halfway."
Compel: higher authorities tend to agree with lower ones, "You can appeal, but I doubt it'll get you anywhere."

Troublemakers Disappear
Invoke: maybe you can get rid of enemies by tipping off the authorities, "Yeah, she told me she had plans to make the government take notice."
Compel: your enemies can turn the tables on you, "I swear! I've never seen those flyers before! I've been framed!"

Some Other Places of Note

Here are some of the interesting locations within the galaxy. These are all in the GCP system; you'll pass through here a lot since you're employed by TransGalaxy, headquartered on Arsubar.

Arsubar

This is the most populous and famous planet in the GCP system. The home planet of the Arsubarans, this world teems with a vast population of nearly every species in the galaxy. Massive cities incrust the surface, and the world imports tons of food and supplies every day just to keep everyone alive. The busy spaceports of Arsubar bring a constant flow of goods and foodstuffs to the planet.

Aspects

TEEMING WITH PEOPLE

Invoke: if you need to find a professional of any stripe, you likely won't have any trouble, "An archaeologist specializing in third century Dolom architecture? Try Professor Grioç at the Arsubaran Polytechnic Institute."

Compel: finding a specific person can be tough, "Gorgor was here a few days ago, but I don't know where he's staying now."

EVERYONE COMES TO ARSUBAR

Invoke: you may see a friendly face, "Doran! I didn't know you were working corporate security now."

Compel: sometimes people come to Arsubar you don't want to see, "Mr. Slightly, fancy meeting you here. Look, I'll have the money soon. That's why I came here, to get a job!"

CONSTANT TRAFFIC

Invoke: it's easy to melt away in the shuffle, "Where'd she go? I can't see her in this crowd."

Compel: chasing after other people is difficult, "Damn it! I got cut off and lost him."

Apollonia

This famed pleasure satellite orbits the planet Arsubar. It's extremely expensive and extremely high class, but it's rumored you can indulge in any vice you like within its quiet and luxuriously decorated halls. Scum is turned away; but if you have enough cash and can clean yourself up, you might be allowed to visit.

Aspects

"LET US MAKE YOU HAPPY."

Invoke: you can get almost anything you want here, "Let us serve you, ma'am. Tell us what you want."

Compel: pleasures of this quality are hard to leave behind, "Good lord! I've been here for two weeks?"

ANYTHING YOU LIKE, FOR A PRICE

Invoke: rare items? No problem, "A bottle of '28 Grrawlr Winery Ryjyllian ice wine? I didn't think there were any of these left."

Compel: the price, "I owe how much?"

ONLY THE BEST

Invoke: high quality service, "I took the liberty of preparing an escape route for you, ma'am. Right this way."

Compel: you aren't the best, "I'm sorry, sir, we simply can't allow you out of the docking area without a change in wardrobe."

G'n'va

This heavily populated planetoid, built up with enclosed habitations, is the largest of Arsubar's moons. Known as the banking moon, G'n'va is home to the Galactic Stock Exchange, or G-SEx, as well as the G'n'va Merchants' Bank, the largest financial institution in the galaxy. Millions of traders and bankers make their homes on the moon and conduct their business at all hours. This place is high class and high income. Rough and tumble outsiders need to keep it in check or they'll find themselves quietly whisked away.

Aspects

FINANCIAL CENTER OF THE GALAXY

Invoke: when you need a lot of cash, "I can finance this little expedition. For a substantial share of the profits."

Compel: some of the sharpest traders in the galaxy are here, "Didn't you read section 12, paragraph 5, sub-clause 6? I believe I *do* have the right."

MONEY NEVER SLEEPS

Invoke: if you need something, the place runs 24-7, "We can certainly accommodate your deposit, ma'am."

Compel: sometimes you have to sleep, "What? It was all moved overnight? Who gave the authorization?"

RICH BY NOON, POOR BY SUNDOWN

Invoke: it's great if it's the noon part, "344% return? This is unbelievable!"

Compel: sundown always comes, "What do you mean out of business? I was just talking to them an hour ago."

Infocity

A massive computer and space station the size of a small moon, Infocity orbits the GCP sun like a planet, just inside the orbit of Arsubar. Outsiders are restricted to a small visitors section and the computers themselves are tended by a monk-like order of Acolytes. The satellite is devoted to the gathering and storage of information. If you need knowledge, this is the place to come. Most computers throughout GCP and even beyond connect to Infocity for archives and data lookups.

Aspects

Infocity Knows All

Invoke: you need to know something, "What's the last survey result for that system?"

Compel: you don't want it to know something about you, "My juvenile arrest record? How did they get that?"

Outsiders Unwelcome

Invoke: you want to keep someone out of Infocity, "They may be Acolytes, but I hear they're expert fighters."

Compel: you want in yourself, "I'm sorry, sir. You may not cross the yellow line."

Vast Stores of Information

Invoke: they really store everything they can, "I don't believe they have financial records for corporate profits from 500 years ago."

Compel: sifting through the truly vast stores of information, "Oh, my God. There are thousands of terabytes of data here. This is gonna take a while."

Job Tower

This satellite orbiting Arsubar is the best place to go when looking to hire someone or when looking for work. The spindle-shaped satellite has a central open area where people can congregate, with smaller rentable rooms and offices above and below for more private meetings. It also includes cheap accommodations for job-seekers. It's a last resort for employment for many, and probably where you found your TransGalaxy job.

Aspects

Find a Job at Job Tower

Invoke: there are loads of jobs here, "I've been looking for an hour and I already have four offers."

Compel: some employers are a bit shady, "Yeah, sign here. You're gonna love it!"

Concentrated Desperation

Invoke: you need something from someone, cheap, "I need some backup. You and you. Fifty credits for an hour's work."

Compel: desperate people are unpredictable, "You tried to fulfill a hit on me for 100 lousy credits? I'm worth more than that!"

Careful: Planetsiders Get Rolled

Invoke: you're a veteran spacer, you know how to avoid these guys, "This section of the station's trouble. Let's go up a level."

Compel: you're naïve, or traveling with someone who is, "Well, well, what have we here? Come straight up from the farm, dirtfoot?"

Stakes

The next planet out from Arsubar in the GCP system, this whole world is dedicated to gambling and entertainment. Basically a low-rent alternative to Apollonia, the place is pretty much run by several wealthy Ken Reeg families. Many diversions can be found here, but don't cross one of the ruling families. People who do tend to disappear.

Aspects

Where Dreams Go to Die

Invoke: you're looking for an entertainer and don't mind if he's washed up, "Hey, that guy used to be Glen Glitter! Get him for the show."

Compel: it's your dreams dying, "I couldn't get anywhere on Arsubar. The only place I can get stage time is at the Obelisk Casino and Revue."

Put Up or Shut Up

Invoke: when you're sick of beating around the bush, "Cut to the chase, Trixie. I'm in a rush."

Compel: you don't have anything to put up, "I believe I'm through with you, Mr. Trevalian. You don't have what I need."

Don't Cross the Families

Invoke: someone else steps on their toes, "Big mistake, Moxie. That was Mr. Quickly's money."

Compel: you cross them, "Hello, Ms. Donovan. I'm afraid you've spent your last hour on Stakes. Pour the concrete, Gog."

Squishy's Scrap Yard

Probably the most famous junkyard in the galaxy, Squishy's sits on the edge of deep space on a frigid hunk of rock orbiting well beyond the farthest planet of GCP. Squishy has a massive collection of junked ships and second-hand parts, paired with a mean and unforgiving negotiating style.

Aspects

Don't Mess with Squishy

Invoke: someone else is messing with Squishy, "I don't think you ought to do that. Squishy won't like it."

Compel: you're messing with Squishy, "You think I'm running a charity? The price just doubled."

Low Prices, Huge Selection!

Invoke: you need a part, and fast, "I found the power coupling!"

Compel: finding the particular part you need, "There must be over half a million ships here. How do we find our model?"

Junk Is Junk

Invoke: you have some scrap you want to unload, "Want to sell? Old Squishy's got you covered."

Compel: you bought some junk and it turns out to be crap, "This thing's a mess! It's completely worn through here."

Organizations and Corporations

Here are a few organizations that are smaller than empires and don't occupy whole zones of space but are still of note.

The Barracado Pirates

There are many pirate gangs in the galaxy, but none more feared than the infamous Barracado Pirates. They appear suddenly and strike ruthlessly, leaving wrecked ships and no survivors. Their distinctive triangular tattoos—over both eyes and the mouth—strike fear into the hearts of even the most veteran spacers. Their base is somewhere among the shattered stars and debris of the Barracado Sector in the Frontier Zone, but no government or bounty hunter has ever discovered its location.

Aspects

Most Feared Pirates in the Galaxy

Invoke: you're using them as a diversion, "See that? Those are Barracado ships. You'd best leave."

Compel: they're after you, "Barracado ships at two o'clock! They're coming in!"

Strike in Force and by Surprise
Invoke: you can tell it's not an attack, "There's only one Barracado ship. They always travel in force; it must be in distress."

Compel: surprise! "Where the hell did they come from? And so many?"

Barracado Tattoos
Invoke: it's hard to hide the fact they're Barracado, "See those tattoos? That guy's wanted, guaranteed."

Compel: you don't have any, therefore you're prey, "Kill everyone who isn't Barracado."

The Fallon Syndicate

Boss Fallon runs a powerful criminal gang based in Job Tower. He has the Tower Administrator in his pocket, and Fallon ensures that things run smoothly on the station, so he's tolerated by the Arsubaran government. He gets a cut of every transaction on the Tower, and people who cross him end up floating home.

Aspects

The Real Boss of Job Tower
Invoke: you need something done for real, you know where to go, "Administration office? No, let's go talk to the real boss."

Compel: he asks a steep price, "I can help you, Ms. Marx, but it will cost."

Fallon Always Gets a Taste
Invoke: so long as Fallon's getting paid, he's on your side, "Stealing my cargo is stealing from Mr. Fallon. Think again."

Compel: you'd like to get the whole payout, "Big mistake. Mr. Fallon always gets a taste. You can explain it to him personally."

An Offer You Can't Refuse
Invoke: Fallon takes care of a problem for you, "Don't worry about the warrant. I've got some friends."

Compel: you can't refuse, "I have helped you, now you must help me."

TransGalaxy PgC

Your boss. One of the largest and most powerful entities in the galaxy. Apart from the empires, Pangalactic Corporations are the biggest and wealthiest institutions anywhere. TransGalaxy isn't just shipping; they have fingers in all sorts of businesses. They also own you for five years. If you cross them, they will utterly destroy you in the coldest, most efficient way possible. Nothing personal. It's just business.

Aspects

"I'm afraid that's policy."
Invoke: you don't want to do something, "I'm sorry, captain. That order violates TransGalaxy ship maintenance directive 1101.62a."

Compel: you want to do something, "I'm afraid shore leave longer than 48 hours is against company protocol."

One of the Pangalactics
Invoke: you've got the authority of a PgC, "I work for TransGalaxy. You wouldn't want to interfere in their business, would you?"

Compel: PgCs aren't noted for mercy, "Violation of terms of service. We're remanding you to galactic authorities for punishment."

Fight for Market Share
Invoke: TransGalaxy really likes it when you make them some money, "Your efficiency increased profits on the last run by 20%. Here's a bonus."

Compel: other companies are competing with TransGalaxy, "Damn it! A crew from Drumå sniped our job!"

Other Snags

As you've seen, aspects can be attached to groups or locations. Aspects can come from other sources as well. The specific environment you're in offers lots of complications, but it can help you as well. Here are a couple of other suggestions for factors that can add aspects to the situation.

Border Crossings

When a delivery is made across an imperial border or from one Frontier Zone world to another, there will generally be a customs check at the destination planet. Most of the time these are routine; but let's face it, you're likely to be carrying illegal goods or contraband. Trouble can ensue. Corrupt local officials also love to "find" something illegal in your hold and demand a bribe.

Aspects

A Little on the Side
Invoke: you can make some scratch in the course of your regular duties, "I've got an angle on something they need at Kronos IX. Not strictly legal."
Compel: a customs official looks too hard, "This hold looks a bit small. What's behind this wall?"

Taste of the Action
Invoke: ease your way through customs, "I'm sure you're a busy man. Here's a little something for your trouble."
Compel: new "contraband" appears unexpectedly, "What's this? Illegal substances? I'm shocked, I tell you!"

Weapons Law

You're a rough-and-tumble spacefarer, usually armed to the teeth. Traveling around as you do, you can run afoul of varying weapons laws. Traveling between jurisdictions brings changing regulations. Some planets allow you to carry just about anything, others limit you to sidearms only, and still others allow no weapons at all. The penalties for breaking weapons laws range from confiscation of illegal weapons all the way up to significant prison time. It pays to double-check local ordinances before going anywhere.

Aspects

License and Registration
Invoke: you have the proper documentation, "I have a permit to carry this weapon, ma'am."
Compel: your weapon happens to be banned, "What's that? Blast weapons are outlawed on this station."

FATE Basics

Gear Up!

You'll need a few supplies along with these rules to play **Bulldogs!** Here's a list of what you're gonna need in your hot little fist, as well as some things that are handy to have.

Stuff You Must Have to Play

- Four Fudge dice for each player and the GM. If you don't have Fudge dice, see Grey Ghost Games (*www.fudgerpg.com*), Indie Press Revolution (*www.indiepressrevolution.com*), or your local RPG dice supplier for a pack.

- A character sheet for each player, or at least blank paper to record characters. Character sheets can be downloaded for free at:

  www.galileogames.com/bulldogs-fate/

- Pencils to write with. You can use pens in a pinch, but sometimes you'll need to erase marks during play.

- Two to six comrades in arms in addition to the GM. You can't play this game by yourself!

Stuff That Makes the Game More Fun

- A set of poker chips or glass beads or something to use as fate points.

- Index cards to write aspects on, to pass notes with, and to make notes on things that come up in play.

- Food for everyone. At least some snacks, if not something more substantial. Also, plenty of drinks. Blasting enemies is thirsty work!

Those Fudge Dice

All right, you've got those Fudge dice we mentioned earlier. Why do you need them to play? Well, in **Bulldogs!** you're extremely likely to be in a situation such as this: Pirates are boarding your ship. You're laying down a withering barrage of blaster fire in the hopes of making them dive under cover, or, even better, end up with a smoking hole through the chest. You'd be happy saying that this happens, but the GM, taking the part of the space pirates in this scenario, prefers it if they overwhelm your position and stick a knife in you. How can we resolve these contradictory desires? That's when you roll dice: Any time you want something and any other character or situation—a black hole, for example—seems to indicate you can't have it.

Fudge Dice: What Are They?

Fudge dice are six-sided dice with different markings than regular dice. Instead of numbers or dots, they have two sides marked with a ⊞, two sides marked with a ⊟, and two sides that are blank ▪. Simple.

When reading the dice, a ⊞ equals +1, a ⊟ equals −1, and a ▪ equals 0. The total of the dice is then added to an appropriate skill to get a result (we talk more about skills later, page 65, *Doing Things* chapter). You can call this result the **effort** made, but sometimes, it's just "the result."

All right, wise guy, you say. I don't have any of these fancy dice. You can still play! Just find yourself some normal six-sided dice, the kind with numbers or pips, and do this: Roll four of them. Any die showing a 1 or 2 gets counted as a ⊟, any die showing a 3 or 4 is a ▪, and any die showing a 5 or 6 is a ⊞.

The Ladder

+8	Legendary
+7	Epic
+6	Fantastic
+5	Superb
+4	Great
+3	Good
+2	Fair
+1	Average
0	Mediocre
-1	Poor
-2	Terrible
-3	Awful
-4	Abysmal

Almost everything in **Bulldogs!** is rated according to the **ladder**.

These adjectives are used to describe important things in the game, such as character skills—someone might be a Good Pilot or Poor at Academics. On this scale, Average represents the level of capability of someone who does something regularly and possibly professionally, but not exceptionally.

While most people in the galaxy are Average at the things they do for a living, you aren't an average person. You live on the edge and push hard at the boundaries of what "normal" people are capable of. You'll most likely be Great or better at whatever your main skill is.

The adjectives and numbers are interchangeable, so if you're more comfortable with numbers, you can say Pilot +3 or Academics –1. We'll use both, as in a Good (+3) Pilot or Poor (–1) Academics.

Beyond the Ladder

It's possible to get results that go past the end of the ladder. You really can't roll below Abysmal (–4), but it's quite possible to get results past Legendary (+8)—sometimes way past it. There are bonuses you can add in—we'll cover these in more detail later in the book. If you happen to have fortune smile so strongly upon you, rejoice! You can just use the number (+9, +10, or whatever). If you feel sad that there's no adjective, make one up. Hell, if you roll that high, you deserve the privilege of assigning an official adjective to the appropriate number!

Rolling the Dice

Whenever a roll is called for, you roll four Fudge dice. You *always* roll four Fudge dice. This gives you a result between –4 and +4. This generally isn't the final result, though. You almost always get to add in some other numbers to modify this roll.

Difficulty

When you make a roll and get a result, you're trying to meet or exceed a target value. The target value is the **difficulty** for the roll. As you might suspect, the difficulty indicates how hard it is to do something. You measure difficulties on the same ladder as everything else. For instance, a gang of thugs is chasing you, meaning to beat you to a pulp with pipes and clubs. You find an old gravsled, but its battery is dead. It might be a Mediocre (+0) difficulty to jumpstart the gravsled, but once you get it going and smash it into the side of a building, repairing the grav drive to get it going again will require a Good (+3) difficulty. You'll find guidelines for setting difficulties in the GM's section (page 153, ***Running the Game*** chapter).

The difference between the difficulty and the result of the roll (the effort) is the magnitude of the **effect**, which is measured in **shifts**. Shifts are used, primarily by the GM, to rule on how effective your efforts are; you can also use them for fancy tricks that aren't directly related to plain old success or failure. We'll talk more about shifts later (page 65, ***Doing Things*** chapter).

Stuff That's on Your Character Sheet

What's all this stuff on the character sheet? It's the most important stuff for you to know. In later chapters we'll cover these in a lot more detail, but here are the essentials.

Aspects

All characters, along with many places and things, have a set of attributes called **aspects**. Aspects can be a bit tricky because they cover a wide range of elements. All your aspects together paint a picture of who your character is, what he's connected to, and what's important to him, in contrast to the "what he can do" of skills. Aspects can be relationships, beliefs, phrases, descriptors, items—pretty much anything that paints a picture of the character. Some possible aspects are shown here.

Sample Aspects

- I've Got an Angle
- Precision Is the Pilot's Friend
- One Woman Wrecking Crew
- Lead by Example
- Everyone Has a Price, Mine Is Just Very Low

These are just a taste, to get you in the groove. We'll talk about aspects more fully in their own chapter (page 53, ***Aspects*** chapter) and in the section describing how to put a character together (page 43, ***Crew Creation*** chapter).

While you're playing, you can use an aspect to give you a bonus when you think it'll help you out in your current situation. This is called **invoking** an aspect and requires spending a fate point (page 54, *Aspects* chapter). It makes you better at whatever it is you're doing, because the aspect in some way applies to the situation in a helpful way (such as PRECISION IS THE PILOT'S FRIEND when you're trying to put your ship down between two tottering spires of rock in a hurricane-force windstorm).

This isn't all an aspect can do. Aspects also allow you to gain more fate points by bringing complications and troubling circumstances into your life. Whenever there's a situation where your aspect could cause you trouble (such as EVERYONE HAS A PRICE, MINE IS JUST VERY LOW when that shady character is bribing you to put a mysterious package on the ship and not tell anyone about it), you can mention it to the GM in the same way you mention an aspect that might help you. The GM can also point out that one of your aspects seems likely to cause you trouble. No matter who calls it, this is called **compelling** an aspect, and it must limit your choices in some way. If the GM initiates or agrees to compel the aspect, you may get one or more fate points, depending on how it plays out.

Skills

Characters have **skills**, like Pilot or Guns, which are rated on the ladder and represent what your character can do. When you roll the dice, you're making a roll based on one of your skills.

Every action that you might undertake is covered by your skills (page 83, *Skills* chapter). When you roll, you add your skill rating to determine the final result. Your skills are all rated between Average (+1) and Superb (+5). You can still try a roll even if you don't have the appropriate skill, but it counts as Mediocre (+0), basically no better than a straight roll of the dice.

Stunts and Species Abilities

Stunts are things you can do which stretch or break the rules—the special tricks you have up your sleeves. Stunts have very specific uses and rules; they're detailed extensively in their own chapter (page 107, *Stunts* chapter).

Alien species have special abilities that act pretty much the same way as stunts—they allow members of that species to stretch or break the rules. Unlike stunts, which anyone can take, only members of the particular alien species have access to that species' special abilities.

Fate Points

Every player begins the first session of the game with a few **fate points**. The exact number varies depending on your choices when building your crew, but you'll never have fewer than one. Fate points give you the ability to take a little bit of control over the game, either by giving your character bonuses when you feel the need, or by taking over a small part of the story. Fate points are best represented by tokens, such as glass beads or poker chips. You may, at any point, spend a fate point to invoke an aspect, make a declaration, or fuel a stunt.

Invoke an Aspect

Aspects (page 53, *Aspects* chapter) are those little phrases that really describe your character and her place in the story. When you have an aspect that's applicable to a situation, you can invoke it to grant a bonus. After you've rolled the dice, you can pick an aspect—one of your own or one on the situation or area—and describe how it'll help you in this situation. If the GM agrees that it's appropriate, you can spend a fate point and do one of the following:

1: Reroll all the dice, using the new result, or
2: Add two to the final die roll (after any rerolls have been done).

You can do this multiple times for a single action as long as you have multiple aspects that apply and fate points to spend. You can't use the same aspect more than once on the same skill use, though you may use the same aspect on several different rolls throughout a scene, at the cost of one fate point per use.

Power a Stunt or Species Ability

Some stunts have particularly potent effects and require that you spend a fate point when you use them. If a stunt requires a fate point to be spent, it'll say so in the description (page 107, *Stunts* chapter).

Make a Declaration

You can simply lay down a fate point and declare something, and if the GM accepts it, it's true. This lets you do small things in a story that would usually be something only the GM could do. You can't use fate points to drastically change the plot or just win a scene. Declaring "Boss Fallon drops dead of a heart attack" right in the middle of your big fight with him is lame and boring, and your GM will rightly kick that idea to the curb. But declarations are very useful for convenient coincidences. Does your character need a flashlight after crash-landing on a strange planet? Spend a fate point and there was one in the ship's emergency kit! Is there something interesting happening and your character isn't there? Spend a fate point to declare you arrive at a dramatically appropriate moment!

Ultimately, your GM has veto power over declarations, but here's a dirty little secret. If you use it to make the game cooler for everyone, the GM will usually grant far more leeway than she will for something boring or, worse, selfish. Also, as a general rule, you'll get a lot more flexibility from the GM if your declaration is in keeping with one or more of your aspects. For example, the GM will usually balk at letting you spend a fate point to have a weapon after you've been searched. However, if you can point to your ALWAYS ARMED aspect, or describe how your DISTRACTING BEAUTY aspect kept the guard's attention on inappropriate areas, the GM is likely to give you more latitude. In a way, this is much like invoking an aspect, but without a die roll.

Refreshing Fate Points

You usually regain fate points between sessions when a **refresh** occurs. If the GM left things at a cliffhanger, she may say that no refresh occurs between sessions. By the same token, if the GM feels that a substantial, dramatically appropriate amount of downtime occurs during play, she may allow a refresh to occur mid-session.

The number of fate points you get at a refresh is called your **refresh rate**. The refresh rate is determined when you build your character (page 45, **Crew Creation** chapter). When a refresh occurs, you bring your number of fate points *up to* your refresh rate. If you went all gangbusters with the compels and you happen to have more fate points than your refresh rate, your total doesn't change—you get to the keep the extras, but you don't add any more, either.

Earning Fate Points

You earn fate points when your aspects create problems for your character. When this occurs, it's said that the aspect **compels** your character. When you end up in a situation where your compelled aspect suggests a problematic course of action, the GM will offer you a choice: You can *spend* a fate point to ignore the aspect, or you can act in accordance with the aspect and *earn* a fate point.

This isn't just the GM's show; you can trigger compels as well either by explicitly indicating that an aspect could complicate things, or by playing to your aspects from the get-go and reminding the GM after the fact that you already acted like you were compelled. The GM isn't obligated to agree that a compel is appropriate, but it's important that you participate here.

Stress

All characters have a **stress track**. Stress is a measure of your ability to shrug off all kinds of punishment—physical, social, or mental—and represents the non-specific difficulties a character might encounter in a conflict. A successful attack on you inflicts a certain amount of stress (page 71, **Doing Things** chapter). In a physical fight, it's bruising, minor cuts and burns, fatigue, and the like. In a social conflict, it's getting flustered or being put off your game. In a mental conflict, stress might mean losing focus or running in circles. Stress can usually be shaken off between scenes, once you have some time to gather yourself.

Resources

Resources represent the cash and credit a character has on hand or can muster to make purchases. All characters begin with one point of Resources. A high Trading or Gambling skill can increase starting Resources (page 94 and page 105, **Skills** chapter). When you make a purchase, Resources can decrease. When you make a big score, Resources may increase. Complete rules on Resources can be found in the **Gear** chapter (page 123).

Alien Species

The galaxy is large and contains a huge variety of alien species. There are ten core species listed below, but these aren't the only ones available as characters and you're encouraged to create your own.

Arsubarans

The human-like Arsubarans' home planet is in the Frontier Zone but, as adventurers and ubiquitous starfarers, they're found everywhere, even deep within the star empires. Arsubarans are adaptable and tough, and they almost seem to like being neck-deep in trouble.

Dolomé

Massive, thick-skinned, and blue, the tripod-legged Dolomé are both physically powerful and mentally acute. A Dolom makes true and loyal friend if you're on her good side, and a terrifying three-armed tsunami of rage if you piss her off.

Hacragorkans

If there's a nose to be punched or an elbow to be thrown, the burly, green, and tattooed Hacragorkans will fight their way to the front. Always ready for a scrap, even when negotiation is called for, the Hacragorkans find a fierce joy in their hand-to-hand fighting abilities.

Ken Reeg

Slick, smooth, and green, the Ken Reeg bring an oily smile and handshake to any meeting. They make voracious traders, slippery salesmen, pitiless lawyers, and ruthless crime bosses. If you've made a deal with a Ken Reeg, prepare to be screwed.

Robots

Where would the galaxy be without the countless anonymous robots performing vast numbers of repetitive and dangerous jobs? Multi-armed maintenance bots, virtually perfect service androids, and tiny spider-like cleaning drones swarm on every inhabited world and space station.

Ryjyllians

Fierce mercenaries from an icy planet, the cat-like Ryjyllians adhere to their clannish code of honor and export their great fighting skills throughout the galaxy. They do not flee combat, and their discipline and professionalism make them the go-to hired army.

Saldrallans

The cold-blooded, snake-like Saldrallans are the founding species of the Union of the Saldralla, and they still strongly influence the imperial culture and government. Their ruthless pragmatism guides the Empire as well as their interpersonal relations.

Templari

Haughty and purple-skinned, the Templari rule the Devalkamanchan Republic, guided by a belief in their own genetic superiority that extends throughout their culture. They would have found themselves destroyed long ago if not for their great skills in military organization and logistics.

Tetsuashans

The slug-like Tetsuashans are unlikely adventurers, but they seem at home in space. Their stoic and inscrutable nature makes the long boredom of interplanetary travel a trivial inconvenience, and they have an affinity for piloting and ship-building.

Urseminites

Whether some genetic engineering project gone horribly awry, or just a cruel twist of nature, the Urseminites are cute and cuddly in appearance and vile and murderous in temperament. They're pests and perennial sources of crime on any planet they call home, so the Urseminites are universally despised.

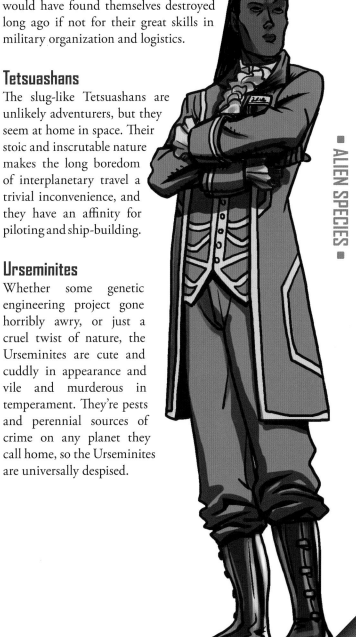

The Building Blocks of an Alien

Species Aspects

Each alien species has a list of six stereotypical aspects. These describe the general reputation and inclinations of the species as a whole and come in three flavors: physiology, history, and psychology. Physiological aspects tell you about the appearance and physical abilities of a species (Never Eat, Never Sleep, Never Stop or Three Powerful Arms). Historical aspects talk about the environment and history of the species (Trust No One or Forged by Struggle). Psychological aspects deal with the typical mental attitude or cultural philosophy of a species (The Stars Call or Code of Honor).

Obviously, individual members of each species vary a great deal from the norm, and that's why individual characters typically have only two of the six aspects that could describe their species (page 46, ***Crew Creation*** chapter).

Species Abilities

Most alien species also have special abilities built into their genetic makeup. You'll find these listed with each of the ten species below. These abilities affect the starting refresh of your character. When you choose a species, you're choosing the package of abilities that comes with the species, so you have to adjust your starting refresh by the amount listed next to the abilities.

All members of a species must have the species-specific abilities listed, unless the ability is marked "Optional" in the description. If there's an optional ability and you choose not to take it, your starting refresh is unaffected by the optional ability's cost.

Arsubarans

Arsubarans are human-like in appearance with a wider variation in hair, eye, and skin color than humans. They describe themselves as adventurous, bold, and clever. Other species describe them as grasping, prolific, and ubiquitous. Arsubarans are, in fact, everywhere. Since the people of Arsubar discovered space travel long ago, they've spread further and faster than any other species. Their omnipresence isn't their only distinguishing trait, however. Arsubarans are also known for their can-do attitude and extreme adaptability. They seem to get along wherever they settle.

Arsubarans have an undue influence on the galaxy considering they've never ruled an empire and, though numerous, they aren't the majority on very many planets. Thanks to their home planet's location in Galactic Central Point, their language is called Galactic and it's spoken throughout the galaxy. In GCP, the Arsubarans do hold the majority, and their distinct influence on the character of the Frontier is greater than their numbers would imply. There are conspiracy theories, especially among the Templari, that the Arsubarans are running a de facto third empire in the Zone, hidden from direct view. The very real chaos of the Frontier seems to belie that idea, however.

On the whole, the other species of the galaxy accept the Arsubarans; really, they have little choice. Although racial tension inevitably arises in many of the places that host Arsubaran colonies, the Arsubarans manage to blend in with the locals for the most part. Arsubarans from the colonies tend to be less domineering and pushy than those from Arsubar itself—at least until they're the majority on any given world.

Arsubaran Names

Arsubaran names are a wide and varied lot, differing greatly depending on clan or planet of origin. They follow a tradition of having a family name passed along the male line to allow genealogical record keeping. Listed are some common Arsubaran names:

Male Names: Aaron, Balthazar, Cantor, Cory, Dag, Devin, Doog, Jonathan, Julius, Karl, Lorin, Ludo, Marco, Mutt, Patrick, Roldin, Sebastian, Skip, William, Zacharias.

Female Names: Amanda, Anna, Belle, Cassandra, Devy, Gabrielle, Heloise, Julia, Kristina, Luca, Marca, Morena, Olga, Sola, Solendra, Tana, Violet, Wanda, Wemy, Wilhelmina.

Family Names: Arsubrian, Bishop, Conner, Elcandur, Farr, Fogel, Golman, Grimm, Hammelin, Kaahn, Kaine, Marcellian, Marx, Pax, Sax, Solar, Solens, Trevalian, Vesper, Wall.

Typical Arsubaran Aspects

NATURAL ADAPTABILITY

Invoke: any time you're trying something new, "I've never done this before, but here goes!"

Compel: your ability causes resentment, "What do you know. The Arsubaran can do it."

WE'RE EVERYWHERE

Invoke: you need a fellow Arsubaran to help out, "There's an Arsubaran outpost near here. Let's head there."

Compel: not everyone's happy that Arsubarans have spread throughout the galaxy, "Another Arsubaran. Haven't we got enough of your kind already?"

CENTER OF THE UNIVERSE

Invoke: you want and deserve attention, "Hey, everyone! Look who's here!"

Compel: you can't stand being ignored, "Hey! I'm still here. Oh. And you still have a gun."

"I'LL DO THAT!"

Invoke: you can step in and do the job better, "Stand aside. I've got this."

Compel: you end up doing things you may not want to, "I'm not sure I knew what I was getting into when I volunteered for the night duty."

THE STARS CALL

Invoke: the starlanes are a comfortable place for you, "Oh, I've been to that planet before!"

Compel: you're not satisfied staying in one place, "Well, I'd love to stay and get things settled here, but the stars call!"

GO ALONG TO GET ALONG

Invoke: not much fazes you, "You guys always eat Selink grubs for lunch? OK, serve me up."

Compel: you don't like to stand out, "Hey, man, I'm just here, doin' my job."

Arsubaran Species Abilities [Total –1]

There's a Familiar Face [–1]

Arsubarans are everywhere. Even on a strange planet or station, an Arsubaran can almost always find another member of her species. When using the Contacting skill, an Arsubaran can make a free declaration that the individual she finds is also an Arsubaran, no matter where in the galaxy she is. Additionally, Arsubarans gain a +1 to social skill rolls when communicating with another Arsubaran (page 84, *Skills* chapter).

Dolomé

In the Frontier Zone, near the GCP, is the planet Dol, populated by a species of large, three-armed, three-legged, blue-skinned creatures. A Dolom is tall—usually about eight to nine feet. Three massive legs in a tripod configuration support a thickly muscled trunk with a strong tentacle-like arm above each leg. A Dolom has three eyes, three nostrils, and one mouth, as well as small ears on either side. The most unique aspect of a Dolom's head is that it can swivel completely around, allowing the Dolom to change directions and orientations extremely quickly, without the need to physically turn around. This quick reaction time contrasts with the Dolom's girth and often unnerves other species the first time they see it.

Despite their strange and imposing appearance, Dolomé are normally gentle and friendly by nature. They're soft-spoken and slow to anger; they tend to treat others as friends and equals unless an individual's actions contradict this stance. Despite their rather long fuse, once a Dolom is roused to anger, he is a creature to be feared. Dolomé possess great physical strength and endurance—when coupled with their deceptively quick reaction time, these attributes can make Dolomé extremely deadly opponents in battle. Dol has rarely been invaded, and those who have tried have always regretted it.

Dolomé are a technically inclined species, possessed of an almost supernatural aptitude for machines and mathematics. In fact, some of the foremost scientists and engineers in the galaxy are Dolomé. The Dolom Academy of Engineering is the famous alma mater of many of the galaxy's best technical workers. Outsiders can attend the Academy, but the course of study is difficult and non-Dolomé are at a distinct disadvantage in the labs if they have fewer than three arms.

Besides strength and technical ability, Dolomé are known for their loyalty to those they consider true friends, and they frequently demonstrate astounding courage when their friends are threatened. One Dolom scientist, when his friends and fellow scientists were trapped within an irradiated laboratory, ripped the door off its hinges and carried the injured and unconscious to safety—thirteen in total—before finally collapsing himself.

Dolom Names

Dolomé use both personal and family names. Examples of their naming conventions can be found below.

Male Names: Aldové, Alvé, Baltus, Barus, Domus, Dorus, Fatus, Galtus, Gomus, Gravus, Hadrové, Hamus, Samus, Secové, Sové, Talus, Tetruvé, Tromus, Truvé, Vové.

Female Names: Adriar, Aliar, Amé, Falé, Famé, Fariar, Galtiar, Halvomé, Hamé, Hamiar, Lalé, Laliar, Maliar, Samiar, Somé, Suldomé, Suliar, Tralé, Tramé, Tromiar.

Family Names: Abrioç, Brioç, Crioç, Curoç, Doroç, Drioç, Duroç, Grioç, Hiloç, Maloç, Moroç, Mrioç, Paloç, Prioç, Salioç, Saloç, Suroç, Trioç, Uloç, Ylioç.

Typical Dolom Aspects

Big and Blue

Invoke: you need to push, smash, or knock through something, "Get out of the way! Here comes Talus!"

Compel: little people seem to design doors and corridors, "Aargh! I can't squeeze through this access hatch!"

Three Powerful Arms

Invoke: an extra hand is always useful, "I've got that. And that. And that."

Compel: maybe they're a bit too powerful, "Let me just get that…damn! I crushed it!"

Technically Inclined

Invoke: you're aces when it comes to fixing things, "A little bonder, a quick application of heat, and there you go!"

Compel: not everyone is interested in the minutiae of your work, "Uh-huh. A triple-whatsis solution. Listen, I see someone I've got to talk to…over there."

Won't Go Down Easy

Invoke: you keep going, and going, "Damn! How much punishment can one guy take?"

Compel: you don't know when to quit, "Come on! We can't take these guys. I said come on!"

Slow to Anger

Invoke: people can't really bait you, "Hmmm. My mother, you say? Doesn't really fit my impression of her."

Compel: sometimes you need to get a little pissed, "I can't believe you're going to let them get away with that."

Fast Friend

Invoke: you stick with your friends, "I've got your back."

Compel: people can get at you through your friends, "I have your little buddy here, so back off!"

Dolom Species Abilities [Total –5]

Thick Skinned [–1]

The high winds common on the surface of Dol gave the Dolomé their sturdy tripod stance as well as the ability to quickly turn their heads away from the wind. It also gave them their thick pebbly skin. They have an automatic Armor: 1 against all hand-to-hand attacks. They don't gain this benefit against ranged attacks—guns are a bit too powerful for their skin to offer much protection.

Third Arm [–1]

Dolomé have long, tentacular arms that can all reach the same side of the body. This, along with their sensitive touch, allows them to perform several tasks at once more easily than members of other species. A Dolom does not suffer a –1 when performing a supplemental action in a round if his third arm can be of use.

Great Strength [–2]

The high gravity of the Dolom home world has made them extremely strong. A Dolom gains a +1 to all Might rolls. Also, although they're a bit slow to get moving, once at a gallop they're very difficult to stop. When running for one exchange to build up speed, the Dolom also gains a +2 to break any physical blocks in his way. This stacks with the Might bonus in the case of inanimate blocks like doors or gates.

Hand-Eye Coordination [–1]

The three eyes of a Dolom combined with her highly sensitive fingers makes her very good at delicate or intricate tasks. When attempting any Engineering roll involving small and delicate manipulation, a Dolom gains a +2 on her roll.

Hacragorkans

The planet Hacragorka is a harsh world with little in the way of natural resources; many dangerous beasts call it home. No wonder its dominant species evolved into such a violent and brutish society. From a young age, Hacragorkans are taught to fight for what they want, whether it's social status, wealth, a mate, or just fun. Say what you want about their social graces—there are few species with more resolve, grit, and pure bull-headedness than the Hacragorkans, and this attitude has gotten them where they are today.

A typical Hacragorkan is tall and thick, usually over six feet and well over three hundred pounds—most of it muscle. Their green skin is rough and bumpy, and their hair is short and bristly. Hacragorkans have a long tradition of tattooing and occasional ritual scarification, and virtually every Hacragorkan is covered in elaborate patterns of swirls and sunbursts. Some of these tattoos and scars signify important events in an individual's life, while others are simply for their aesthetic value—tattoos and scars are, in fact, one of the few aesthetic art forms that exist on Hacragorka.

Hacragorkan society places little value on "frivolous" pursuits such as academic learning, science, and most art (with the notable exceptions of body art and music); instead, they place the greatest value on physical strength and battle prowess. For this reason, ritual combat and blood sports are common on Hacragorka, and gladiatorial fighters are actually one of the planet's chief exports, next to mercenaries and weaponry. Despite their love of battle, Hacragorkans disdain guns. They'll use them when the situation calls for it— they're a pragmatic people—but they prefer hand-to-hand combat or, failing that, the use of knives, axes, and swords.

Hacragorkan Names

Hacragorkans have both personal and family names traced through the female line. Their names are short, grunting sounds. Here are some examples.

Male Names: Barg, Berg, Bor, Bug, Burg, Dor, Drub, Durb, Durg, Gar, Gerb, Gor, Grub, Gub, Thar, Thrub, Thub, Thurg, Tor, Torg.

Female Names: Arbra, Arga, Barba, Bruba, Brunda, Burga, Darga, Dorba, Druga, Durba, Golba, Gorba, Grorba, Gurga, Horga, Thorda, Thubra, Truga, Turga, Urga.

Family Names: Abragag, Agab, Azog, Bagagob, Bargab, Borgab, Drabag, Gabog, Gagab, Gagog, Gog, Gogagog, Golbarg, Gozagag, Grabag, Guldag, Gurbag, Magog, Zagog.

Typical Hacragorkan Aspects

Can Take a Hit

Invoke: you don't go down on one blow, "That all ya got?"

Compel: that many blows to the head can cause problems, "Wait. Explain that again."

Big, Meaty Fists

Invoke: pow! "There's one! And two! You want some more?"

Compel: not all problems can be solved with these, "Jeez, man. You knocked him out. I still had questions."

Battle-Scarred

Invoke: you are one bad mofo, "Let's steer clear of this guy."

Compel: maybe you lost some stuff that was important, "See that damage on his left eye? Take him from that side."

Forged by Struggle

Invoke: hardship doesn't mean much to you, "Extreme heat, little water, no food. What's the problem?"

Compel: you had to fight for everything, now you can't stop, "Don't touch that last fillet or you'll lose your arm."

Mix It Up!

Invoke: a fight! Great! "All right! Let's go!"

Compel: you jump into a fight when there're other things to do, "Another bar fight? Leave her there to sort it out. We've got work to do."

"You talkin' to me?"

Invoke: you know how to start something, "I don't see anyone else here, so you must be talkin' to me!"

Compel: you're always starting something with the wrong guy, "Shut up, Durb! That's the customs inspector!"

Hacragorkan Species Abilities [–2]

Quick Healers [–2]

Hacragorkans are back on their feet and ready to fight faster than most other species—which is good, since they're usually suffering from one injury or another. Out of combat, Hacragorkans recover physical consequences as if they were one level lower (a moderate recovers as if it were mild, etc.). This doesn't apply to extreme consequences. Additionally, in combat *once per scene* a Hacragorkan may clear away a mild physical consequence with a supplemental action.

Dangerous Bearing [–1]

Hacragorkans are intimidating just by their very nature. A Hacragorkan gains a +2 when attempting to intimidate an opponent with the threat of force. They also gain a +2 when attempting to resist intimidation backed by a physical threat by any opponent.

Pugnacious [+1]

Hacragorkans are easily provoked into physical conflict. The GM can compel this attribute as if it were an aspect *once per session*. If the player wishes to avoid this compel, she must spend *two* fate points to refuse. Check out the **Aspects** chapter for more on compels (page 55).

Ken Reeg

There's some dispute as to the origin of the Ken Reeg as a species. Most people think the Ken Reeg are an offshoot of the Arsubaran species, either due to natural evolution or genetic augmentation. Apart from a few things, they're physically identical to Arsubarans. The most obvious difference is their green skin, but most notable is the fact that Ken Reeg have no need for sleep. Few other species can claim such a thing. The Ken Reeg, of course, vehemently refute any assertions that they share a common ancestry with the Arsubarans, maintaining that they are a unique and separate species.

As a species, the Ken Reeg have a reputation for being good with numbers and rules. Ken Reeg are frequently found in the gambling dens of the planet Stakes (this, in fact, is considered by many to be the Ken Reeg home planet, though it's unlikely that they originated there), as well as in the fields of law and accounting. In addition to skill with figures, Ken Reeg have a reputation for being morally and ethically flexible. Many other species view Ken Reeg with distaste, seeing them as nothing but con artists, gamblers, silver-tongued lawyers, and snake-oil salesmen. The Ryjyllians, in particular, have an intense dislike for the Ken Reeg due to their "lack of honor." The Ken Reeg, for their own part, dislike nobody, preferring instead to keep their options open. After all, if you burn too many bridges, the money can't get in from anywhere.

If you know a Ken Reeg, it's unlikely that you truly know him. Most Ken Reeg have two separate aspects to their personality: the face and the name. According to Ken Reeg custom, the face is what you present to those you don't fully trust, and although Ken Reeg are often exceedingly friendly to people they just met, they're slow to trust. A Ken Reeg's face is his outward demeanor; it's how he presents himself in public. Typically this includes an air of respectability, a hard work ethic, and a willingness to get the job done. The name, on the other hand, is the facet of the Ken Reeg's personality that only his inner circle—those he truly trusts—sees. Some Ken Reeg never share their name with anyone, not even their families.

This slowness to trust is so culturally ingrained that even the Ken Reeg language—Reegi—is known almost exclusively to Ken Reeg; sharing the Reegi language with non-Ken Reeg is, in fact, considered grounds for social ostracism and enormous loss of status. This secrecy surrounding the language is so great that most people believe that Ken Reeg use Galactic as their native language and have no language of their own. The Ken Reeg wouldn't have it any other way.

Ken Reeg Names

Ken Reeg names—at least any you've ever heard—sound Arsubaran, but with a personal flair. Their names sound like nicknames, because that's what they are—nicknames for the face of the Ken Reeg.

Male Names: Benny, Billy, Dizzy, Dougie, Droobie, Fennie, Henny, Iggy, Izzy, Jimmy, Lolly, Mickey, Morrie, Morty, Paulie, Sammy, Sonny, Telly, Tony, Willy.

Female Names: Babe, Bonnie, Candy, Della, Donna, Doxie, Holla, Honey, Lana, Lonnie, Mixie, Moxie, Nixie, Noxie, Sloopie, Solla, Sugar, Trixie, Tutti, Twinks.

Family Names: Action, Flash, Glitter, Happy, Magic, Quickly, Rainbows, Razzle, Sharps, Shine, Slick, Slightly, Snappy, Snaps, Stardust, Sweets, Trick, Twinkle, Twist, Wonder.

Typical Ken Reeg Aspects

"COMMERCE NEVER SLEEPS."

Invoke: your business can take place anytime, "Let's meet at 03:00 in Docking Bay 13."

Compel: you might miss a deal if you're complacent, "Sorry. I sold it off six hours ago."

SLIPPERY AS A SNAKE

Invoke: it's hard to pin you down, "Wait. What do you mean about the fine print?"

Compel: people don't want to trust you, "I know all about you, Noxie. No deal."

TRUST NO ONE

Invoke: it's hard to pull a fast one on you, "Nice try. That's why I recorded the whole thing."

Compel: you can't tell when someone is being sincere, "If you had only trusted me. Now it's too late."

"THERE'S ALWAYS A LOOPHOLE."

Invoke: no contract is ironclad, "I think you forgot about a little thing called sub-paragraph 3, section B, article 1."

Compel: your own deals are not always airtight, "You left in the escape clause. Now I can sell it to Greenway."

VORACIOUS GREED

Invoke: if you want it, you'll go to any lengths, "You may have disabled my ship and put a warrant out, but this deal was too good to pass up."

Compel: the things you want might cause you trouble, "That necklace is worth a fortune. I've got to get it for myself."

"LET'S MAKE A DEAL."

Invoke: you can finagle your way out of almost anything, "I think there's some way to resolve this to our mutual benefit."

Compel: other people can get you to cut deals even when you shouldn't, "I know I murdered your brother, but isn't there some way we can settle this with cash?"

Ken Reeg Species Abilities [+1]

Never Sleep [0]

Ken Reeg have no need for sleep. They still grow fatigued from physical activity and need to rest, but they never actually fall asleep. A Ken Reeg can be considered alert at all times. Additionally, any task that would normally take a few days or longer gets reduced one step on the time scale (page 65, ***Doing Things*** chapter) if the Ken Reeg decides to devote himself to it full time.

Dealmaker [+1]

The Ken Reeg are notoriously grasping and are always willing to make a deal. The GM can compel this attribute as if it were an aspect *once per session*. If the player wishes to avoid this compel, she must spend *two* fate points to refuse. Check out the ***Aspects*** chapter for more on compels (page 55).

Robots

Robots aren't a true species, nor do they have a shared history or culture. Robots are usually viewed as little more than expendable tools and thoughtless automatons. While it's true that many robots are merely mechanical devices with no true sentience, some are more than that. It's commonly thought that a robot that's been around long enough starts to become self-aware, and as the ghost in the machine starts to become more and more powerful, that robot can become a fully developed personality with desires and agendas of its own. Of course, nobody likes to think about that; after all, if robots were sentient beings, they'd have to be freed from bondage.

Most robots are effectively slaves, and most robots aren't even aware of this fact. There are, however, a few robot communities in the galaxy, clusters of robots who have developed varying degrees of sentience and banded together for mutual protection and support. The largest of these is the Collective, a self-proclaimed safe haven in the Frontier Zone for free-thinking robots from anywhere in the galaxy. The Collective is scoffed at by many, and now and then the occasional government tries to squash it out. Most of these attempts have simply failed, with the aggressors being turned back by the superior robot numbers and organization. A few have managed to destroy the community, but the Collective always returns a few years later, in a different location but with the same individuals behind it. Some theorize that the Collective's members upload and store their minds to some undisclosed location; when they're destroyed they simply find new bodies.

The other major robot community is much smaller than the Collective, but much better known. The robots of the System see themselves as the immune system for the galaxy—each individual robot an antibody and each organic creature in the galaxy a virus. Their stated goal is to eradicate the "organic plague," as they call it, one creature at a time. Besides hunting down and killing organics, robots of the System also "liberate" non-sentient robots by capturing them and reprogramming them—they call it "Awakening"—to swell their ranks.

By and large, though, these two communities are not the norm, even for sentient robots. Most sentient robots try to better themselves and explain to their organic masters that they are living beings, too. Some lucky ones manage to find groups of organics willing to accept them for what they are.

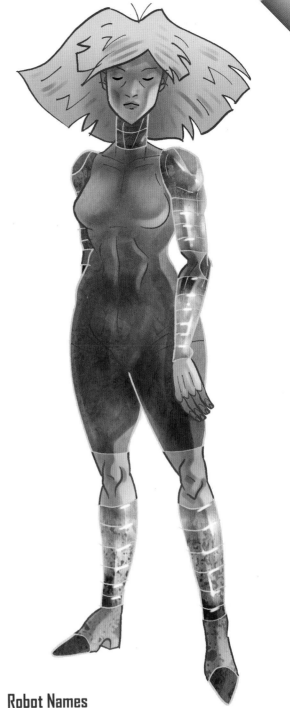

Robot Names

Robots are named by their manufacturers—usually a model number and a unique identifier. Robots that work in close proximity with biological beings are often given a nickname, as well.

Names: Acme TB-M Class FF5094, Aldo-Maxo 2000 Series X1, Blackhawk Warbot 12-004, BotTech 3000 J1-9941, Mechtech DGL 1106, Mnemo Devices MMO-001L, Quality Robots Mobile Toolkit 1101Y, Snappy Robots Posh Series C1L, Tomol Industrial Machines Mechbot TIM-M-0062, Unicorp Heavy Machines XL-2014.

Nicknames: Bluey, Boltbucket, Buzz, Clunky, Electro, Gearhead, Glitch, Happy, Knuckles, Lady, Maitre D, Ol' Grim, Princess, Rover, Rusty, Shorty, Sonny, Stilts, Wrench, Zippy.

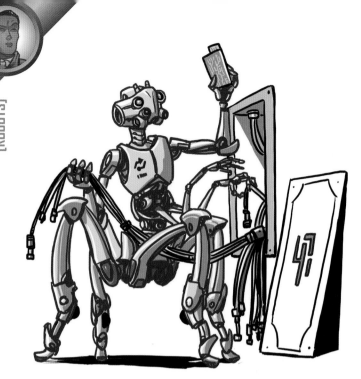

Typical Robot Aspects

Never Eat, Never Sleep, Never Stop

Invoke: you need to get something done, "I can't believe it's been working on that for three days straight."

Compel: you aren't an organic being, "We're all going to dinner. Look after the ship, Chippy."

Fully-Equipped

Invoke: you have the right tool for the job, "I just happen to have a bone saw handy, sir."

Compel: you always think *you're* the right tool for the job, "Hey! I was fixing that."

Just a Machine

Invoke: you want to be overlooked, "No one here. Just a robot."

Compel: you want to be taken seriously, "I'm sorry, you're equipment. You can't report a crime."

Form Follows Function

Invoke: you can fight in a tight spot, "That access hatch is too small. Hey, look at that, the robot fits."

Compel: you're ugly, "Don't bring that thing. It looks like a cross between a scooter and a spider."

Slave to Programming

Invoke: it's hard to stop you from doing your job, "Hey! Come back here! You're a hostage!"

Compel: you have to do what your programming instructs, "I'm sorry, that violates protocol 1.1.7.9."

Newly Awakened

Invoke: you have a mind of your own, "Protocol calls for me to sacrifice myself, but I think I'll follow you."

Compel: you don't like being ordered around, "I'm afraid I can't do that, Dave."

Robot Species Abilities [–1 to –7]

Reprogammable [–2]

A robot's mind isn't fixed—they can be reprogrammed to perform other tasks. If an engineer spends a few days working on the robot, she can completely rearrange the robot's skill configuration with a Good (+3) Engineering check, including completely removing a skill or adding new ones. The only restriction is that the robot must retain the same number of skill points. The robot can perform this task on itself but must *spend a fate point.*

Never Sleep [0]

Robots don't sleep. If they have sufficient fuel or a recharge they can continue working indefinitely, not counting wear and tear. Robots must spend some down time defragmenting their systems, reinitializing their code, and recharging their batteries, but a robot can be considered alert at all times. Additionally, any task that would normally take a few days or longer gets reduced one step on the time scale (page 65, ***Doing Things*** chapter) if the robot decides to devote itself to it full time.

Don't Breathe [–1]

Robots don't need to breathe. This means that they're able to function in any atmosphere—even liquid ones—and are also unaffected by a complete lack of atmosphere.

Machine Resistance [–3]

Robots are resistant to extreme heat, cold, and vacuum conditions. Robots can operate easily in temperatures down to freezing and heat well above a biological comfort level. Extreme cold or extreme heat can still damage a robot's parts by freezing its fluids or melting insulation or internal plastic. A robot can survive a vacuum indefinitely, although sudden decompression may cause damage. A robot can't be affected by diseases or poisons that infect biological beings. A robot may ignore any environmental aspect that the GM rules wouldn't affect a robot.

Immortal [–1]

With regular maintenance, a robot is effectively immortal. Robots are unaffected by the ravages of age during play and may have been around for hundreds of years.

Electro-Magnetic Vulnerability [+1]

Robots are particularly vulnerable to electro-magnetic attacks. When hit with an electro-magnetic attack of any kind, the attack gains Damage: 2.

No Natural Healing [+4]

Robots can't heal damage. Stress boxes and physical consequences require outside intervention for recovery. An Engineering check is needed to clear most damage from a robot—use the regular healing rules but substitute Engineering for Medicine.

Anti-Robot Prejudice [+1]

Robots are treated like slaves or furniture in most parts of the galaxy. They aren't considered to have free will, so most beings don't care if they're rude to a robot. A robot suffers a −1 penalty whenever making social interaction rolls with characters who aren't robots.

Extra Limbs [−1] (Optional)

Robots are often fitted with extra limbs to help them do their jobs. During a round, robots with more than two manipulating limbs may take two actions that require a hand without the normal −1 penalty for the second action.

Additional Sensory Apparatus [−1] (Optional)

Some robots are equipped with additional senses, such as sonar, heat sensing, or sensing vibrations through the ground. Pick one type of additional sense for the robot. Any scene aspect that restricts vision or other senses must directly block this additional sense; otherwise the robot can ignore the aspect.

Extra Speed [−1] (Optional)

Some robots are built with multiple limbs dedicated to locomotion or with tires or treads to increase speed. When moving as part of another activity, a robot with this equipment may move one additional zone without taking the −1 penalty for a supplemental action.

Hover [−1] (Optional)

Some robots don't actually walk or roll in order to move around; instead they hover above the ground with built-in anti-gravity. Robots with this feature don't leave tracks and don't trigger any sensors that require weight to activate. They can also easily access a zone directly above them, an action that would be off-limits to a ground-based being without a jump.

Programmed [+1] (Optional)

Non-Awakened robots cannot act contrary to their programming. The GM can compel this attribute as if it were an aspect *once per session*. If the player wishes to avoid this compel, she must spend *two* fate points to refuse. Check out the **Aspects** chapter for more on compels (page 55).

Ryjyllians

Ryjyl, an icy planet in the Frontier Zone, is home to a species of warriors without peer. To a Ryjyllian, honor is everything. Honor is primarily gained through battle. Therefore, battle is everything. The Ryjyllians are known throughout the galaxy as some of the most skilled and vicious warriors around, and they're feared for their short tempers. However, it's also commonly known that a Ryjyllian would rather die than bring shame upon her clan; for this reason, most other species view the Ryjyllians with a healthy respect that's tempered by caution.

Ryjyllians have cat-like eyes, retractable claws, pointed ears atop their heads, and fur. Ryjyllian fur is thick—the better to withstand the cold climate of their homeworld—and typically ranges from dark gray to bright white, though variations from this norm aren't uncommon. Ryjyllians of both sexes have thick manes that they grow long and braid; these braids often have some significance, though the meaning varies from clan to clan.

Unlike many other starfaring species, Ryjyllians value the ties to their families more than ties to their species. To a Ryjyllian, the clan is everything. There are countless clans of varying sizes throughout the galaxy (though most of them are still based on Ryjyl), and each operates as an independent nation-state. There are alliances between clans, and occasionally smaller clans merge into a larger clan, but for the most part, they're separate entities. For this reason, people sometimes find it difficult to deal with Ryjyllians; signing a treaty with one clan doesn't mean that another clan will honor it.

Ryjyllians, in general, follow a very strict warrior code; while clans sometimes have variations on this code, the basics are fairly universal. Ryjyllian honor forces fair combat, even between bitter enemies, and a Ryjyllian must give quarter to an enemy that surrenders. These rules apply to all conflicts between Ryjyllians, but the rules are somewhat more lax when it comes to members of other species. The code says that most non-Ryjyllians are without honor, and therefore will not participate in honorable combat or dealings when given the chance. Most Ryjyllians will give a non-Ryjyllian the benefit of the doubt once, but if the caution proves to be warranted, a non-Ryjyllian can expect little in the way of honor or even civility from that individual or her clan.

Ryjyllian Names

Ryjyllians have round, yowling names, reflected by their native tongue. All Ryjyllians identify their ancestors back several generations when making a formal introduction. Such a recitation generally sounds like a catfight to outsiders.

Male Names: Awrlol, Awrrl, Awyawl, Brawrlal, Brrawl, Grawl, Grawyawarl, Grrawal, Hsbrawrl, Hsyrrl, Mawl, Mrryawl, Mrryrl, Prawl, Prbrawl, Prrmrrl, Waryall, Wawarrl, Yall, Yawawl.

Female Names: Bawrgrr, Brrwr, Gbrowr, Gbrywr, Grrawr, Hsbrrwr, Mawr, Mrrawr, Prrbrawr, Prrbrwr, Prrowr, Rorlawr, Rrowr, Srrbrrawr, Wrrawr, Yawbrowr, Yibrowr, Yowr, Yowrmrr, Yrrbrr.

Family Names: Ryjyllians don't have family names per se, instead listing their ancestors. The term "awp" indicates descent, and the more prestigious parent (male or female) is typically listed. A formal Ryjyllian name looks like this: Yall awp Yibrowr awp Awrlol awp Gbrywr.

Clan Names: The clan name isn't part of the personal name; most Ryjyllians can recognize what clan another Ryjyllian comes from on sight. A Ryjyllian will offer her clan if asked, but she'll usually assume that it's obvious. The five largest clans are Hawp, Hwrrr, Mrrr, Myip, and Yowrrr.

Typical Ryjyllian Aspects

Cat-Like Reflexes

Invoke: for quick acrobatic moves, "I can't believe she made that jump!"

Compel: not everything cats do is great, "Do you need to sharpen your claws on every damn tree we pass?"

Short Temper

Invoke: when someone has pissed you off, "I'll mail your head back to your mother!"

Compel: if you want to keep your temper, "That's done it!"

Warrior of a Warrior People

Invoke: great for fighting, "Don't you know not to go in against a Ryjyllian?"

Compel: fighting is in your blood, "Well, it would have been nice if we could've turned him in for bounty instead of killing him in a duel."

Loyal to My Clan

Invoke: when acting in a way that will bring honor to your clan, "No Myip clan warrior has ever fled a battle!"

Compel: your clan calls on you, "The Mrrr clan has attacked our territory. I have to go home."

The Ryjyllian Code of Honor

Invoke: you show no fear, "I care nothing for odds, only honor."

Compel: opponents can exploit the code, "Wait! I beg for quarter!"

Last to Retreat

Invoke: you won't run from a fight, "I'll cover you if you wish to flee, but a Ryjyllian fights to the end!"

Compel: sometimes discretion is the better part of valor, "I couldn't get her to come. Now her position's been overwhelmed."

Ryjyllian Species Abilities [–3 to –4]

Acute Hearing [–1]

Ryjyllians have extremely keen hearing. When making any perception related skill checks, Ryjyllians gain a +2 if hearing matters.

Claws and Fangs [–1]

A Ryjyllian is never unarmed. They have retractable claws in their fingers and sturdy and deadly fangs in their jaws. These natural weapons inflict Damage: 1 and use the Fists skill for their attack.

Low Light Vision [–1]

Ryjyllian eyes are better than average at seeing in dark conditions. Ryjyllians have a +2 bonus against any penalties imposed by darkness aspects, except for aspects coming from the complete absence of light (such as Pitch Black).

Ryjyllian Combat Focus [–1] (Optional)

Some Ryjyllians train in special combat techniques that allow them to enter into a sort of battle trance that inures them to pain. It also makes them more deadly combatants. Once per session, the Ryjyllian can *spend a fate point* to enter a battle trance. While in this state, the Ryjyllian automatically generates one extra shift on any attack roll intended to deal stress. In addition, the Ryjyllian gains two additional physical stress boxes, which can be filled as normal. However, if either or both extra stress boxes are filled, when this state ends the Ryjyllian takes an immediate mild consequence. If mild is already filled, this consequence rolls up normally. The Ryjyllian can exit this state at any time; otherwise it lasts until the end of the scene.

Example: Mawr goes into a fight. Her player spends a fate point to activate the Ryjyllian combat focus. Mawr's stress track, normally four, gains two additional boxes:

☐☐☐☐(☐☐)

Mawr gets hit several times during the fight. None of the attacks is enough to force her to take a consequence, but she's hit for two, four, and five stress. When the fight wraps up, her stress track looks like this:

☐☒☐☒(☒☐)

Mawr then exits the combat focus, losing the two additional stress boxes. The five box was filled, so she suffers a mild consequence.

Saldrallans

There are two major empires in the galaxy; the Templari rule over one, while the other empire is ruled—at least mostly—by the Saldrallans. The two empires are an exercise in contrasts. Where the Templari Empire is racially homogeneous (for the most part), the Saldrallan Empire is diverse and cosmopolitan. The Templari Empire is warlike and totalitarian, while the Saldrallans are pragmatic and egalitarian, if ruthless at times. Indeed, the Saldrallan Empire contains representatives of every major species—and many minor ones—in various positions of authority.

Saldrallans can be somewhat unnerving to members of other species. The upper body is a torso with arms, while the lower body trails off into a snake-like tail. The entire body is covered in fine scales. They have ophidian heads—complete with poisonous fangs and, in some cases, hoods like that of a cobra. Lacking eyelids, they never blink and they sleep with their eyes open. A Saldrallan also possesses heat-sensing organs beneath his eyes that allow him to see the heat emanating from living creatures; this gives him the ability to detect them in the dark and even track them for short distances by their heat signature. Perhaps the thing that makes Saldrallans the most alien to other species is their ability to change their gender, seemingly at will; for this reason, Saldrallans have no preconceptions based on gender, and often can't even tell the difference between a male and female of a different species.

Despite their somewhat unnerving appearance and mannerisms, most people find Saldrallans to be fairly agreeable creatures once they get to know them. Saldrallans are famously pragmatic, to the point where species is rarely a concern when it comes to advancement in the Saldrallan Empire. The Saldrallans are, first and foremost, concerned with their Empire running efficiently and continuing to grow. To this end, they make efforts to ensure that members of all species are happy within the Empire, because a happy citizen is usually a productive one. Exceptional members of other species can climb quite high up the political ladder; there have even been a few non-Saldrallan emperors in the past, though this is the exception rather than the rule.

Despite this apparent acceptance of all beings and creeds, these policies aren't motivated by morality. Indeed, Saldrallan morality is a flexible thing and can be boiled down into the idea that you should always do that which is most expedient and benefits the Empire (or company, or army, or other organization) most. The ugly side of this is that those who get in the way of prosperity and progress often don't last long. At best, these people are quietly disappeared; at worst they are made a public example.

Saldrallan Names

Saldrallans have personal names and clan names. Each of the Saldrallan clans has its own reputation and status that's well known to other Saldrallans. When a Saldrallan introduces himself formally, he always names his clan, then himself. A Saldrallan introduction sounds like this: "I was hatched for the Shass clan, I am called Hessien." Saldrallan names don't distinguish gender. They can tell by smell what gender another Saldrallan currently belongs to; since this is changeable, they don't find the distinction important.

Personal Names: Hasses, Heshesh, Hesshes, Hessien, Hessnss, Hessshlss, Hessshssk, Hssk, Sassask, Sasses, Sassless, Shesshesh, Shesslss, Shissien, Shshk, Shsss, Sissik, Sissnak, Sssiss, Sssk.

Clan Names: Aash, Hash, Hess, Hiss, Husss, Huush, Sess, Shass, Shul, Shuss, Ssesh, Sssek.

Typical Saldrallan Aspects

Exothermic

Invoke: you can lie very still and quiet when resting, "Holy crap! I didn't see that Saldrallan there!"

Compel: you're sluggish in cold weather, "It must be 10 degrees in here. I think I'll take a nap."

Lidless Gaze

Invoke: this can really freak people out, "OK, I'll tell you! Just stop staring at me."

Compel: you seem weird and scary, "I don't want to talk to you. Just go away."

Ruthless

Invoke: no one can tug your heartstrings, "Damn. I can't believe you shot him down like that."

Compel: you'll cut even friends loose if you need to, "Sorry, there's no time to wait for you."

Efficiency, Expansion, Power

Invoke: you're relentless in pursuit of what you want, "This is what it takes to succeed."

Compel: your desire for success can strain your friends, "Again? I'm getting tired of doing all this work."

Tolerant

Invoke: you can get along with anyone, "I don't mind his peculiar habits. He has an excellent eye for investigation."

Compel: you may miss problems that actually demand attention, "Hmm. His gambling wasn't an issue before."

Flexible Morality

Invoke: doing bad things just doesn't bother you, "This may be illegal, but the net gain is quite high."

Compel: you don't understand why it's bad, "I am confused. You didn't want to sell your vintage discs? The profit was exceptional."

Saldrallan Species Abilities [−2]

Heat Sense [−1]

Saldrallans have heat organs underneath their eyes that allow them to see in the thermal spectrum. Any scene aspect that restricts vision or other senses must directly block this additional sense, otherwise the Saldrallan can ignore the aspect.

Poison Bite [−2]

Saldrallans possess long fangs that can inject poison into an opponent. Once per fight, in addition to any normal damage, a Saldrallan may place an immediate consequence on an opponent (Poisoned, Spreading Weakness, etc.) if Fists is used for the attack. Only the lowest available consequence is used, and you must successfully strike your opponent to use this ability.

Cold Blooded [+1]

Saldrallans require external heat or cooling sources to regulate their body temperature. The GM can compel this attribute as if it were an aspect *once per session*. If the player wishes to avoid this compel, she must spend *two* fate points to refuse. Check out the **Aspects** chapter for more on compels (page 55).

Templars

The Templari Empire is feared by most denizens of the galaxy, and for good reason—it has arguably the best, most efficient, and most effective military in the galaxy. This is largely because the Templari value war and conquest above all else. In fact, they're commonly known as the Devalkamanchans, a combination of the names of the two war gods they worship: Deval and Kamanch.

Although they look remarkably like Arsubarans in many ways, Templari are tall, generally a few inches taller than Arsubarans. They are completely hairless, and their purple skin and pointed ears further distinguish them from Arsubarans. Physical perfection is important to Templari, and most are well-muscled and athletic due to constant physical training; it's extremely rare to see a Templar that's overweight or underweight.

The Templari society is perhaps the most xenophobic society in existence. Templari believe that their species is superior to all others and that other species were created specifically to be conquered and to serve them. They do not allow any non-Templari into the military or government. Rather than incorporate and assimilate the way the Saldrallan Empire does, the Devalkamanchan Republic subjugates, oppressing members of other species and keeping them under heel. Only the military is authorized to own weapons of any kind within the Templari Empire; thus, only the Templari have weapons—at least, legal weapons.

Understandably, Templari relations with other species are strained. The Saldrallans regard them warily, and the Templari eye Saldrallan space with hunger. Templari see the Arsubarans as upstarts, but also as threats because of their numbers and ability to integrate into other cultures. Even the other warrior species—the Ryjyllians and the Hacragorkans—are seen as inferior and are typically exterminated rather than subjugated when they're encountered; the Templari have found that such fierce people make poor subjects.

Templari Names

Templari names have many clipped syllables and glottal stops. They have family names that they trace through the male line. Listed are some common Templari names:

Male Names: Akryl, Avaar, Bal'n, Darv'n, Devaar, D'kryl, Draf'n, Gar'n, Gavanch, Jal'n, Jocaar, Kamanch, Lar'n, Locaar, Rabl'n, Racaar, Savaar, Tamaar, Tamanch, Trom'n.

Female Names: Anaa, An'k, Belaa, Bel'n, Beval, Danaa, Deval, Falaa, Fr'n, Jacaa, Jan'k, Javal, Jr'n, Kr'n, Salaa, Selaa, Sel'n, Seval, Talaa, Tr'n.

Family Names: Baan, Baf't, Bel'd, Durv't, Fal'n, Gaf'd, Gref'd, Hal't, Harn, Kaf't, Kal'n, Kran, Laf't, Saan, Tran, T'rbrik, Tref'd, Vaan, Var'd, Varn.

Typical Templari Aspects

Superior Species

Invoke: you are flat-out better than everyone else, "Of course I made it. I'm Templar."

Compel: others are resentful of your natural superiority, "Everyone but the Templar can come in."

Imperfection Is Unacceptable

Invoke: you do everything perfectly, "I hold myself to the highest standard."

Compel: it's unacceptable if you fail, "I failed? This isn't possible."

"Submit, or be crushed."

Invoke: drive your enemies before you, "You have chosen to resist. So be it."

Compel: your need for victory prevents you from cutting your losses, "But they are not yet utterly defeated. We can't withdraw!"

To the Purple Be True

Invoke: your actions bring glory to your species, "I will show you how a true Templar behaves!"

Compel: you give fellow Templari preferential treatment, "I had to go with her. She's purple."

Arrogant

Invoke: you demand respect, "Of course they let me in. Anything else would be laughable."

Compel: being full of yourself pisses people off, "That jerk. I'll take him down."

Martial Discipline

Invoke: there's a precise and orderly way to do things, "Stay together and strike here; that's their weak point."

Compel: you're accustomed to following orders, "We were instructed to stay here. That order hasn't changed."

Templari Species Abilities [0]

The Templari are an example of a species with no special abilities outside the norm. They're already special enough; they don't need anything extra.

Tetsuashans

The planet Suash is a damp, swampy, bug-ridden, dark planet. Few go there willingly if it can be at all avoided. It's widely theorized that the planet's native species, the Tetsuashans, were driven to excel at space travel because of their unpleasant homeworld. However, the Tetsuashans are puzzled that many consider their homeworld unpleasant; to them, it's simply home. Despite this, Tetsuashans can be found nearly everywhere else in the galaxy. It's said that only the Arsubarans are more numerous than the Tetsuashans in the galaxy; it's actually more likely that the Tetsuashans outnumber the Arsubarans, but nobody notices them most of the time.

A Tetsuashan is small, usually only about three feet high. Their bodies are slug-like, composed entirely of muscle and organs, completely without bone. They have no feet or legs, moving instead on a muscular pad; however, they do have two arm-like pseudopods with grasping digits. A Tetsuashan has a relatively featureless face, with only a small mouth and a single eye directly above it. Tetsuashans are usually a grayish brown in color, and their skin glistens in the light, though they're not slimy to the touch. They're asexual beings that reproduce through a process they call "seeding" in which a lump is expelled through the Tetsuashan's skin which quickly develops into a clone of the original Tetsuashan; therefore, the concept of gender is completely alien to Tetsuashans. This causes some consternation amongst other species, as many forms of humor and innuendo are frequently lost on these creatures, and interpersonal relationships take on a very different dynamic with them.

For the most part, Tetsuashans manage to exist below the radar of the rest of the galaxy. Most people pay them no mind, taking their presence for granted; the Tetsuashans do little to combat this, seeming content with the lack of attention. These creatures are extremely resilient, both mentally and physically, and these reserves of endurance and willpower often surprise people not familiar with Tetsuashan stoicism. Tetsuashans show little emotion, so it's difficult to truly know what they think of other species; they do, however, treat all species with the same apparent indifference.

Tetsuashan Names

Tetsuashans have mushy, round sounding names. They have no family name, nor do they trace bloodlines. Each Tetsuashan is considered a sole individual, although they're aware that all Tetsuashans are genetically identical.

Names: Blorb, Blub, Blurb, Boog, Foosh, Furb, Glub, Glurp, Goo, Goosh, Gum, Gurb, Moosh, Mub, Oorb, Shoob, Sloosh, Splurb, Squishy, Urp.

Typical Tetsuashan Aspects

Short of Stature, Strong of Will

Invoke: you're a tough little sucker, "Even with those injuries, it got up and flipped the switch."

Compel: things might be out of reach, "It seems the key component has been placed above my reach. I will need assistance."

Slug-like Form

Invoke: useful for getting weird places, "How'd it get in here? I thought the door was locked."

Compel: other species find you a bit disgusting, "Ugh. Another slime trail? Can we get rid of this thing?"

Space Is Home

Invoke: you can do all sorts of space things, "It slipped right out the airlock and then came back in the other side. Didn't expect that."

Compel: you can't stay too long planetside, "This dry city has become unpleasant. I am returning to the ship."

Omnipresent

Invoke: you can always find another Tetsuashan, "Their engineer is a Tetsuashan. We had a chat."

Compel: people ignore you, "Is someone talking? Oh, I didn't see you there."

Fearless

Invoke: nothing fazes you, "It walked right into their line of fire. No fear."

Compel: sometimes you should be afraid, "Shut up, Goosh! That guy's gonna kill us."

Inscrutable

Invoke: other species have trouble reading you, "Is it pissed? Happy? I can't tell."

Compel: you have trouble conveying emotion, "OK, Sploog. We'll get to it later."

Tetsuashan Species Abilities [–3]

Slime Trail [–2]

Tetsuashans move using a pad or "foot" that allows them to cling to sheer surfaces. They may climb any normal surface as if they were walking at their normal slow pace without needing to make an Athletics roll, and they gain a +4 to Athletics when climbing a surface that's slippery, slick, or completely upside-down. They exude a gooey slime to ease their travel and leave wet trails behind that gradually dry into a crust and eventually a powder.

Squish [–2]

A Tetsuashan lacks bones and can squeeze its body down to an extremely small size. It can fit through very small or narrow openings easily, without the need for an Athletics roll.

Resilient [–2]

Tetsuashans heal far more quickly than the norm. This healing ability doesn't apply to extreme consequences, but all lesser damage heals at a faster rate. Out of combat, Tetsuashans recover physical consequences as if they were one level lower (a moderate recovers as if it were mild, etc.). Additionally, in combat *once per scene* a Testuashan may clear away a mild physical consequence with a supplemental action.

Regenerative Powers [0]

No wound is permanent for Tetsuashans. Even extreme consequences will heal given enough time—usually a couple of years, but sometimes as fast as a few months. Even lost limbs or organs will regrow.

Poisoned by Salt [+2]

Salt is extremely toxic to Tetsuashans. Just coming in contact with salt causes 1 stress, and every round a Tetsuashan remains in contact, the salt continues to inflict 1 additional stress. If attacked with salt, the Damage is increased by 1.

Reduced Speed [+1]

The Tetsuashan method of locomotion, while useful for climbing, is particularly slow. Moving even within the same zone in combat, such as to take cover, requires a supplemental action. Moving more than one zone requires all of the Tetsuashan's concentration and an Athletics roll; no additional actions may be taken. Tetsuashans may not move more than two zones in a single round no matter how high they roll on Athletics.

Urseminites

No species is quite as reviled as the Urseminites. This fact is at odds with an Urseminite's first impression—at least if that first impression involves only seeing the creature. An Urseminite is small, about three or four feet tall, and looks remarkably like a living teddy bear. They're short and pudgy, covered in soft fur that ranges from pink to brown, and everything about their physical appearance is completely non-threatening. They have no claws and their teeth aren't pointed.

It's widely theorized that the Urseminites are a genetically engineered species, created for the express purpose of being pets or perhaps nannies. This seems likely, because nobody knows of an Urseminite homeworld—these creatures live in small communities on various worlds, as well as in the space lanes themselves—and nobody really knows anything about Urseminite history or heritage. However, if they were engineered for domestic purposes, something went horribly wrong with the process, because their personalities could not be more contradictory to their appearances.

Urseminites revel in vice. They smoke huge, disgusting cigars that they roll themselves; they drink to excess; they hit on everything that moves; they pick fights; they lie, cheat, steal, and kill—all for amusement and personal gain. Urseminites are supremely selfish creatures; there's a theory that something within the Urseminite brain prevents them from empathizing with other creatures, prevents them from realizing that other creatures aren't mere playthings for their own grotesque amusement.

Most species want nothing to do with these cuddly villains, giving them wide berth when they see them. Some individuals recognize, however, that the Urseminites do have their uses. For all their small and non-threatening stature, Urseminites are notoriously vicious in battle—packs of them can take down seemingly superior foes in a surprisingly short time. They are often pirates and mercenaries, and there are some who take advantage of their willingness to undertake any job, turning a blind eye to the Urseminites' methods.

Thankfully, compared to the other major species of the galaxy, Urseminites are rare. They have no homeworld, and groups of Urseminites larger than five or six are almost unheard of. It's likely that these creatures even begin to hate each other after a while, and this, fortunately, prevents them from amassing any kind of sizable force. Their small numbers are suppressed further by the Templari and the Saldrallans, both of whom frequently put bounties on the heads of Urseminites. The Saldrallans specify that these Urseminites must be proven pirates or criminals, since there are a rare few who do legitimate work for the Empire. The Templari, however, make no such distinction and are content to try to hunt the Urseminite species into extinction. So far, they haven't been successful.

Urseminite Names

Urseminites don't take family names. As befits their general attitude, the individual is all that matters. Here are some sample names.

Male Names: Bres, Corl, Doom, Doonfa, Drevid, Falik, Grevid, Gun, Hebrid, Kalik, Korvid, Lar, Mar, Murd, Palik, Par, Sar, Savid, Trun, Van.

Female Names: Bada, Bandi, Bedla, Blada, Caldi, Dani, Drandi, Folli, Goll, Hansi, Horra, Mala, Meda, Moll, Piska, Slandi, Terra, Tora, Tori, Traski.

Typical Urseminite Aspects

Cute as a Button

Invoke: lull their suspicions, "Aww, how cute! Ow, crap, she stabbed me!"

Compel: it's really hard to take something as adorable as you seriously, "You just stay here, I wouldn't want you to hurt your widdle hands."

Short and Round

Invoke: you're small enough to fit strange places, "That cabinet's too small for anyone to hide in. You've got something to tell me?"

Compel: not the best body shape for great feats of athletics, "Can't reach the switch? I guess you're too short, sucker."

"Never met a vice I didn't try."

Invoke: high tolerance levels for all sorts of things, "How are you still awake? There was enough in there to knock out an elephant."

Compel: it's easy to find vices to try, "Gambling? I'm in."

Selfish

Invoke: sometimes it helps to look out for number one, "I got clear, let's go!"

Compel: it's mean to leave your friends behind, "You left me to rot on that rock, you little jerk."

Vicious Little Bastard

Invoke: go ahead, cut 'em, "Holy crap! That thing jumped at me like a mad dog!"

Compel: unnecessary cruelty, "Man, you could have just killed him. You didn't need to do *that*."

"Empathy is for suckers."

Invoke: it's hard to appeal to your good side if you don't have one, "Mercy is for chumps. So long, sucker."

Compel: one more reason people don't like to be around you, "I hate that little SOB. Go ahead and shoot him."

Urseminite Species Abilities [–1]

Thick Fur and Fat [–1]

Urseminites are very durable for their size and shape. Their bodies are insulated with thick fur and a layer of fat that protects them from damage. Urseminites have Armor: 1 against hand-to-hand damage.

Hard to Kill [–2]

Urseminites are sturdy little buggers with a great resistance to pain. Urseminites automatically gain an additional stress box. They can also take an additional mild physical consequence.

No Natural Weapons [+1]

Since the Urseminites were genetically engineered to be physically inoffensive, they have no natural weapons. Their nails and teeth are blunt and their thick layer of fur cushions even a punch or kick. An Urseminite's Fists skill may never be higher than Fair (+2).

Universally Despised [+1]

Every species in the galaxy hates the Urseminites. The only beings who don't despise them have never met one. Urseminites suffer a –1 penalty whenever making social interaction rolls with characters of a species other than their own. This penalty doesn't apply to Intimidation rolls.

Creating Your Own Species

What's a galaxy without a vast menagerie of weird aliens? **Bulldogs!** doesn't restrict you to a few alien species; you can also create your own. The ten canon species offer good examples of what you can do.

Creating your own species is a lot like creating a character. You need to think a bit about your species' background, motives, general appearance, and capabilities. The process of creating a species works best if you have an idea of what sort of creature you want to come up with. This section is a toolkit for building a species of your own invention, but you need a vision in your head to start. Make sure you and the GM are on the same page as you develop your alien species. Don't bring in something that doesn't fit in the **Bulldogs!** world of high action—this should be a collaboration between the player and the GM.

As with character creation, species creation goes through a number of phases. Each phase prompts you to think about where your species comes from and what they're like rather than what they do mechanically, but each phase leads to some game rule effects.

Phase 1: Physiology

What does your species look like? Do they tend to be tall? Short? Lithe? Muscular? Do they have any odd appendages, like wings or tentacles? Are they even Arsubaroid in shape, or do they have some other, non-standard shape, like a giant amoeba or a six-winged bird? What colors are they, usually? Are they extremely hardy? Are they known for their strength or intelligence? Think about what your species is like in a purely physical sense, in terms of appearance, capabilities, locomotion, powers, and so forth. An obviously physical thing like wings or great strength would fit into this phase, but so would something innate but mental, like psychic powers.

When you're done answering some of the questions above, come up with two aspects based on how you described your species. If your species is capable of something that's too powerful or complex for an aspect to describe, a species ability might be appropriate in addition to the two aspects you choose.

Example: Max decides to create his own species rather than use one of the ones listed. He decides he'd like his species to be humanoid in shape, but with bony ridges and horns on their heads. He'd also like them to be tough, fast, and strong. He wants this species to be somewhat predatory, so he decides that they probably eat normal food but also require something else: the psychic energies given off by the deaths of sentient beings. He chooses the aspects PREDATOR'S PHYSIQUE and PSYCHIC HUNTER and creates an ability called PSYCHIC VAMPIRISM to represent their unusual source of sustenance.

Phase 3: Psychology

During this, the final phase, you get to really delve into what kinds of creatures these are that you're creating. The psychology and personality of your species should be informed by both its physiology and its history—both nature and nurture. During this phase, you can also decide how these people view other species, and how those species view them.

You should choose the final two aspects for the species based on their psychology. Again, you might want to create a species ability if an aspect just doesn't seem like the right fit.

Example: The Molodocs, being a fierce people, see others as either threats or prey. As such, relations with other species are strained at best and hostile at worst. This doesn't much bother the Molodocs, Max decides, because the fact that they've survived this long has made them an extremely proud species; they tend to look down on other species (who are, after all, potential meals). However, when a Molodoc truly trusts someone, he considers that person to be part of his clan, and thus worthy of both respect and protection. Max chooses the aspects TRUST BRINGS YOU INTO MY CLAN and HUNGRY EYE.

Creating Abilities

When creating your own species, you might find that you need to come up with some special abilities unique to your species. A lot of the powers and abilities shared by a particular species don't really fit as stunts, either because all members of the species have these abilities or because they go slightly beyond what a stunt can do for a character. Not all abilities are advantages, either. Some are detrimental to the species as they travel the star lanes.

When building a new species, use the three-phase creation system as a guideline for what sorts of extra abilities the species might have. Each ability either lowers a character's starting refresh pool or adds to it. Those that add to the refresh pool are detrimental abilities, while those that lower it give the species special powers beyond the norm. Keep an eye on the starting power level of your game when designing a species. No character is allowed to begin the game with a refresh pool lower than one, so make sure the net cost of a species' abilities doesn't drop the refresh pool below what's available at your power level. See **Crew Creation** for more on power levels (page 45).

Here's a list of abilities that you can pick and choose from, or use these as inspiration when creating your own. Some abilities are listed with a cost of 0. These tend to be less heroic or exciting abilities and more in the realm of interesting details. You can take only one of these abilities at no cost. Each 0-point ability taken after the first costs −1 instead.

Phase 2: History

Where does your species come from? During this phase, it's a good idea to decide what kind of planet your species lives on; this should be informed by choices you made in the previous phase. For example, a strong, solid species might live on a high-gravity homeworld, while a species that's highly resistant to cold likely lives on an ice planet. You should also use this phase to come up with some defining moments in the species' history; you don't have to come up with the details right now, just a few broad strokes. This is also a good place to come up with a name for your species, if you haven't already.

During this phase, you should choose two more aspects relating to the species' history. If any other special species abilities seem likely to arise from this phase, set those up as well.

Example: Max's species, which he's calling the Molodocs, is starting to come into focus. He decides that their homeworld is harsh and dangerous, and that many of the predatory animals on the world are sentient, even if they aren't that advanced technologically or socially. In order to survive in this harsh environment, the Molodocs have had to become supreme hunters, the better to hunt those creatures that try to make meals of them. He decides that there have been several wars in Molodoc history, and that this has caused the species to become fractious and clannish. He chooses the aspects TO THY CLAN BE TRUE and ONLY THE FIERCE SURVIVE.

Amphibious [–1]

This species is equally at home in air or liquid environments. Members of this species must still breathe air, but they don't have to make an Athletics roll for normal swimming movements and they can move at their normal rate through liquid.

Note: This ability doesn't confer the power to breathe liquid; the species must still breathe regular air unless another ability (such as Breathe Unusual Atmosphere) is purchased that states otherwise.

Aquatic [+1]

Some species are completely aquatic and can't survive outside a liquid environment. Such species can only breathe the particular liquid that makes up their home atmosphere (usually water). Outside of their liquid environment they will begin to suffocate. When they're out of water, they can hardly move and must make an Athletics roll to move even within their own zone. Special accommodations must be made for this species, such as setting up pools, channels, or tubes of water to enable them to move around. Outside of a liquid environment, members of this species need to walk around in an encounter suit all the time; this could cause problems if the suit is breached.

Armor Bonus [–1 to –5]

Some species have a shell or tough hide that's resistant to damage. The cost for this ability varies based on how effective the armor is against attack. Each point of Armor costs –1. Armor only applies to a certain type of damage: energy weapons, projectiles, or hand-to-hand damage. A species can't have more than Armor: 5 against any particular attack.

Restriction: If the armor's only effective against a narrow range of damage, such as only blunt melee attacks, the restriction counts as a +1 against cost. There's a minimum –1 cost for the ability, however. So the cost for Armor: 3 against only blunt melee attacks is –2.

Blindsight [–1]

Some species can "see" using another sense, such as sonar, heat sensing, psychic senses, or sensing vibrations through the ground. Any scene aspect that restricts vision or other senses must directly block this additional sense or the aspect can be ignored by members of this species.

Breathe Unusual Atmosphere [0]

This species can breathe an atmosphere that isn't comprised of the usual oxygen/nitrogen mix. This could be water, chlorine gas, or any other specified atmosphere. The species has no difficulty breathing a normal atmosphere as well. To create a creature equally at home in water and on land, specify water and pair this with the Amphibious ability. Strange creatures dwelling on gas giants or planets with unusual atmospheres also qualify. Additional atmospheric types may be purchased by taking this ability multiple times, but each additional atmosphere beyond the first costs –1.

Chameleon [–1]

Members of this species have the ability to change the color of their skin to blend in with their surroundings. They gain a +2 to all hiding-related Stealth checks.

Cling [–2]

This species has claws or suction pads or some other structure that allows them to cling to sheer surfaces. They may climb any normal surface as if they were walking without needing to make an Athletics roll, and they gain a +4 to Athletics tests when climbing a surface that is slippery, slick, or completely upside-down.

Cold Blooded [+1]

Cold blooded species need external heat or cooling sources to regulate their body temperature. The GM can compel this attribute as if it were an aspect *once per session*. If the player wishes to avoid this compel, she must spend *two* fate points to refuse. Check out the **Aspects** chapter for more on compels (page 55).

Communication Restriction [+2]

Some species can't communicate using normal means. They either lack the apparatus to form words or they can't hear what's said to them. In normal circumstances, this is inconvenient. In emergencies, it can be disastrous. When attempting to communicate with anyone outside their species, beings with this restriction suffer a –2 on all social rolls. In addition, the GM can compel this attribute as if it were an aspect *once per session*. If the player wishes to avoid this compel, she must spend *two* fate points to refuse. Check out the **Aspects** chapter for more on compels (page 55).

Contortion [–2]

Species with this ability can squeeze their physical body down to an extremely small size. They can fit through very small or narrow openings easily, and they don't need make an Athletics check to do so.

Damage Resistance [–1, –2 or –4]

Some species are just particularly tough. Maybe they have a sturdy physical structure; maybe some body part can be discarded and regrown; maybe they just have a great resistance to pain. At a cost of –1, members of this species may take an additional mild physical consequence. At a cost of –2, members of this species gain an additional stress box as well as the extra mild physical consequence. At a cost of –4, members of this species gain two additional stress boxes in addition to the extra mild physical consequence.

Disease/Venom Immunity [0]

Some species are highly resistant to disease or poison. A species with this ability must choose either disease or poison. To be immune to both, the ability costs –1. A member of the species is immune to damage, consequences, or environmental aspects related to disease or poison.

Disease Vulnerability [+1]

This species is particularly susceptible to disease. Members of the species suffer a –2 penalty when attempting to resist the effects of diseases. Additionally, the GM can compel this attribute as if it were an aspect *once per session*. If the player wishes to avoid this compel, she must spend *two* fate points to refuse. Check out the **Aspects** chapter for more on compels (page 55).

Electro-magnetic Vulnerability [+1]

Members of this species are particularly vulnerable to electro-magnetic attacks. When hit with an electro-magnetic attack of any kind, the attack adds Damage: 2.

Environmental Immunity [0]

Some species aren't affected by certain types of harsh environment, such as freezing temperatures, extreme heat, or vacuum itself. When taking this ability, choose one or more of these types of environment. A member of the species is immune to damage, consequences, or environmental aspects related to the chosen environment. To be immune to more than one or all of these environments, the ability costs –1.

Extra Limb [–1]

Some species have additional limbs with prehensile abilities. It's not necessary to take this advantage for extra legs, only for limbs that have the ability to manipulate objects. During a round, members of this species may take two actions that require a hand without the normal –1 penalty for the second action.

Extra Speed [–1 or –2]

Some species are particularly fast, either because they have multiple limbs dedicated to locomotion or because they possess much quicker reflexes than the galactic norm. When moving as part of another activity, a member of this species may move one additional zone without taking the –1 penalty for a supplemental action. If this ability is taken at a cost of –2, members of this species gain an additional +2 to Alertness for the purposes of determining initiative.

Fast Healing [–2]

Species with this ability heal far more quickly than the norm. This healing ability does not apply to extreme consequences, but all lesser damage heals at a faster rate. Out of combat, members of this species recover physical consequences as if they were one level lower (a moderate recovers as if it were mild, etc.). Additionally, in combat *once per scene* a member of this species may clear away a mild physical consequence with a supplemental action.

Flight [–2]

Some species have the ability to fly. They have wings or some other method for true flight and can move freely about in the air. When in flight, a member of this species may move one additional zone without taking the –1 penalty for a supplemental action. Also, species with this ability only suffer a –1 penalty on zero-gravity movement and action.

Glide [–1]

This species has wings or other structures allowing it to glide. While they must take off from a spot that's some height above the ground, with a proper launching point this species may glide for long distances. While gliding, a member of this species may move one additional zone without taking the –1 penalty for a supplemental action. Species with this ability only suffer a –1 penalty on zero-gravity movement and action.

Healing Restriction [+2]

Some species recover from damage very slowly. Members of this species recover physical consequences as if they were one level higher (a mild recovers as if it were moderate, etc.). A severe consequence doesn't act like an extreme, but it can take months or years to recover from a severe consequence.

Hover [–1]

This species doesn't actually walk in order to move around; instead it hovers above the ground, either through some internal lighter-than-air chambers or natural anti-gravity abilities. Members of this species don't leave tracks and don't trigger any sensors that require weight to activate. They can also easily access a zone directly above them, an action that would be off-limits to a ground-based being without a jump.

Immortal [0]

Some species are extremely long-lived, perhaps to the point that they are effectively immortal. Members of these species aren't affected by the ravages of age during play, and it's possible they've been around hundreds or even thousands of years.

Incorporeal [–3]

Some species have no physical body—they may be extra-dimensional, gaseous, or made of pure energy. Such beings are immune to physical attack. Incorporeal creatures have one type of attack that will still affect them, such as electro-magnetic energy, lasers, or wooden weapons. This must be specified when building the species. An incorporeal being can move easily through incredibly tiny spaces, but normally not through solid objects. A being of this type can't pick up, hold, or interact with any corporeal item.

Invisibility [–4]

Some species are completely undetectable by normal sight. This grants members of this species a +4 to Stealth rolls. Beings that use sight in combat suffer a –2 penalty when attempting to hit a member of this species in hand-to-hand combat and a –4 when attempting to hit with a ranged weapon. Beings that use senses other than sight are unimpaired.

Keen Sense [–1]

Many species have far greater ability with a particular sense than the galactic norm. Pick a particular sense. When making any perception related skill rolls, a member of the species gains a +2 if using their chosen sense. Multiple senses may be enhanced by taking this ability more than once.

Leap [–1]

Some species can leap prodigious distances. Members of this species gain a +2 bonus when using Athletics to jump.

Low Light Vision [–1]

Many species have eye structures that are better than average at seeing in dark conditions. Species with this ability can ignore darkness aspects, except for aspects coming from the complete absence of light (such as PITCH BLACK).

Missing Sense [+1]

Not all species share the same senses. Some lack hearing or sight. This restriction can be taken for multiple senses, granting a +1 refresh for each sense. The GM may assess penalties up to –4 whenever the character is attempting something that requires the missing sense.

Natural Weapon [–1 to –5]

Some species are equipped with fangs, claws, spines, or other natural weapons. At a cost of –1, the species has some natural weapon that inflicts Damage: 1. Each additional –1 increases the damage rating, up to Damage: 4. If the attack is ranged, such as spines that can be flung at an opponent, this ability has an additional cost of –1.

Never Sleep [0]

Some species don't need sleep. Members of these species can be considered alert at all times. Additionally, any task that normally takes a few days or longer is reduced one step on the time scale (page 65, ***Doing Things*** chapter) if the character devotes himself to it full time.

No Arms [+4]

Some species have no limbs capable of grasping and manipulating objects. This causes the obvious disadvantages, and the GM can assess penalties of up to –4 when such a being attempts a task that normally requires arms.

No Natural Attack [+1]

Some species have no natural weapons, not even hard bone to make a fist. These species may not raise their Fists skill above a rank of Fair (+2).

Poisoned by Substance [+1 or +2]

Some normally harmless substances are poisonous to particular species. The amount of refresh this grants depends on how common the substance is. Something that's relatively rare—a particular plant, chemical, cleaning solution—grants a +1, while something common—salt, plastic, glass—grants a +2. Just coming in contact with the substance causes 1 stress, and every round the creature remains in contact continues to inflict 1 additional stress.

Psychological Weakness [+1]

Many species share a biological propensity for certain mental states, which can be a disadvantage at times when dealing with other species. The particular weakness should be determined for each species—a tendency to get in fights, an inability to resist a reward, etc. The GM can compel this attribute as if it were an aspect *once per session*. If the player wishes to avoid this compel, she must spend *two* fate points to refuse. Check out the ***Aspects*** chapter for more on compels (page 55).

Reduced Speed [+1 or +2]

Some species are particularly slow, either because they lack normal means of locomotion or because they have unusually poor reflexes. Moving even within the same zone in combat requires a supplemental action, and moving just one zone requires all of the character's concentration and an Athletics roll. No additional actions may be taken. Characters with this ability may not move more than two zones in a single round. If this ability is taken at a cost of +2, members of this species have an additional –2 penalty to Alertness for the purposes of determining initiative.

Regeneration [0]

No wound is permanent for species with this ability. Even extreme consequences will heal given enough time—usually a couple of years, but sometimes as fast as a few months. Even lost limbs or organs will regrow.

Shapeshifting [-1, -2, or -4]

Some species can radically change their form. There are three separate abilities that fall under this heading. Changing shape requires a supplemental action (page 70, *Doing Things* chapter).

Single Form Shapeshift [-1]: Members of this species can transform from one form into a single other form. Determine what the secondary form is and create a new skill configuration that applies to this form. The primary and secondary forms must have the same power level (page 51, *Crew Creation* chapter). Use the same number of skills as the primary form, but reassign the skills higher or lower. Once set, this skill configuration doesn't change except through advancement.

Mimicry [-2]: This species is adept at mimicking observed forms. A member of this species can change shape to mimic the appearance of another species or individual, so precisely that a casual observer won't be able to tell the difference. The shapeshifters can't change mass, but they can do tricky things like increase or decrease density to take larger or smaller forms. The mimicry is good enough to grant a +4 to Deceit rolls when trying to convince others that you're the being whose form you've taken on. Mimicry has no affect on a character's skill configuration.

True Shapeshifting [-4]: This species is a true shapeshifter, able to change form into any object or being at will. Members of the species can take on the shape of virtually any living or nonliving thing; however, as with mimicry, they can't change mass. A character with this ability gains a +4 to Deceit or Stealth rolls when attempting to avoid detection using shapeshifting. For each form, true shapeshifters can also shuffle their skill configurations just as with the single form version.

Short Lived [+2]

Some species have very short lifespans. They typically only live for a few years before dying of old age. If a game lasts longer than a few years of in-game time, any character from this species will pass away before the game is over.

Social Disadvantage [+1]

Some species suffer from a disadvantage when dealing with other species in a social setting. This can be because of a particularly pungent smell, an unusual linguistic mindset that leads to constant misunderstandings, or just a bad reputation in general among other galactic species. The character suffers a −1 penalty when making social interaction rolls with characters of a species other than her own.

Special Attack [-2]

Some species have exceptional dangerous abilities for self-defense, such as emitting a scent that incapacitates most other species, a piercing shriek that deafens another being, or the ability to blind an opponent. Poison bites or claws also fall into this category, including species that can infect others with a rare disease. Once per fight on a successful hit, characters with this ability may place an immediate consequence on their opponent related to the special attack type (POISONED, DEAFENED, etc.) in addition to any normal damage. Only the lowest available consequence will be used.

Specialized Respiration [+1]

Some species must breathe a particular combination of gases that differs from the normal oxygen/nitrogen mix found on most inhabited planets and aboard space stations and star ships. Such species must carry their particular breathable atmosphere with them in some way or they will begin to suffocate.

Stunt [-1]

Any species ability that is the equivalent of a stunt may be taken for a −1 cost. A species may take an existing stunt as an ability, or create a new stunt using the rules in the Creating Stunts section (page 107, *Stunts* chapter).

Unable to Move [+2]

Some species have no means of locomotion. They must have some artificial device to aid them or be assisted by another being in order to move at all.

Vulnerability [+1 to +3]

Some species are particularly vulnerable to damage. The cost for this ability varies based on how vulnerable the species is. This vulnerability applies only to a certain type of damage—energy weapons, projectiles, or hand-to-hand damage. Each point added to refresh by this vulnerability represents a +1 Damage added to attacks of that type. A single species cannot have more than a +3 Damage applied to a single attack type.

Restriction: If the species is only vulnerable to a narrow range of damage, such as only stabbing melee attacks, the restriction counts as a −1 against cost.

Crew Creation

To play **Bulldogs!**, you get together with the rest of your group to create your ship, its captain, and the crew. As a player, you'll be taking the role of one of these crew members. The crew creation process gets you thinking about who this character is, where he or she came from, what his or her goals and ideals are, and so forth, as well as what he or she is good at doing.

Some details get determined collectively by the group:

Ship: determine what type of ship your crew is aboard, and what its strengths and weaknesses are.

Captain: who's the captain of your ship? This individual will have a lot of influence over the characters after play begins.

Power Level: this determines the starting skill level and refresh rate of the characters in your game.

Each player, except the GM, creates a single character to play:

Species: choose an alien species to which your character belongs. This is important later when you're building character aspects and stunts.

Aspects: come up with ten aspects for your character. These aspects are the most important facet of character generation, as they shape the story of who your character is.

Skills: decide what your character is good at and not so good at.

Stunts: pick special abilities that modify your skills.

> The Crew Creation section assumes a couple of things about your crew:
>
> 1: They're all flying around the galaxy on a ship.
> 2: They're employed by TransGalaxy in Class D Freight.
>
> These two things are the default assumptions to start playing **Bulldogs!**, but they're not necessary to play. For advice on creating different types of games, take a look at *Other Campaign Settings* (page 161, ***Running the Game*** chapter).

Ship

This decision should be made by the entire gaming group—GM included—and everyone should have some input. After all, your characters will be spending at least half their time aboard your starship. Your characters will be flying a Class D freighter. TransGalaxy, an interstellar shipping company, runs a cargo operation they call Class D Freight. The company buys cheap ships, crews them with anyone who applies, and insures the hell out of them. These ships run high-risk cargo—hazardous or volatile materials, deliveries to hot zones or hostile planets, etc. The idea is to make good money on the deliveries that actually arrive, and to collect insurance on those that fail. The crews of these Class D ships are nicknamed "bulldogs" because of the Class D Freight logo. Class D crews also have a reputation for not letting go once they've got hold of a job.

Your crew starts on a freighter of dubious space-worthiness. In this step, you collectively determine the specifics of the ship, represented as aspects. All of the players, including the GM, participate in this process. No one player, even the GM, has a final say.

Your ship gets three aspects. Answer the following questions, creating a ship aspect for each one.

Concept: The first aspect describes the ship generally. Is it an old clunker? A newer ship with something wrong with it? Cobbled together from scrap? Choose an aspect that gives a good general description of the vessel.

Problem: Next, decide what's wrong with this ship. No Class D ship is in tip-top shape. Does the power cut out at inconvenient times? Is the ship particularly slow? Do parts just fall off? Choose an aspect related to the biggest problem the ship has.

Strength: Finally, all ships have some redeeming features. What's this ship's secret strength? Does it have some extra juice right when you need it? Are there hard-to-find nooks and crannies where you can stow contraband? Is it deceptively fast or maneuverable? Can it stand up to massive punishment? Choose an aspect that describes the ship's hidden strength.

Example: A group of players sits down to create a Bulldogs! crew. The first step is to generate their ship. They start to brainstorm about what type of ship they want.

Michael (the GM): So, this is Class D, the ship will be in bad shape.

Alison: Yeah, I'm thinking a real junker. Something that's been flying for a really long time.

Nick: An old ship that's got so many recycled parts that it barely resembles what it was when it came off the line. That sounds good.

Eryn: For the first aspect, how about "THIS THING STILL FLIES?"

Michael: Cool. For the problem aspect, let's go with what Nick said. How about NO ORIGINAL PARTS.

Eryn: That's good. This thing is a flying hunk of junk. So what should be its one redeeming feature?

Alison: Maybe it's got some hidden reserves of speed. Given its overall crappiness, I'd like to be able to get away from a fight rather than have to stay with the ship falling apart all around us.

Nick: How about DECEPTIVELY FAST?

Michael: Awesome. Let's note down all of these aspects on the character sheets, and I'll fill in the ship sheet. How about a name?

Alison: Something that sounds way cooler than this ship deserves. We get to name it, right?

Michael: Your captain does, anyway. You guys as players get to decide right now what it's called.

Eryn: How about the *Black Watch*?

Michael: Sounds cool. If everyone is agreed, that's the name.

Captain

This is the second step that all of the players complete collectively. The ship's captain is usually portrayed by the GM. This is because the crew of a Class D vessel generally doesn't have much of a say in where they go and what they do. A certain adversarial relationship usually exists between a Class D captain and his crew.

Assuming the captain is a non-player character, answer the following questions, creating an aspect for the captain for each one.

Concept: Who is the captain? When deciding this, think about these questions. What kind of person ends up as a captain in Class D? What sort of past did this person have that got him or her here? How did the captain's past actions lead to this? No one aspires to be in Class D, not even the captain. This first aspect should give a glimpse of the person behind the office and describe the captain in a short phrase.

Trouble: All Class D captains cause problems. How does the captain make life difficult for the crew? Does the captain have personal habits or quirks that cause trouble? Does the captain's past come to haunt the entire ship's crew? This should be a very compellable aspect.

Leadership: Finally, a captain is in charge. The question is, how does the captain lead? Is the captain a strict disciplinarian? Completely lackadaisical? Does the captain play favorites? This aspect describes the main relationship the captain has with the crew.

We're assuming that your captain is a non-player character. This works well for an initial **Bulldogs!** game because the GM can use this captain character to create more problems and interesting situations for the players. Although the group has a bit less autonomy, they'll end up trying to do their best in a situation where the captain is more of an adversary than a team member.

You can have a player take the role of the captain if you like. Just make up the captain as a normal character using the rules in this chapter. Make sure you choose the player taking this role carefully. If the player isn't comfortable with a leadership role or if the other players are going to have issues with taking orders from this player, it'll create a bad situation. Ensure that all the players are on board with having one character have authority over the rest, and that the captain player is comfortable being in charge.

Michael: Now we need to generate our crew's captain. Again, this is Class D, so this guy is down on his luck.

Eryn: I'm thinking a former military officer. A real hard-ass.

Nick: I like that. Let's make him a Templari, then he's got a real reason to be desperate. Nobody in the Frontier Zone likes those guys.

Alison: Cool. He's got a military tattoo on his scalp, right behind his left ear. All Templari ex-military guys have those.

Michael: Did you just make that up? I'm writing that down. I like that detail. So what's the concept aspect we want for this guy?

Eryn: I guess it's a guy.

Michael: Sounds like it, so far. Everyone OK with that?

Eryn: Sure. I just wanted that out there. Here's my idea for the first aspect: EX-NOVA LEGION OFFICER.

Nick: That's good, but why's he in Class D? Why did he leave the Nova Legion?

Alison: Maybe we don't know. I doubt he's the sharing type. He's been disgraced in some way, but it's a secret.

Eryn: OK, DISGRACED EX-NOVA LEGION OFFICER.

Michael: So noted. How about problems?

Nick: Here's a hint for why he's disgraced: the trouble aspect MEAN DRUNK.

Alison: Awesome! That's going to cause problems, all right.

Michael: Now for his leadership style. He's ex-military, and he's now in charge of a ship that's bottom of the barrel. They let anyone aboard these things. How does he handle that?

Eryn: I'm thinking STRICT DISCIPLINARIAN.

Alison: Not hard enough. How about BETTER TO BE FEARED THAN LOVED?

Eryn: Oh, yeah. That's better than mine.

Michael: Everyone agree? Great. Note all of these down on your character sheets. I'll flesh him out a bit more later. I'll just pick a name from the Templari lists: Jocaar Laf't.

Power Level

You can customize the power level of the characters in your game. Starting lower gives your character a lot more room to grow before becoming a planet-killing super man, but it can be fun starting at a high power level as well. Each level indicates three things:

Refresh: Your character's starting refresh is the number of fate points you have in a pool at the beginning of play. Starting refresh goes down depending on the alien species and stunts you choose, later in the process. You never start with a refresh less than 1.

Skill Points: The number of skill points determines how powerful your character is at the beginning of play. The more points you have available to spend, the higher your character's skills will be.

Skill Cap: This is the maximum level your top skill can be as a starting character. The GM can raise the skill cap later through advancement, but for now your character can't exceed this maximum skill level.

Fresh Meat
6 refresh, 20 skill points, skill cap at Great (+4)

At this level you're just getting started with your adventuring life. You're Fresh Meat. As Fresh Meat you're going to have to work hard to keep yourself alive. On the other hand, you've got a lot of potential for growth; characters starting here can run for many sessions in a long campaign before they start to seem overpowered.

Trouble
7 refresh, 25 skill points, skill cap at Great (+4)

Now you know just enough to be dangerous. Now, you're Trouble. You might not be all that experienced, but at least you have a bit of a reputation to maintain. You still have good growth potential but aren't wet behind the ears. Take it easy on big threats, but you can at least hold your own.

Hard Boiled
8 refresh, 30 skill points, skill cap at Superb (+5)

At this point, you're a known quantity in the star lanes. You're a Hard Boiled spacer. You're likely extremely good at what you do and have a reputation for doing it. You can take on heavy hitters and likewise attract a lot of resistance. There's less room to move up, but you won't have to worry too much about lesser threats.

Serious Badass
10 refresh, 35 skill points, skill cap at Superb (+5)

You're a major-leaguer; you're one of the guys they send in when it hits the fan. You are a Serious Badass. There's very little in this galaxy that you need to fear. They should fear *you* instead. It's hard to move up from this level; you're already one of the galaxy's best. This level is great for a short game or a one-shot, however.

Example: The group now decides on the power level for their characters.

Eryn: I don't want us to be too new, so I don't like Fresh Meat. On the other hand, I'm not sure I want to be marauding around at the top level right at the start.

Michael: So no Serious Badass either. What does everyone think between Trouble and Hard Boiled?

Nick: Well, I'm thinking we should be relatively new. I'm leaning toward Trouble.

Michael: Any objections? All right, Trouble it is. Make sure you note down the refresh level on your sheet; that's going to be important as we continue making characters.

TRANS
GALAXY

Species

Check out the list of alien species in the ***Alien Species*** chapter (page 19) and pick one of these species for your character. If you don't see one you like, you can create your own using the rules at the end of that chapter. Your species gives you some special abilities that change your starting refresh. Adjust your refresh according to the cost listed next to species abilities, and note down the special powers you have based on your species. Your species is important once you start choosing aspects, as well.

Example: Nick now starts on his own character. The players have discussed the various roles on board the ship—pilot, engineer, etc. Nick's character is the pilot.

Now that he knows his role, his first step is to choose a species. He thinks briefly about being an Urseminite, but he'd like to be a little more heroic than that, and he doesn't want to play against type quite that much. He decides he'd like to be a Ryjyllian.

He notes down the Ryjyllian species ability. He's starting with 7 refresh since the group chose the Trouble starting power level. The base Ryjyllian package costs –3 and Nick decides not to get the optional RYJYLLIAN COMBAT FOCUS ability. As a pilot, he's not going to need that much fighting power, and Nick wants to keep his refresh up a bit. He notes that his refresh rate is 4 after choosing his species.

Aspects

Your aspects should give a sense of who your character really is. They describe her origins, the things that are important to her, aspects of her personality (like a bad temper or a strict code of honor), and so forth. Because aspects are so important in defining who your character is, we devote more time—and more structure—to coming up with aspects than we do for other parts of character creation. Choosing your aspects should be done before you choose your stunts or skills. It's broken down into several steps.

If you're familiar with another FATE game like **Spirit of the Century** or the **Dresden Files RPG**, you're probably used to a more backstory-based, collaborative method for choosing aspects. In **Bulldogs!** we've made this process more individualized. We still recommend creating characters together, but you can generate characters almost completely on your own using the system in this book.

There are two reasons for this. First, **Bulldogs!** characters often don't have an extensive shared history. Their history together is mostly aboard their current ship, and this method allows you to start from the moment the crew is pulled together. Second, the collaborative method is a bit more time-consuming and doesn't have as much guidance in how to create character aspects. The process in **Bulldogs!** is much faster and most players have an easier time coming up with aspects using the process here.

Heritage

Choosing or creating your species is a major decision. A Hacragorkan is significantly different in tone and feel from an Arsubaran, and both are significantly different from a Saldrallan or a Tetsuashan. Different species have different role-playing implications based on racial history and cultural norms. Your species shouldn't be a straitjacket, however. While your species suggests certain aspects, you're by no means restricted to choosing from the list presented for your species; feel free to come up with your own aspects that are similar in nature or implied by the species write-up.

Player Rules: Choose two aspects from the list presented with your species write-up, or choose two aspects of your own that stem from your racial background. It's possible, for example, that an Arsubaran might choose FORMER SLAVE as a species aspect, if he came from a world where Arsubarans are treated as slaves.

Example: Nick's character is a Ryjyllian, so Nick has to decide on two Ryjyllian aspects to add to his sheet. He doesn't want to venture too far afield, so he picks two off the list: CAT-LIKE REFLEXES and SHORT TEMPER.

Character Background

While your species defines your character to a certain extent, nature only extends so far before nurture kicks in. Your character's personal past—the events and people that got her where she is today—is far more important than her ethnic background and therefore generates more aspects.

Player Rules: Choose four aspects based on your character's background. If you need some help thinking about your character's background, follow these steps:

Homeworld: What planet did your character grow up on? This isn't necessarily the world that your species calls home, and it might not be a planet at all. Some people are raised on space stations, moons, asteroids, or even on starships. Choose one aspect based on your homeworld.

Personal Strength: What is your character really good at? Is he unusually resilient? Does he have a nose for finding the truth? Is he good with machines? Good with people? An ace pilot? Does he know games of chance inside and out? Choose one aspect based on your personal strength.

Personal Weakness: Everyone has flaws; what are your character's? Does he drink too much? Gamble too much? Is he sickly, or gullible? Does he have trouble holding onto money? Does he have an unusual body odor? Choose one aspect based on your personal weakness.

Former Associates: While your character was growing up, she was bound to meet other people. Who are they? A former associate can be anyone—a family member, a good friend, an illicit contact, someone to whom you owe a great deal of money, or that guy who wants you dead. Choose one aspect based on your former associates.

> The Former Associates aspect is great for introducing elements of your character's past that the GM can use to generate adventures that are personally engaging for your character. You want these characters to be interesting and to cause the right kind of complications, since they're certain to show up in your character's future story.

Example: Nick decides his character, who he's named Prbrawl, came from the Ryjyllian homeworld. Ryjyl is described as an icy planet, so Nick thinks that the harsh conditions on the planet have shaped Prbrawl's character. He picks the aspect TOUGH IT OUT as the homeworld aspect.

As the pilot of the *Black Watch*, Nick decides Prbrawl is a natural leader. For his strength, Nick chooses the aspect LEAD BY EXAMPLE.

Now for Prbrawl's personal weakness. As a Ryjyllian with the difficult childhood implied by the first aspect, Nick decides Prbrawl's main problem is that he holds everyone to his own high standards. He chooses NO TIME FOR WEAKNESS as the aspect for this step.

For the last part of this section, Nick decides that Prbrawl's prickly nature has led to some problems with crewmates in the past. His short temper combined with contempt for others who don't live up to his standards seems a recipe for resentment. Nick chooses an aspect that gives Prbrawl some old rivals and enemies, OLD UNDERLINGS OUT FOR REVENGE. These underlings aren't named and the aspect is vague, so there could be more than one. This should give the GM a lot to work with.

Sample Background Aspects

Some Homeworld aspects:

Born on the Ass-End of Space

Invoke: you know a lot about your obscure corner of the galaxy, "Oh, sure, everyone knows about the Gelnyki System."

Compel: you're a galactic hick, "Wow, Arsubar sure does have a lot of people. Where's my wallet?"

"You call this cold?"

Invoke: the harsh conditions on your home world have toughened you up, "I know we don't have any winter survival gear, but I can probably reach there in an hour. I won't freeze."

Compel: you've got no time for coddled weaklings from more hospitable worlds, "Come on, it's only 30 degrees below. A walk in the park!"

Used to Fighting Gravity

Invoke: everything else seems easy by comparison, "It's like walking on air up here!"

Compel: sometimes you overestimate the force required, "A good strong push and—whoops! Sorry about the bulkhead."

Pleasure Station Outlook

Invoke: you know what people want, "I know the signs. He's in withdrawal."

Compel: lack of a cushy lifestyle now, "I haven't had my hair done in days! This is intolerable!"

Some Personal Strength aspects:

"Keys? Who needs keys?"

Invoke: you can get things started without keys, "Just attach this, plug this in, tap here, and…voila!"

Compel: when you do need keys, "You forgot the keys again, didn't you."

Discipline Is Power

Invoke: your self-discipline enables you to succeed, "You don't understand. I'm in control, that's why I win."

Compel: chaos can wreck your strength, "We have no control over the situation! I don't know what to do!"

Fear Is for the Weak

Invoke: you feel no fear, "I don't care about the odds."

Compel: when you feel fear, you feel weak, "I can't believe it. I'm afraid of her."

Could Sell Salt to a Tetsuashan

Invoke: you're the greatest salesman that ever lived, "One time only, get it while it's hot."

Compel: Tetsuashans get pissed when they realize they just bought salt, "It was just a misunderstanding! No need to get hot under the collar."

Some Personal Weakness aspects:

Hopelessly Addicted

Invoke: you'll do anything to get what you need, "I need this paycheck, so I won't quit."

Compel: you can't do without the stuff, "I'm almost out. This is a disaster!"

Small and Insignificant

Invoke: nothing to see here, "No. Nobody's here."

Compel: you can't get people to notice you, "Excuse me! Excuse me! Oh, never mind."

Rubs People the Wrong Way

Invoke: if you want to get someone's dander up, "What's the matter? Can't take a little criticism?"

Compel: you need a friend, "What? We're not pals?"

Stalked by the Reaper

Invoke: when you want to kill someone, "You messed with the wrong guy."

Compel: your buddies keep dying all around you, "Oh, no, Mercury! Not you, too!"

Some Former Associates aspects:

Friends in Low Places

Invoke: low places are sometimes where things get done, "Don't worry. I know a guy."

Compel: the authorities view you as a person of interest, "We knew you were in town, and that's why we knew you were up to something."

Ryjyllians Don't Like Me

Invoke: you want to piss off a Ryjyllian, "What's that, cat face? Got a problem?"

Compel: Ryjyllians can be bad news, "Oh, man. That's Leo's Legion. They hate me."

Arrik Maspeth Killed My Father

Invoke: you finally got the son of a bitch in your sights, "I have you now, Maspeth."

Compel: Maspeth wants to finish the job, "Ah, the Valerian brat. I can finally tie up loose ends."

Jolek Owns My Debt

Invoke: people don't want to cross Jolek, "Wait, aren't you the guy who's in Jolek's pocket? Never mind."

Compel: Jolek calls it in, "Time to settle up, my friend. Or take a trip to the bottom of the Gorth Sea."

Current Berth

Now that you've thought about how you got to where you are now, it's time to think about where you are now. Collaborate with the other players on this section—after all, you *are* all signed on to this berth. This doesn't mean that you should give up on a really cool idea; in fact, if you have something unique in mind for your character, work with the rest of the group to make it happen in a way that complements their characters' stories, rather than limiting them.

Player Rules: Choose four aspects based on your current berth. If you need some help, you can use the following steps:

Desperate Situation: No one joins Class D on a whim or because they're seeking adventure. The only people in Class D are those who are so desperate they have no other choice. What led to this? What problem is your character running from? Why couldn't you find a job on any other ship? Are you traveling under an assumed name? What happened that was so terrible you signed your life away for five years?

Job: What do you do in your current berth? Are you the first mate? The cook? The captain? A stowaway? The muscle? What you do for a living is important, even if it's a short-term job. If it *is* a short-term job, you might choose an aspect based on having a string of such jobs.

Shipmates: Who do you spend your days with? What kind of people are they? Who are the people above you, and who do you have authority over? Do you travel with pirates or honest merchants? Do you trust your shipmates? Do you like them? Think about the people you interact with on a regular basis. Who are your co-workers, your friends and acquaintances, the people you avoid, and the people who tell you what to do?

Captain: Who are you working for, anyway? Even if you don't answer directly to the captain, it's still important to think about this. A no-nonsense, humorless authoritarian runs a very different ship than does an easygoing rebel. What kind of relationship do you have with him? Are you a trusted ally, or simply another fare to ferry from one destination to another? Does your captain inspire confidence? Are you the captain?

Example: Nick continues creating Prbrawl's aspects. He figures that some of those old underlings from the previous aspect got one in on his character, bringing proceedings against Prbrawl in the Pilot's Guild and securing a judgment against him. He creates the aspect BLACKBALLED BY THE PILOT'S GUILD as a Desperate Situation.

Despite his prickly personality, Prbrawl's a good pilot. Nick assigns PRECISION IS THE PILOT'S FRIEND as his Job aspect.

Now the group discusses Shipmates aspects. Nick sees Prbrawl as taking a bit of a fatherly role aboard the ship, maybe more than his crewmates prefer. The other players are good with that. One of the other players is building a character named Annabelle Quinn, a new crewmate with secrets to keep, so Nick puts SHIELD QUINN FROM THE CAPTAIN as his Shipmates aspect.

Lastly, Nick thinks that Prbrawl's relationship with the captain is relatively good. He's proven himself to the drunken Templari, so he chooses AT LEAST PRBRAWL IS RELIABLE as his Captain aspect.

The Shipmates and Captain aspects should have the most crossover with other players. If your Shipmates aspect doesn't mention another player character by name, you may want to rethink it. This helps tie your character to the rest of the group and strongly influences how the game goes once you start.

If the captain is a non-player character, take a look at the aspects that were established for her in the earlier section. How will your character interact with this captain? If the captain is another player's character, think about your unique relationship with that character.

If a player takes the role of the captain, her Shipmates aspect should deal with her attitude toward the whole crew. Her Captain aspect then refers to her own relationship with her job.

Sample Current Berth Aspects

Some Desperate Situation aspects:

APPARENTLY, MURDER IS A CRIME

Invoke: when you want to kill someone, "I cut that guy down on Arsubar, I don't mind doing it here."

Compel: there's also a bounty, "You're worth a lot of money, buddy, so get comfortable."

"I GOTTA GET AWAY FROM DROOGIE."

Invoke: you keep things moving, "All done! Let's pack up and get out of here."

Compel: Droogie will find you eventually, "Hey, doll. Remember me?"

THROWN OUT OF THE ACADEMY

Invoke: you got in in the first place, "I really am brilliant."

Compel: your methods are unconventional to say the least, "Don't worry about side effects, I'm sure it'll be fine."

NO ONE WANTS A BLIND PILOT

Invoke: amazingly, you can still fly, "She has an instinctual way with the controls. Uncanny."

Compel: you're still a blind pilot, "Look out! I mean, uh, listen to the proximity alarm!"

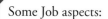

Some Job aspects:

Baddest Captain Around
Invoke: no one holds a candle, "That's why they pay me the big bucks."
Compel: your crew doesn't appreciate it, "We're sick of your crap, captain."

I Keep This Clunker Working
Invoke: they need you in Class D, "How did you get this thing off the ground?"
Compel: you're a busy man, "Smithy! That power coupling cable on deck two went out again!"

"You won't get past me."
Invoke: best protection around, "Going somewhere?"
Compel: crewmates may not like you, "The captain says you're staying aboard."

I Know All the Hidey-Holes
Invoke: help the crew earn a little extra cash, "I've got a nice stash of banned Ryjyllian ice wine we can unload at our destination."
Compel: you hid something you shouldn't have, "Oh, yeah. Looks like some of the contraband got loose."

Some Shipmates aspects:

"Rolley's my brother"
Invoke: you've got his back, always, "Behind you, Rolley! I've got him!"
Compel: they can get at you through Rolley, "We have your friend. Come alone."

Me and Mrioç, We're Unstoppable
Invoke: nothing can stop you, obviously, "Let's take 'em down!"
Compel: not even your employer, "Wait! Get back on this ship! Stop!"

"I like these people, but I don't trust them."
Invoke: they're Class D, not really trustworthy, "Nice try, Benny. Put the card back up your sleeve."
Compel: you can't let them guard your back, "No way. If I go, we all go."

Secretly in Love with Dahlia Sohn
Invoke: you're inspired by love, "I saw him sneaking up on you, Dahlia."
Compel: she'll never know, "I saw this cute guy on station. See you later!"

Some Captain aspects:

"I'd follow Barrett into Hell."
Invoke: you are inspired, "Barrett says go, we go!"
Compel: he might just lead you into Hell, "In here? If you say so."

I Should Be the Captain
Invoke: take a chance to win big, "I say leave him behind. Who's with me?"
Compel: you undermine him every chance you get, "We haven't been paid lately. I can't be the only one who's noticed."

Looking for Someone to Follow
Invoke: and you'll take whoever looks likely, "You've got a plan? OK, I'm in."
Compel: who you follow changes often, "We did it your way last time. This time I like Coran's plan."

Ship, Crew, Everything Else
Invoke: you'll keep this thing together, "I don't give a damn about TransGalaxy. We get off this rock now."
Compel: in that order, "You've jeopardized this ship. That means you've got to go."

Skills

Aspects flesh your character out and give an overall sense of his personality and capabilities. However, skills really determine what your character is good at, and what he's not so good at. Nearly any action you take in the game requires a skill roll, so it's important to choose skills that are both useful to you and representative of the kind of character you want to play. During crew creation, you can choose skills for your character according to the following guidelines. Any skills you don't explicitly choose default to a rating of Mediocre (+0).

The complete list of skills and their descriptions is found in its own chapter (page 84, **Skills** chapter).

Skill Packages

Depending on the power level of your game, a character gets between 20 and 35 skill points to spend. You may not buy any skills at a level higher than the skill cap for your game's power level. Take a look at your game's power level (page 45) and choose a package from one of the following lists.

Fresh Meat

These are the 20 skill point packages you can choose from:

Well-Rounded: 11 total skills: 3 at Good (+3), 3 at Fair (+2), 5 at Average (+1).
Strong Focus: 10 total skills: 1 at Great (+4), 2 at Good (+3), 3 at Fair (+2), 4 at Average (+1).
Extra Focused: 8 total skills: 2 at Great (+4), 2 at Good (+3), 2 at Fair (+2), 2 at Average (+1).

Trouble

These are the 25 skill point packages you can choose from:

Wide Ranging: 13 total skills: 4 at Good (+3), 4 at Fair (+2), 5 at Average (+1).
Focused: 14 total skills: 1 at Great (+4), 2 at Good (+3), 4 at Fair (+2), 7 at Average (+1).
Dual Focus: 12 total skills: 2 at Great (+4), 2 at Good (+3), 3 at Fair (+2), 5 at Average (+1).

Hard Boiled

These are the 30 skill point packages you can choose from:

Jack-of-All-Trades: 15 total skills: 5 at Good (+3), 5 at Fair (+2), 5 at Average (+1).
Well-Rounded: 14 total skills: 2 at Great (+4), 3 at Good (+3), 4 at Fair (+2), 5 at Average (+1).
Strong Focus: 12 total skills: 3 at Great (+4), 3 at Good (+3), 3 at Fair (+2), 3 at Average (+1).
Expert: 10 total skills: 2 at Superb (+5), 2 at Great (+4), 2 at Good (+3), 2 at Fair (+2), 2 at Average (+1).

Serious Badass

These are the 35 skill point packages you can choose from:

Jack-of-All-Trades: 19 total skills: 5 Good (+3), 6 Fair (+2), 8 Average (+1).
Well-Rounded: 17 total skills: 3 Great (+4), 3 Good (+3), 3 Fair (+2), 8 Average (+1).
Expert: 15 total skills: 1 Superb (+5), 2 Great (+4), 3 Good (+3), 4 Fair (+2), 5 Average (+1).
Acknowledged Master: 14 total skills: 2 Superb (+5), 2 Great (+4), 2 Good (+3), 3 Fair (+2), 5 Average (+1).

Example: The group chose Trouble as their starting level, so Nick looks at the skill packages available. He wants Prbrawl to be an effective pilot, but also an effective leader. He chooses Dual Focus to get two Great (+4) level skills.

Stunts

Once you have your skills, choose stunts for your character. Each stunt you choose reduces your character's refresh by one. At the beginning of each session and at any refresh point during a session you'll get fate points up to your refresh level—refresh you spend now means fate points you'll have to earn later (page 17, **FATE Basics** chapter). Keep in mind that you can't reduce your character's refresh to less than one. In general, consider spending close to half of your remaining refresh allotment on stunts.

Stunts let you use your skills in ways that go beyond the typical rules; they're discussed more fully in their own chapter (page 107, **Stunts** chapter). You usually choose stunts that are associated with your character's best skills, but you can take stunts tied to any skill— even ones left at default.

Example: Nick takes a look at stunts for Prbrawl. Each character started with a refresh of 7. The Ryjyllian package of species abilities costs –3. Nick chose to forego the Ryjyllian Combat Focus ability, saving him a point of refresh. Prbrawl's refresh is currently 4. If he spends half of this on stunts, he can get two stunts and still have a refresh of 2 when starting play.

Aspects

Characters have a set of attributes called **aspects**. Aspects cover a wide range of elements and should collectively paint a decent picture of *who* your character is, what he's *connected* to, and what's *important* to him. By contrast, skills could be said to paint a similar picture of what your character can *do*.

Aspects can be:

- Relationships (IN TIGHT WITH DOVAN; I'LL GET ONE OVER ON TRISK)
- Beliefs (I AM THE LAW; HIT 'EM WHEN THEY LEAST EXPECT IT)
- Catchphrases (YOU DON'T TOUCH A CORINN; YOU START IT, I END IT)
- Descriptions (UGLY SOB; BIG, MEATY FISTS)
- Items (STARSMITH RIFLE; MY OWN SPECIAL DON JON CUBES)
- Any other phrase that helps paint a picture of your character (LAST SON OF SOLON; READY FOR ACTION)

In terms of game rules, aspects are the main avenue by which you gain or spend **fate points**, a kind of currency that you can spend for bonuses or that you can earn when aspects cause problems for your character.

Your character has ten aspects, as you probably already observed from the previous chapter (page 46, *Crew Creation* chapter). Your ship and your captain have three aspects apiece.

You'll also encounter temporary aspects during play. These could be aspects that apply to the location where you find yourself (for examples, see page 8, *The Galaxy* chapter). They can also be aspects on the scene, such as BROKEN FUEL HOSE or RAGING BLAZE. You can also have temporary aspects placed upon you through maneuvers (page 84, *Skills* chapter) or consequences (page 71, *Doing Things* chapter).

Here's a summary of how aspects can be used in the game:

Invocation

You can invoke an aspect by *spending a fate point*. When you invoke an aspect, explain how it's helpful to you in your current situation. You may then either re-roll all your dice, or add +2 to the roll.

Declaration

You can invoke an aspect outside of a roll by *spending a fate point* to make a **declaration** (page 84, *Skills* chapter). This allows you to add a detail to a scene without making a roll.

Compel

When your aspects put you at a disadvantage, they can be compelled. If you accept the compel and allow the aspect to complicate your choices, you receive a fate point. To refuse a compel, you *spend* a fate point instead.

Tag

On any aspect you create or discover in a scene, you get the first invocation for free—i.e., you don't have to spend a fate point to invoke it.

Using Aspects

To use an aspect, either the player or the GM declares that the aspect is relevant. The next step is to determine if the aspect's relevance works for or against the character who has the aspect. As a general rule of thumb, if it's *for*, the owner spends a fate point. If it's *against*, the owner gains a fate point unless he pays a fate point to avoid it. This is the guiding principle that all specific uses of aspects—invoking and compelling—start from.

Invoking Aspects

When one of your aspects applies to the situation you're in, it can give you a bonus. Doing this requires *spending a fate point* and is called **invoking the aspect**. In this context, the aspect makes your character better at whatever it is he's doing, because the aspect can somehow have an influence on the outcome of the situation. Invoking an aspect can be used to either:

1. Pick up all the dice you rolled and re-roll them, or
2. Leave the dice alone and add +2 to the result.

It's possible to use more than one aspect on a single roll, but you can't use the *same* aspect more than once on the same roll or action; even if you've re-rolled the dice, that's still the same roll. Re-rolls are riskier than just taking the +2 bonus—you can always end up worsening things or not making much improvement—but when a lot of ▬ dice hit the table, a reroll can be a much cheaper way to recover.

The GM is the final arbiter of when an aspect is or is not appropriate. Usually this means you must invoke an aspect that's appropriate to the situation at hand. If you want to invoke an aspect that doesn't immediately seem appropriate, you'll need to describe how the aspect actually does apply to the situation. The GM's priority here isn't to strictly limit the use of aspects; instead, she should encourage their appropriate use by encouraging players to make decisions that keep their aspects interesting.

You aren't limited to invoking aspects on your own sheet. You can invoke aspects on another character, on the scene itself, on the general environment—such as the system or planet where you are—or on the room or ship around you.

Example: Ship grav temporarily fails and a massive pallet of hazardous waste shifts across the cargo bay, directly towards Quinn the co-pilot. Prbrawl sees Quinn about to be pasted and leaps out to push Quinn out of the way of the two ton pallet. He uses his Athletics skill but the dice don't cooperate; he gets a ▬▬▬▬. Prbrawl has an aspect called CAT-LIKE REFLEXES, and it's perfect for this type of physical action. Nick, Prbrawl's player, spends a fate point, invoking Prbrawl's CAT-LIKE REFLEXES, and re-rolls the dice.

This second roll is better: ▣▬▬▣. But Nick knows that a +1 isn't going to be enough to get both Prbrawl and Quinn out of the way of the oncoming pallet. He can't use CAT-LIKE REFLEXES again on the same action, so Nick spends a fate point and tells the GM he wants to use his SHIELD QUINN FROM THE CAPTAIN aspect, since he figures the captain will be angry if Quinn gets hurt. The GM doesn't think this really applies, so Nick needs to pick another aspect instead. He chooses TOUGH IT OUT, changing tactics slightly so that he's less concerned about his own safety, focusing on getting Quinn out of the way.

The GM agrees, and Nick spends another fate point to invoke TOUGH IT OUT for a +2 to the result. His Athletics roll is now a +3, and he's pretty certain he'll be able to knock Quinn out of the way of the oncoming pallet. Getting himself out of this situation is his next dilemma.

Declaration

You can also invoke an aspect to make a **declaration**, using it add something to the story that isn't tied to a die roll or skill use at all. This costs a fate point like any other invocation does. For example, you could invoke a MADE MAN IN THE FALLON SYNDICATE aspect to declare that the gang has some interest on this particular planet.

You can spend a fate point to make a declaration without using an aspect (page 84, **Skills** chapter) but if you invoke one of your aspects you're allowed to do a bit more. For example, if the GM looks skeptical over whether or not you can spend a fate point to declare that you arrive at the exact right moment, invoking your SWOOP IN TO THE RESCUE or GRAND ENTRANCE aspect should remove any of the GM's doubts. That said, this isn't a method for you to get away with anything; as always, aspect invocation is only allowed when the GM approves.

Compelling Aspects

An aspect can also allow you to gain more fate points by bringing complications and troubling circumstances into your character's life. When this occurs, it's referred to as **compelling the aspect**. Usually only one aspect is involved in a compel, but in some unusual circumstances more than one can be compelled for a bigger payout.

The GM often initiates compels. When she compels one of your aspects, she's indicating that your character is in a position where the aspect could create a problem or a difficult choice. However, you can also cause the GM to compel another character's aspects with a similar rationale and results. Sometimes, a compel will even happen by "accident" when you just naturally play out your character's aspects and cause bad things to happen.

When you're the target of a compel, you can negotiate the terms a bit, especially if the compel is going against your vision of your character. For the most part, compels make the story much more interesting, so don't turn every compel into an opportunity for an extended argument. Once the terms are set, you have a choice. You can *spend a fate point* and ignore the aspect, or take the consequences and limitations on your choices and *receive a fate point*. When you accept the fate point, the aspect is officially **compelled**.

> **GMs:** Be familiar with your players' aspects and compel them during play. This is how you make the story interesting and you shouldn't be shy about leaning hard on your players' compellable aspects. They'll thank you for it!
>
> **Players:** If there's an aspect that could be compelled, remind the GM about it. This is how you get fate points!

There are a few ways an aspect can complicate a character's life via compels—it limits responses available to a character in certain situations, it introduces unintended complications into a scene, or it provides inspiration for a plot development or a scene hook for the character.

Limitations

An aspect may limit actions and choices. If your character is in a situation where he would normally have a number of choices, and limiting those choices to act in accordance with his aspect is going to make more trouble for him, that's grounds to compel the aspect.

It's important to note that an aspect may dictate the *type* of action, but it usually shouldn't dictate the *precise* action, which is always the player's decision. In this way, the compel highlights the difficulty of the choices at hand by placing limits on those choices.

Example: Brunda has an aspect indicating her PUGNACIOUS nature. The customs officer is giving her a hard time about paperwork, probably angling for a bribe. Brunda could lose her cool over the bureaucratic BS, pissing off the customs officer and causing big problems for the delivery, so the GM compels her PUGNACIOUS aspect, saying, "His weasel face keeps yammering. It's setting you off. Maybe you should tell him what you think of his rules…" and sliding forward a fate point.

If Brunda accepts the fate point, her PUGNACIOUS aspect dictates how she'll respond in this situation, limiting her choices. Maybe she'll tell the customs guy where to stick it, or maybe she'll pop him in the face—that's her choice—but however she reacts, her tendency to be PUGNACIOUS should dominate her actions.

Then again, she's already in dutch with the captain, and she knows her crewmates won't appreciate it if she assaults a port official; she may not want that kind of trouble, so maybe she should spend a fate point and choke down her rage…

Complications

An aspect may also *complicate* a situation, rather than directly limiting a character's choices. If everything is going along normally and the aspect makes things more difficult or introduces an unexpected twist, that's also grounds for a compel. In come cases, complications may suggest that certain consequences are mandated, such as failing at a particular action without a skill roll—perhaps the character would succeed at a defense roll against a Deceit action, but his BORN ON THE ASS-END OF SPACE aspect is compelled, forcing a failure if he accepts it.

Example: Annabelle Quinn has the aspect PLAGUED BY POOR JUDGMENT. The crew is attempting to track down an elusive passenger when Quinn meets a shifty fellow who claims to know where the passenger is. His condition is that Quinn follow him down this dark corridor, alone. The GM puts down a fate point, saying, "Sounds good to you; why don't you go with him and turn this into a PLAGUED BY POOR JUDGMENT moment?"

Quinn's player, Alison, considers this. She's running low on fate points, and this guy doesn't look all that dangerous. Quinn's an ex-pirate and handy with a gun. On the other hand, he may have accomplices, and this is likely to lead to the rest of the crew having to come find her, if it turns out she can't handle it by herself.

Alison decides she can live with that and takes the fate point. "That's great, pal! Lead the way."

GM-Driven Compels

Some compels are used to directly drive the story in one way or another and, as such, are really the province of the GM. The aspects of the player characters offer great ideas for creat adventures and provide the basis for scenes.

This means that sometimes an aspect may add a complication "offscreen," such as when the GM decides to use a character's personal nemesis as the villain for a session or to give the character an unpleasant responsibility or assignment. She might also use a character's aspect to justify a particular "hook" for a future scene. When this happens, it counts as a compel.

GMs shouldn't rely on a player's *particular* response to this kind of compel to drive a plot—remember, *the purpose of a compel is to create drama, not force people into things.* Keep in mind that a player can always negotiate the terms of a compel—he might have an even better idea for a dramatic way to start a scene or move the story along.

Sometimes, it may seem as though there's no practical way to buy out of a "scenestarter" compel. Suppose you have the aspect MY DEAR BROTHER, and the GM proposes a compel with, "Hey, so you find your brother beaten to a pulp and left in your airlock, with a note that says 'Don't plan on taking any long trips' on him." It would be pretty lame to spend a fate point and suggest that it doesn't even happen.

Keep in mind, though, that when you buy out of a compel, you're really buying out of the potential complication that could arise from what's proposed. You're giving yourself the option of a response that's not as dramatic. So you don't have to say, "No, my brother doesn't show up in the airlock." You might say, "Man, I've got a lot going on right now in this story… look, here's a fate point, and let's say I call station security and just get him to the medical bay."

Example: Prbrawl has the aspect BLACKBALLED BY THE PILOT'S GUILD which is what kept him from finding a real job and landed him in Class D. The Guild isn't happy that he's still flying a ship, so any Guild pilots he runs into are likely to be hostile. The Guild itself can cause problems for him through official channels as well.

Prbrawl pilots the *Black Watch* in and out of Job Tower all the time, and the local Guild Master decides to make Prbrawl a personal project. As the *Black Watch* comes in to dock, Prbrawl receives an official message from the station master that a complete review of crew qualifications will be required to dock at the station. The GM suggests that this is a compel based on Prbrawl's BLACKBALLED BY THE PILOT'S GUILD aspect. This bureaucratic headache won't leave many options. Prbrawl's player, Nick, accepts and the GM gives him a fate point.

There are a couple of ways that Nick can fulfill the terms the compel. He can go ahead and dock at the station, triggering the review and probably causing a massive red tape tangle for the ship and his captain, or he can reroute the ship to a different port nearby. That means he has to explain the problem to the captain or try to keep him in the dark with some excuse. Either way, he's got a problem on his hands.

Say Yes, Roll the Dice, or Compel

You may have gathered this already, but just to be clear, there's a chance that a compel could happen any time you might otherwise pick up the dice. Usually, when you as a player want to try to do something, the GM will have you roll dice if she has an interesting idea of what might happen if you fail. If she doesn't, there's really no reason to roll at all.

But, if there's a good opportunity for your action to complicate things, she might "trade in" the dice roll in favor of making up something that's interesting and engaging. This is great stuff to make dramatic moments with, and it's definitely something *you* can use as well—as long as you're willing to deal with the potential complications, you might be able to succeed at an immediate task in exchange for future problems.

For example, Prbrawl could point at his SHORT TEMPER and say, "I'm not gonna take that kind of lip. I punch him in the face." The GM will say, "OK. This is going to start a general brawl," and accept it as a worthy compel, handing Prbrawl a fate point without the dice ever getting involved. Prbrawl isn't even trying to resist the provocation; instead, he's just rolling with it.

Situations like this can really help inspire players to get involved in the evolving story.

"Accidental" Compels

Sometimes characters simply play to their aspects without thinking to compel them. When that happens, the GM should make a note of it (sometimes with the player reminding her) and, if possible, award the player with a fate point retroactively. If it's too late for that, the GM should make a note to give that player an extra fate point next session.

It's important that the GM keep in mind what sorts of things would normally constitute a compel. Compels happen in order to make certain choices or situations more difficult or more dramatic for the compelled character. Certainly, staying in character and playing in a way that's appropriate to a character's aspects should be praised; but it should be rewarded only when the player's aspect-consistent play has actively made his character's choices more difficult.

Negotiating a Compel

In play, players and the GM can both initiate compels. When the GM initiates a compel, the process is very simple. The GM remarks that the aspect might be appropriate here and offers you a fate point. Of course, in a perfect world, the GM would always be aware of all aspects and always know when they should be compelled and rewarded. In practice, the GM is keeping track of a lot of stuff and may not realize that you have an aspect that's appropriate to the situation.

When this happens, you should feel free to capture the GM's attention and point to the appropriate aspect, holding up a fate point and raising your eyebrows or giving some other signal to indicate you thinks it's time for a compel.

When you call attention to one of your character's aspects, it may be as formal as "I think my GREEN EYES OF JEALOUSY aspect applies here," or it may be conversational, like, "Boy, that guy talking to my girl is pretty suave, as I watch them with my GREEN EYES OF JEALOUSY" (brandishing a fate point). There's no one way to do it and your group can fall into whatever pattern is most comfortable for all of you.

After a player or the GM suggests a compel, the immediate next step is to negotiate over the terms. Usually, the person who suggests the compel has an idea in mind already, but that doesn't mean things are set in stone. Remember: compels are supposed to make things more dramatic and interesting, not force people into boxes. So, you should feel free to suggest alternate details, offer a suitably dramatic counter-proposal if you feel it'd be more in keeping with your character, and so on. Likewise, GMs should feel free to turn up the heat on a player who's proposing a weak compel.

Example: Quinn is left alone aboard the ship with Captain Laf't while her crewmates go out to retrieve the cargo. After they're gone, Alison holds up a fate point and says, "This is going to be awkward because I DON'T THINK THE CAPTAIN LIKES ME."

The GM recognizes one of Quinn's aspects and agrees. "Yes, Captain Laf't emerges from his cabin and looks into the cockpit. Spotting you, his eyes narrow, and he barks, 'Quinn! Stop lollygagging and see to your duties!' He's going to send you outside to clean the blast marks off the exterior of the ship. Right where you're likely to be seen and identified by dock hands who know your old associates."

Alison says, "I'm not sure I want that complication right now. How about I get into it with the captain since I'm performing pre-flight duties in the cockpit? I know he won't like it if I talk back to him."

The GM says, "That's going to cause issues. Let's do a full-on argument with the captain here; he'll roll Leadership and you can try to resist. Either way, a black mark is going down on your ledger in his eyes. He'll get you for this later, even if he gets his way."

What's a Weak Compel?

When judging whether or not a compel is "worthy," the primary thing to look for is whether the outcome provides a palpable sense of consequence to the character and/or the story. If the outcome isn't going to create something that'll matter much in the grand scheme of things, then it probably isn't enough to work as a compel. Making a compel more worthy might mean that the GM changes the circumstances of a conflict to be less advantageous to a character; it might mean that the session suddenly takes a stunning new direction plotwise; or it might mean that the character has an additional problem to deal with that he didn't before. As long as it's an effect you can feel in play, it's probably good enough.

Compelling Multiple Aspects

Occasionally, a situation comes up in play that seems to be relevant to more than one of your character's aspects. This shouldn't be seen as a problem—rather, it's an opportunity for high drama.

When a situation is complicated enough to involve more than one aspect, then each of the aspects is subject to a compel. You decide how to deal with this—after negotiating, you can take every compel for a large payout, or take only a certain number and then buy out of the rest. This might mean that you ultimately break even on fate point gain, but that's okay—it still shows your character's priorities in a dramatic moment, which is a successful compel.

Keep in mind that there should be a clear complication or limitation offered by each aspect; one complication that references two aspects shouldn't give you two fate points unless it's a really, really big deal.

Example: On Hacragorka, the crew of the *Black Watch* has come under fire during the delivery. This is Brunda's home planet and some of her relatives have been helping the crew out. Just as the firefight breaks out, Brunda realizes that her favorite cousin is nowhere to be seen.

The GM looks at Eryn, Brunda's player, and says, "This is a compel of your I CAN'T KEEP TRACK OF MY COUSINS aspect and your THEY NEED MY HELP aspect. Your crew needs you but your cousin is also in trouble. You need to decide which way to go."

Eryn thinks about it and says, "I need to stick by my crew. They really do need my help. I'll have to go after my cousin after I deal with this, and someone's going to regret messing with my family."

The GM decides that both aspects are certainly complicating Brunda's life. He slides over two fate points—she's going to need them.

Encountering Other Aspects

You can potentially use aspects besides those your character has. Your fellow players' characters have aspects, of course, as do many non-player characters; sometimes even the *scene itself* may have aspects, like DARK or CLUTTERED. Ships and planets also usually have aspects. Entire regions of space have aspects.

To invoke an aspect other than your own, your character needs to directly interact with the object, location, or person that has the aspect you want to invoke, in a way appropriate to the action in progress.

Let's say a scene has the aspect POISONOUS ATMOSPHERE since it's on a hostile planet; not only does that mean characters can be described as needing breathing apparatus, but characters can invoke the POISONOUS ATMOSPHERE aspect when they do something that exposes an enemy to the planet's air.

Your character also needs to have reasonable access to the aspect in question, meaning your character needs to know that the aspect is there. With scene aspects, this is easy—if your character is present in the scene, that'll usually do it. There are several ways you can gain access to an aspect that's on another character or scene:

- Discover it via **assessment** (page 83, *Skills* chapter)
- Create it with a **declaration** (page 84, *Skills* chapter)
- Establish it with a **maneuver** (page 84, *Skills* chapter)
- Inflict a **consequence** (page 71, *Doing Things* chapter)

If your character can interact directly with the owner of the aspect in an appropriate manner and can reasonably know about the aspect in question, you may use that aspect in a number of different ways.

Invoking Other Aspects

Invoking an aspect that isn't on your character is precisely the same as a regular invocation—just declare how that aspect is relevant, spend a fate point, and take a +2 or a reroll. The only thing to keep in mind is that, if you're invoking an aspect on another player character or on a non-player character to gain an advantage over them, that character will *receive the fate point you spent*, either at the end of the exchange (page 67, *Doing Things* chapter) or at the end of the scene (outside of conflict).

You can also invoke other aspects for effect, allowing you to use someone else's aspect or a scene aspect to make a declaration. All the guidelines for invoking (page 54) apply here.

Example: Prbrawl's player, Nick, knows that Captain Laf't has the aspect DISGRACED EX-NOVA LEGION OFFICER since that was established at the beginning of the game during crew creation. The captain has decided to punish the crew, and Prbrawl steps up to deflect the blow. He describes Prbrawl using a military manner and respectfully reminding the captain of TransGalaxy regulations, all while standing in parade rest and dutifully staring directly ahead. He spends a fate point and adds a +2 to his Rapport roll to convince the captain that the crew has done nothing wrong.

Since he's using one of the captain's own aspects against him, that fate point gets added to Laf't's pool. This will most likely come back to bite Prbrawl on the ass later.

Tagging

A **tag** is a special move that you may be able to do when you're invoking aspects other than your own. Whenever you make a roll to gain access to or create an aspect, *you may invoke it one time, and one time only, for free*—as in, you don't spend from your pool of fate points to take advantage of the aspect. If you invoke that aspect a second time, you'll need to pay the fate point as usual.

A tag is subject to one key limitation—it must occur *almost immediately* after the aspect has been brought into play. Some minor delay is OK, but should be avoided if possible. At worst, a tag should happen sometime during the scene in which it was established. Some assessments are an exception to this time limit (page 83, ***Skills*** chapter).

If you wish, you can allow another character to use the tag for an aspect you've discovered or introduced. This allows for some great set-up maneuvers in a fight; you can maneuver (page 84, ***Skills*** chapter) to place an aspect on a target, then pass the tag to an ally who attacks, using the advantage on his own roll. This can only be done, however, if it's reasonable that the advantage could be passed off. A sniper who uses a maneuver to aim his rifle at a target, putting an IN MY SIGHTS aspect on it, can't pass the advantage to someone else—the aspect placed is specific to him. But if Prbrawl uses a maneuver to put a BLINDED BY HOT STEAM aspect on a pirate, he could reasonably pass the advantage to Brunda, who moves in for the knockout blow.

Tags, even when they're detrimental to a character, don't award a fate point like a normal invocation would. If no fate point was spent, there's no fate point to pass around.

Tagging often involves temporary aspects that result from maneuvers. Make sure you have a grasp on how temporary aspects behave (page 63).

Example: Brunda just punched a dockworker in the face, using her Fists skill to put a maneuver on him so he's STUNNED. Her next move is to pick him up and hurl him at the rest of the dockworkers who are attacking her and her crewmates. She tags the STUNNED aspect to give her a +2 to this roll.

The throw takes out several of his cohorts, but this particular dockworker stands up, trying to shake off the attack. If Brunda decides to put him down for the count and invokes STUNNED again, she'll have to pay one fate point for the privilege since she's already tagged it.

Compelling Other Aspects

Interacting with the aspects of others creates a powerful opportunity for the clever player to set up another character to be compelled. If you're aware of and can access an aspect on another character or non-player character, you may spend a fate point to try to trigger the circumstances of a compel (page 55) on the target. If the GM decides this is a compel-worthy circumstance, she takes the offered fate point and proceeds with a compel, running it as if she had initiated the compel herself.

This is a chain reaction—the first player calls for the compel, and if the GM accepts it as valid, she negotiates it with the player of the target character, who either decides to accept (gaining a fate point) or avoid (spending a fate point). Once the initiating player spends the fate point, *he does not get it back even if the target buys out of the compel*.

As with a normal compel, the final result can be negotiated as much as necessary.

Scene Compels

Scene aspects may imply some circumstances that will befall any (or many) of the characters in the scene—EVERYTHING'S ON FIRE! is a classic example. In such a case, it's entirely apropos to act as if that aspect is on each character's sheet and compel the aspect for each of them, dishing fate points all around and nicely covering the effects the aspect has on the characters in the scene.

Technically speaking, a player could try to use a scene aspect to initiate a mass compel, but it'd be a pretty expensive proposition—he'd have to spend a fate point for every character he wants to be affected by the compel.

Game Aspects?

Some GMs may wish to step things up to an even more "meta" level and allow for a game session or even the entire campaign to have aspects on it (**game aspects**), like WE CAN'T CATCH A BREAK or INTERSTELLAR WAR. Such aspects should be used sparingly, since their omnipresence will strongly shape the face of the game. When adding a game aspect to your campaign, ask yourself: Am I okay with this showing up in nearly every scene or session (or at least the majority of them)?

Picking Character Aspects

More than anything else, aspects are a player's most explicit way of telling the GM, "This is the stuff I want to see in the game." If the player picks an aspect like DEATH DEFYING, then he should be able to fully expect that the GM will put him in death-defying situations. Every aspect you give to a character influences play. You, the GM, and the other players will all invoke and compel these. They'll come up again and again.

Creating aspects can be one of the hardest things to do when creating your character. Aspects are basically catchphrases or short descriptions that colorfully describe your character or her relationships. An aspect should be short and punchy—when writing an aspect, if the text starts to get longer than about six words or so, it's too long. Of course, a really good, vibrant phrase is an exception to this rule, but as a guideline, keep them short.

Aspects come up often in play, so make sure they're very descriptive and evoke your character. The best aspects give a vivid picture of your character's personality or relationships. Someone reading the character's list of aspects should have a pretty accurate idea who that character is.

Why Would I Want a Bad Aspect?

You may have noticed that a number of the aspects throughout **Bulldogs!** are "bad" aspects—they indicate a downside for a character, either in their directly negative connotations or in their two-edged nature. Aspects like OBNOXIOUS DRUNK, BACK-PLANET RUBE, I WON'T BACK DOWN, and I STAND BY MY WORD all suggest situations where the character will have to behave a certain way—making an ass of himself at an important social function, falling for a line of bull, pushing a volatile situation too far, or keeping a promise rashly made.

So why put such aspects on your sheet if they're only going to make trouble for you? Simple—you *want* that kind of trouble. On a basic, game-rules footing, "bad" aspects are a direct line to getting you more fate points—and fate points are the fusion core that powers some of the more potent *positive* uses of your aspects. We'll get more into how aspects can generate and use fate points later on in this chapter.

Outside of just the rules, a "bad" aspect adds interest and story to a character in a way that purely positive aspects don't. This sort of interest means time in the limelight. If someone's trying to take advantage of the fact your character's a BACK-PLANET RUBE, that's an important point in the story, and the camera's going to focus on it. "Bad" aspects also immediately suggest story to your GM; they tell her how to hook your

character in. From the perspective of playing the game to get involved and have fun, there's nothing but good in this sort of "bad."

Clever players will also find positive ways to use "bad" aspects. Prying eyes might dismiss the OBNOXIOUS DRUNK as "just a drunk;" someone who WON'T BACK DOWN will be more determined to achieve his goals. This brings us the "secret" truth about aspects—the ones that are most useful are the ones that are the most *interesting*. And the most interesting aspects are *neither* purely good nor purely bad.

As a rule of thumb, when picking an aspect, think of three situations where you can see the aspect coming into play. If you've got one reasonably positive situation and one reasonably negative situation out of that set, you're golden! If they're all of one type, you may want to reconsider how you've worded your aspect—try to put a little of what's missing in there. Ultimately, though, one aspect that's "all good" or "all bad" isn't that much of a problem, as long as you have a good mix throughout your whole set.

Aspects That Kick Ass

Aspects are one of the major sources of flavor for your character; they're the first thing your GM will look at on your sheet when she's trying to work out what sort of stories to throw you into. This is strong stuff, and the best part is, you're in *total* control of it with the words you choose for your aspect.

Whenever you're writing down the name of an aspect, ask yourself, "How much attitude does this aspect suggest?" If it seems rather timid, then you might well be off the mark, and it's time to rethink it. Certainly, don't feel like you have to do this with every aspect you take, but if your character is described as "Mr. Milquetoast," you may discover that your GM is at loose ends for keeping him involved in the story.

A few "good—better—best" examples are listed here.

Wimpy	Cool	Kick Ass!
STRONG	STRONG AS A TENEBRIAN OX	STRONGEST ARSUBARAN IN THE GCP
CRIMINAL PAST	FORMER PIRATE	NO ONE QUITS THE BARRACADO PIRATES
BRAWLER	BARROOM SCRAPPER	"YOU TALKIN' TO ME?"

In each of these cases, the Wimpy option certainly suggests its uses, but it doesn't really jump off the page as something that suggests story. The Cool option is better because it's more specific; both GM and player can see some potential story hooks in these, and they serve to differentiate themselves interestingly from their more demure predecessors. But the Kick Ass! options are where it's at.

STRONGEST ARSUBARAN IN THE GCP could easily be the phrase others use to identify the character, and it suggests more applications than simple strength. NO ONE QUITS THE BARRACADO PIRATES names the gang of pirates the character was once a part of, creates built-in enemies pursuing her, and starts to put some non-player characters onto the map. "YOU TALKIN' TO ME?" gives the character more than just a history of brawling; it gives him attitude and presents lots of situations where he'll be belligerent even if that might be unwise. So when you pick an aspect, ask yourself: Is this Wimpy, is this Cool, or is this Kick Ass!?

Example: When Nick created his pilot, he wanted to give Prbrawl an aspect that would help him in his duties; he chose EXPERIENCED PILOT as his job aspect. The GM knows where Nick is going with this, but feels the aspect isn't as kick ass as it could be. She suggests PRECISION PILOTING as an alternative.

Nick likes this. The aspect now implies that Prbrawl is a bit of a perfectionist, but he doesn't see how this could cause him problems down the line. It's pretty cool, but not kick ass. He and the GM discuss this a bit and settle on PRECISION IS THE PILOT'S FRIEND. With this aspect, Prbrawl can invoke it for piloting tasks, but it can also be compelled when he might be more careful and precise than a situation warrants, slowing down response time and causing problems. That kicks ass!

Story Vs. Situation

In addition to positive and negative, aspects tend to divide into another set of two camps—**story** and **situation**—and it's a good idea to make sure you have aspects of each type.

Story aspects suggest sources for stories that involve your character by bringing in an external element from the world at large. They're most easily identified by asking yourself if the aspect, independent of the character, is something other characters might interact with, affect, and change. Gangs of criminals, lost items, enemies, hidden treasures, strange planets, spouses, and so much more all fit into this category.

Situation aspects suggest the *kind* of situations your character might get into much more than they suggest the *origin* of those situations. Situation aspects make a statement to your GM about the style of stories you wants your character to be in. Aspects like NICK OF TIME, I WON'T BACK DOWN, and LAST MAN STANDING all suggest vivid situations—ones which should rightly repeat themselves over the course of playing the character—but they don't really suggest the *context* of those situations.

We're focusing on the split between story and situation aspects because it's an easy one to miss if you're not looking for it. You can very easily fall into the trap of creating a character who only has situation aspects. On the surface, situation aspects may be more attractive since they usually apply in a multitude of circumstances; certainly, you'll want to have at least a few situation aspects in your repertoire.

But if situation aspects are *all* that your character offers to the game, you run a real risk of being difficult to hook into the bigger storyline. Fundamentally, story aspects offer easy hooks to your GM to pull you into her story. You want this, since you came to the party to play the game. But it's more than just that. By providing story aspects, you're providing some things that exist separately from your character. At the core of it, this means you're helping to build the game world. You've got ownership and stakes in the bigger picture. The GM will be grateful to you for it, and that kind of gratitude pays out in the form of a more satisfying game.

Getting On the Same Page

You may have noticed that, so far, we're using a lot of ink to talk about how your aspects communicate things about your character to the GM. We mean it. Out of all the things in the game, aspects are probably the clearest message you can send to the GM about what you want from the game, short of walking right up to the GM and saying so. Also, in all likelihood, the GM will have copies of your character sheets when you're not around, so the aspects you've picked are going to represent you in absentia. Once you've picked all the aspects for your character, take a step back and look at them as a whole. Ask yourself if they paint the kind of picture you want them to. If they don't, change them!

By themselves, aspects can't say it *all*, of course, and it's important to remember that. Short of making each aspect a paragraph or essay, you're dealing with a few short, catchy phrases and names here. You want them short, because you want to be able to talk about them casually without running out of breath. But the brevity of an aspect's name means some things are left unspoken. Take the time with your GM to speak these unspoken things when you can. Both you and your GM should look at an aspect not as the end of an idea, but the start of one. You both bring your own ideas of what the aspect means to the table and, at least to some extent, you're both right. Usually this works out fine—the combined perspectives make the whole greater than the sum—but sometimes you and the GM may have a radically different idea of what the aspect entails. Be clear with one another and figure out how to iron out any differences—ideally *before* the fate points start flying.

That said, after you've gotten some sessions of play under your belt, you might feel like you've picked one or more aspects that don't "feel right." We're sympathetic to that, and your GM should be, too. If an aspect doesn't seem to be working out well for you, you should feel free to ask your GM if you can change it.

Creating and Discovering Aspects in Play

There are several ways that previously unknown or nonexistent aspects can show up in play. Here, we'll discuss the methods.

Guessing Aspects

Sometimes, you might want to use an aspect that's on a scene or character—except that you don't actually know if the target has the aspect in question. In other words, you're making a *guess*—maybe, just maybe, an aspect fitting a particular description is there—and, while guesses are allowed, they're subject to some special rules.

One way to make a guess is to roll it as an assessment action (page 83, *Skills* chapter); if it's successful, the GM can reveal whether or not the target has a similar aspect. The good part about this option is that, even if your guess is wrong, you'll still get an aspect from the target if the action succeeds. The bad part is that the target usually gets a roll to defend himself from being assessed, and therefore the attempt might fail.

Another route is to spend a fate point and try to guess the aspect, explaining how you intend to use the aspect if it exists. This is basically "gambling" with an invocation or compel. You're committing your fate point on the possibility that your hunch about the target's aspects is correct. You won't get another aspect from the target if you're wrong, but because you're spending the fate point, the target doesn't get the option to defend against you.

If, conceptually speaking, the guess hits reasonably close to the mark—even if it doesn't match the aspect's exact name—the GM should exercise some flexibility and allow it.

Example: Quinn is sneaking into a warehouse to ambush some smugglers. Her player, Alison, might guess that the scene has a DARKNESS aspect on it and spend a fate point, asking if she can invoke it for her Stealth roll to get near the smugglers undetected. The scene has the aspect SHADOWY CORNERS instead; but Alison's guess is reasonably close to the mark, so the GM reveals that the aspect is SHADOWY CORNERS and allows the invocation.

If the guess just plain misses the mark, and the fact that the mark was missed doesn't amount to a significant and potentially secret piece of information, you should get the chance to reconsider your guess and take back the fate point you spent.

Example: Same as before, but this time, the GM's idea of the warehouse is that it's actually pretty well-lit—big lights hanging from the ceiling, etc. When Alison spends the fate point and explains her intent, the GM holds up her hand: "It's actually pretty well lit in here. There are big lights everywhere, most of them turned on." Alison takes back her fate point, since this wasn't a particularly secret bit of information—it just hadn't been brought up yet.

If the guess misses the mark, but missing the mark tells you something significant and potentially secret, the fate point is still spent. This sort of circumstance almost never comes up with scene aspects, but it *can* come up when guessing at aspects on another character and may even amount to a "reveal" (page 83, *Skills* chapter) of the target's true aspect.

Example: Prbrawl's trying to reason with the dispatch official at the local warehouse; he spends a fate point to guess at an aspect on the guy, I'M A REASONABLE MAN. The GM smiles darkly and shakes her head. "No; the more you talk to this guy, the more you realize he can't stand his job or scummy pirates like your crew. The more you talk with him, the more pissed he gets." The fate point stays spent—Prbrawl has learned some valuable information about this obstacle to his immediate plans; he may even be able to guess at the existence of a HATES CLASS D SCUMBAGS aspect that he could invoke later on. He could try to sweet-talk the GM into considering this to be a reveal of such an aspect, allowing for a tag (page 59).

In the worst case scenario, your guess misses the mark because you've been duped. This most often happens as the result of a Deceit action (page 90 XX, *Skills* chapter), although it might arise from other circumstances. In such a case, the deceiver can either return the spent fate point to you or leave it spent.

If he leaves it spent, you just learned you were duped— you don't get the benefit of tagging the aspect, but you've learned something significant about your target. The deceiver doesn't get this spent fate point for himself, either—it's simply gone.

If the deceiver returns the fate point to you, things may actually be a bit worse for you—the deceiver gets to place a temporary aspect on you (and tag it), representing how he managed to snooker you.

Example: Brunda is talking to a client, a smooth Ken Reeg called Sparkle Twist. Twist knows quite well what's contained in the cargo she wants to load on the *Black Watch*, but she's convinced Brunda otherwise. Her earlier Deceit roll was designed to get Brunda to underestimate her, thinking she's NOT AS SHARP AS SHE THINKS SHE IS. Brunda, certain there's something fishy going on, wants to make Twist doubt herself; she uses Rapport to try to convince her something's up. Brunda's player invokes Twist's NOT AS SHARP AS SHE THINKS SHE IS aspect in the process.

Twist's confidence won't be shaken in the least, but she decides to play along; she returns the fate point, putting the aspect SNOWED BY TWIST on Brunda.

Regardless, guesses can't, and shouldn't, be made willy-nilly. There must always be a justification for making the guess. If the guess seems unjustified—if the player is "shotgunning" guesses to randomly try to figure out another character's aspects—the GM is completely justified in shutting that player down cold.

Temporary Aspects

Unlike the "permanent" aspects built into a character's sheet, **temporary aspects** are introduced to—or inflicted upon—a character or scene by the actions of a character in the game, but they fade over time. Temporary aspects differ in terms of the duration and the tenacity with which they stay on the recipient.

Most commonly, a temporary aspect results from a successful maneuver (page 84, *Skills* chapter). If you get no shifts (page 65, *Doing Things* chapter) on a maneuver roll, the maneuver is successful, but the aspect is considered **fragile**—that is, it can only be tagged once and then it goes away. Fragile aspects are usually described as very momentary changes of circumstance—if you use Guns as a maneuver to aim at a target and you don't get any shifts, you might call that aspect A QUICK BEAD. When you attack the target, you can tag it; but then you lose your bead on him for some reason, like he shifts position or slips behind cover or something else.

If you get shifts on a maneuver roll, the resulting aspect is said to be **sticky**—in other words, it "sticks" to the target until something can be done about it. Sticky aspects don't go away after they're tagged, allowing people to spend fate points to continue invoking them. These are usually described in more severe terms than fragile aspects, to represent that they're a tangible problem or advantage for a character. If you get shifts on a Guns maneuver to aim, you might call that aspect RIGHT IN MY SIGHTS—essentially, you can hold a steady aim on your target until he does something drastic to throw your aim off.

Sticky aspects may be easier to place on a location or scene rather than on another character, because the scene can't roll to defend against your maneuver. This is especially true when they potentially offer complications to everyone present—on both sides— such as with a maneuver to add a THE BUILDING'S ON FIRE! aspect to a scene.

Getting rid of a sticky aspect requires making a successful maneuver roll to cancel the effects of the maneuver. If a character is in a position to stop you from getting rid of the maneuver, he can try to make an appropriate defense roll to oppose you. If he succeeds, the aspect remains. If you succeed, it goes away. If no one's in a position to stop you from getting rid of the maneuver, it's very easy—you just have to make a roll against a difficulty of Mediocre (+0). Temporary aspects that result from maneuvers always go away at the end of a conflict or scene.

Some temporary aspects have real staying power and have the ability to outlast a scene; they may even stay fixed to the target for as long as a session (or more) of play. Those kinds of temporary aspects are called **consequences**, and each character has a certain limit on how many he can take, based on his skills. They represent lasting effects such as physical wounds, psychological problems, and so forth. These aspects usually can't be removed by normal means—they require appropriate justification to remove, as well as a certain amount of recovery time (page 73, *Doing Things* chapter).

Assessments

Sometimes you may use your skills to make a careful **assessment** well in advance of taking action—maybe as part of putting together a plan, or simply observing the target long enough to learn something that would be a critical advantage. This approach is most often used with skills that have an element of perception—such as Investigation and Empathy—but knowledge skills could also be applied to discover "knowable things." Here, the skill isn't used to place a temporary aspect on the target so much as to discover an *existing* aspect on the target that may have been hidden or secret.

Because this aspect is freshly introduced into play by your action, you should be able to tag this aspect. However, you're often going to use assessment as a way to prepare for a future encounter, which may not happen for several scenes. So, if you've discovered an aspect this way, *you don't have to worry about the usual time limit for tagging until the first scene where you encounter the target of your assessment.* Aspects discovered in this fashion are still present after these time limits expire, so they can still be invoked later.

All assessment efforts require the use of a significant chunk of time, usually indicated in the skill write-up. However, this time invested in preparation allows these skills to come to bear in more time pressured environments—like a fight—where they wouldn't typically be useful.

Example: Prbrawl does a full scan of the pursuing pirate vessel, trying to see if there are any weaknesses in the ship's defenses. He rolls his Pilot skill to make an assessment against the difficulty set by the GM. He gets a success and learns that their engines are RUNNING TOO HOT.

Declarations

Traditionally, perception and knowledge skills focus on the discovery of what already exists ("knowable truths"). But in **Bulldogs!**, these skills also allow for **declarations**. That is to say, you can use these skills to introduce entirely new facts into play and then use those facts to your advantage. These new facts might also take the form of an aspect. For example, if your character has a strong Alertness or Investigation skill, you might use a declaration to add features to a scene for you to use to your advantage—when the fire starts, your character just "happens" to notice that the janitor left a bucket of water in the hallway.

As with maneuvering (page 84, *Skills* chapter) and assessment (above), the resulting aspect can be tagged. Unlike assessment, declaration doesn't take any actual in-game time at all—just successful use of a knowledge skill at the right moment.

Example: Quinn is running from some of her former pirate associates through the halls of a space station. The pirates got the drop on her; now she really wants to just get away from them, at least until she has some backup from her crew. Alison decides to invent some details about the local environment so Quinn can take advantage of them. She uses her Alertness skill to declare that the access corridor she's in contains STEAM PIPES. The GM thinks this is reasonable and will cause an interesting scene, so she sets a low difficulty for the roll. If Alison's roll succeeds, knocking a hole in one of the pipes will create a blast of hot steam that will make the pirates pause in their pursuit.

Many skills allow for some kind of specialized knowledge—for example, you might use your Guns skill to make some declarations about the firepower an opponent is carrying.

As with assessments, aspects created with declarations don't go away after being tagged, as long as circumstances make it reasonable that they hang around. This does mean that occasionally assessments and declarations can backfire on the character establishing them—other characters might use the same aspect, or the GM might bring that aspect back around to complicate the character's endeavors.

Example: Alison has declared the STEAM PIPES in the corridor, and now she's reached the end and needs to climb up out of an access hatch to make good her escape. "That's great," the GM says, "But steam pipes are very hot. Make an Athletics roll to climb up there without burning yourself." Alison sighs and picks up the dice.

Doing Things

Characters in your games are going to do a lot. For most things they do, there's no real need for rules. Characters can stand, walk, talk, and otherwise do normal things without needing to roll dice. They can even take actions that use their skills, like accessing a public terminal or driving a hovercar, without worrying about the dice. The dice only come out when there's an interesting challenge with meaningful consequences.

On the simplest level, when a character rolls the dice, if he matches or exceeds the difficulty, he succeeds; if he doesn't, he fails. If the issue is simple, this may be all that's necessary; but sometimes you also need to know how well a character did or did not do. Clearly, if a character rolls three higher than the target, that's better than rolling only one higher.

The result of the roll is called the **effort**. Each point that the effort beats the difficulty by is one **shift**. If a roll is below the target difficulty, it's a failure and it generates no shifts—there are no "negative" shifts (although, if you flip the perspective, the opposition could be said to generate shifts). If a roll matches the target difficulty, it's a success but generates no shifts. If it beats it by one, it generates one shift; if it beats it by two it generates two shifts, and so on. The number of shifts generated by a roll is used as a measure of many elements; it's referred to as the **effect**.

Example: Prbrawl rolls his Pilot skill to land the ship in inclement weather. The difficulty of this Pilot roll is Great (+4). He has a Great (+4) Pilot skill and he rolls a ⊞⊟⊞⊞. His effort is Fantastic (+6) and he generates two shifts.

Using Shifts

You can spend shifts to affect the outcome of a roll. Often, your GM will implicitly spend shifts in accordance with how you've described your character's actions. Sometimes, you might explicitly spend shifts as well. Basic uses for one shift include:

Reduce time required: Make the action take less time.

Increase quality of outcome: Improve the quality of the job by one step.

Increase subtlety: Make the job harder to detect by one.

Exactly how you can apply the shifts towards quality and subtlety depends on the skill; this is detailed in the write-ups of the individual skills (page 85, *Skills* chapter).

Time

When you take an action that isn't instantaneous, it's expected to take a certain amount of time; this usually ranges from a few moments to a few days. Sometimes you need to take longer to do something or you want to do something a little faster. When that happens, take a look at the following chart and determine how long the task should take. Each shift you put towards doing something more quickly makes the task happen one step faster.

Example: The guidance system on the *Black Watch* has shorted out and Prbrawl is attempting to fix it with an Engineering roll. The GM tells him that it will take a day to repair. Unfortunately, the cargo they're carrying is going to spoil if they're delayed that long. Prbrawl makes his roll and generates three shifts. Looking at the time table, he's able to reduce the required time from a day to an hour.

Time Increments

Instant
A few moments
Half a minute
A minute
A few minutes
15 minutes
Half an hour
An hour
A few hours
An afternoon
A day
A few days
A week
A couple of weeks
A month
A few months
A season
Half a year
A year
A few years
A decade
A lifetime

Spin (Optional)

Spin is an optional rule that creates a special effect when a character scores a significant or better success (3 shifts or more). If you understand how it works and want to use it, that's awesome. However, be aware that some players find it confusing and complicated. If players have a hard time with this rule, just ignore it.

The special effect caused by spin may simply be color—your character looks particularly cool doing whatever he's doing or perhaps he's due some recognition for excellence. In some cases, as outlined in skills and elsewhere, gaining spin can result in an actual game effect. In combat, for instance, if a character gets spin on a defensive, he can add a +1 to the very next action that occurs—even if it's not his own. You'll find other applications of spin throughout the text; in general, it serves as an easy way of noting that a character has done particularly well. Whenever your character rolls well enough to generate spin, it's time to sit up, pay attention, and spice up the details.

Remember, every three shifts generated on a roll gives your character one point of spin.

Example: Big Brunda is fighting with a knife-wielding assassin. She uses her Fists skill to defend herself against the man's attack and gets an Epic (+7) result. The assassin only had a Good (+3) attack, so Brunda beats him by four shifts. Three of these shifts give her a point of spin, and she gets a +1 on her next turn to brain him with a pipe using her Weapons skill.

Taking Action

You'll roll dice in three types of situations:

Simple Actions: The character rolls against a fixed difficulty.

Contests: Two characters each roll; the high roll wins and generates shifts.

Conflicts: Two or more characters act in direct opposition to one another, but the resolution isn't as simple as a contest.

Simple Actions

Simple actions are rolled against a difficulty set by the GM; they're used to simply see if a character can do something and, possibly, how well he can do it. The GM describes the situation; the player chooses a skill to apply to it and rolls against a difficulty determined by the GM (page 153, *Running the Game* chapter). The default difficulty is Average (+1). Some sample simple actions include:

- Climbing a wall
- Looking up obscure planetary survey data
- Searching the scene of a battle for evidence about the combatants
- Shooting a (non-character) target

Contests

Contests are very much like simple actions in that they are easily resolved one way or another, except the action is in direct opposition to someone else instead of against a set difficulty. Each party rolls the appropriate skill, and the high roll wins as though it beat a difficulty equal to the low roll. A tie means both succeed, but whether that means the outcome is a tie or if it calls for another roll depends on the situation. Some sample contests include:

- An arm wrestling match
- A footrace
- A drinking contest

Conflicts

Conflicts occur when two or more characters are in opposition in a way that can't be quickly and cleanly resolved. A conflict is broken down into a number of exchanges where each party attempts to achieve its goal, taking turns to act. Anyone affected by that attempt may be called upon to roll a response, such as defending against an attack. Each party accumulates success in the form of stress on their opponents. Eventually, one of the parties accumulates enough stress or suffers enough consequences to be taken out; alternatively, opponents may preemptively offer a concession.

Conflicts are the most involved actions in the game, and an entire scene may revolve around a conflict. Conflicts include:

- Any kind of fight scene
- A financial negotiation
- A long, tense staredown
- Trying to talk your way past a security guard as he tries to scare you off

Conflicts are complex enough that we're going to give you an entire section detailing how they're handled.

Running Conflicts

Once a conflict begins, follow these steps:

1. Frame the scene
2. Establish initiative
3. Begin the exchange
4. Take actions
5. Resolve actions
6. Begin a new exchange

Framing the Scene

During a conflict, elements in the scene might play a part in how the conflict unfolds. When framing the scene, the GM declares if there are any aspects on the scene, laying them out for the players. (Using scene aspects is discussed on page 58, *Aspects* chapter.)

If the scene takes place over a broad area, the GM also describes the **zones** the scene will be occurring in. Each zone is a loosely defined area; characters can directly interact with anyone else within the same zone (which is a nice way to say talk to or punch them). You need to determine who is in what zone so you know whether characters can punch each other or if they need to throw things or use ranged weapons. Determining which zones characters start in should be reasonably intuitive, but if there's a question, the GM can rule on where the character starts.

If you're looking for a quick rule of thumb, remember that people in the same zone can "touch" each other, people one zone apart can throw things at each other, and people two or three zones apart can shoot each other. A scene shouldn't involve more than a handful of zones. Considering that some guns can easily operate up to three zones, and occasionally a few more, a comfortable number of zones for the scene is usually three to nine zones—but don't feel like you need to cram in more zones than the area readily supports. More detailed information on how to create a map for a conflict is found on page 154, *Running the Game* chapter.

Establish Groups

Your opposition might all be detailed characters like the players' characters, but often minions, goons, or other faceless supporters are there to help out the opposing force. These supporters are collectively called "minions" and they're handled slightly differently than other characters (page 78). Minions usually get divided into a number of groups equal to the number of opposing characters. If the players' opposition is composed of a mix of non-player characters and minions, enemy characters may "attach" themselves to a group of minions, directing it and taking advantage of its assistance.

Dealing with large groups is a potentially complex exercise for the GM. Later in this chapter we have several recommendations and strategies for making this a lot easier (page 79).

Establish Initiative

The order of characters' actions is determined at the beginning of the conflict; this is referred to as the order of initiative (i.e., "who takes the initiative to go when"). In a physical conflict, characters act in order of highest to lowest Alertness skill; in a social conflict, it's based on Empathy.

Ties in initiative are resolved in favor of characters with a higher Resolve. Any remaining ties are in favor of the player closest to the GM's right.

When a character is attached to a group of minions, use the character's initiative. Otherwise the group of minions has initiative based on the quality of the group (as determined in "Minions," page 78).

Once that order is established, that's the order in which actions are taken for the duration of the conflict. When the last person has gone, the exchange ends, and a new exchange begins with the first character acting again, and everyone else acting in the same order.

An Alternative to Skill-Based Initiative

Some groups may find the idea of using particular skills to determine initiative "unbalancing," or at least unpleasant, in that it tends to give certain skills particular prominence. Also, some GMs don't like keeping track of a detailed order of actions.

If your group doesn't like skill-based initiative, use this alternative method instead:

- At the beginning of each exchange, the option to go first moves one player clockwise around the table.
- Initiative for that exchange proceeds clockwise (and includes the GM).
- Thus, the person who went first on the prior exchange goes last on the next one, and the others get their turn one step sooner.

This simple method makes sure that everyone gets a chance to go first over the course of a game, and it doesn't require players to make any special initiative-based decisions in their skill selections.

Taking Action

When it's your turn in the conflict, you describe what your character's doing and, if necessary, roll an appropriate skill. Each action you take within the conflict is resolved as either a simple action (if there's no opposition), or as a contest, with the details depending upon the specifics of the action.

Most actions in a fight will be either attacks or maneuvers.

Attacks

An attack is when you attempt to force your agenda on a target—by attempting to injure him, by bullying him, or by some other means. An attack is rolled as a contest, with the attacker attempting to beat the defender in an opposed skill roll.

Not all attacks are necessarily violent. An attempt to persuade or distract someone is also a kind of attack. When determining whether the attack rules apply, see if you have two characters in conflict, an agenda (or "want") pushed by the acting character, and a target or obstacle to that agenda (the defending or responding character). The skills used to attack and defend depend on the nature of the attacker's agenda. Here are some examples.

The attacker wants...	So he uses...	And the defender can use...
To physically harm	Fists, Guns, Weapons	Fists, Weapons, Athletics
To deceive	Deceit	Resolve, Empathy
To scare	Intimidation	Resolve
To charm	Rapport	Resolve, Deceit
To force movement	Might	Might

If the attacker wins the roll, he inflicts stress on the defender (see "Resolving Actions," page 71). If the defender wins, the attack fails; if the defender wins significantly, he may even earn spin (see "Spin," page 66), which he can use to his advantage.

Example: Big Brunda knocks a guy in the head with a pipe, an attack using Weapons. She gets a Superb (+5) result and his defense roll was only Fair (+2). She got three shifts on her roll and inflicts three physical stress on her opponent.

Maneuvers

A maneuver is an attempt to change the situation in some way, affecting the environment or other people, but without damaging or forcing the target—if force is used or damage is dealt, it's an attack.

Some examples of maneuvers are jumping to grab a rope, throwing dust in your enemy's eyes, drawing all eyes to you in a ballroom, or taking a debate down a tangential path.

A maneuver that doesn't target an opponent is resolved as a simple action. In most simple maneuvers, you roll against a GM-set difficulty; the resulting shifts give you an idea of how well you succeeded. A maneuver can also target an opponent; if successful, it places a temporary aspect on him. Either kind can place a temporary aspect on a scene. See the "Resolving Maneuvers" section later in this chapter (page 74) for details.

Example: Quinn's under fire and wants to get to a better position. There's a pile of crates nearby, so she tries to jump on top using Athletics. This is a simple action, since no other character is impeding her, and the GM says it has a Fair (+2) difficulty. Quinn succeeds in her roll with a Good (+3) result and tells the GM she has an aspect called HOLDS THE HIGH GROUND.

Special Actions

FREE ACTIONS

Some actions are "free"—they don't count as the character's action during an exchange, regardless of whether or not a roll of the dice is involved. Rolling to defend against an attack is a free action. So are minor actions like casting a quick glance at a doorway, flipping a switch right next to your character, or shouting a short warning.

There's no limit on the number of free actions a character may take during an exchange as long as the GM agrees that each action is free; the GM should feel free to impose limits if it seems like someone is taking excessive advantage of this rule.

Example: Brunda is being pressed back by a mob of attackers. She's using all of her actions in attack and defense to keep them at bay, but she knows her shipmates are behind her, unaware of the oncoming horde. She uses a free action to shout over her shoulder, "Close the airlock!"

FULL DEFENSE

You can opt to have your character do nothing but protect himself for an exchange. By foregoing your normal action, you gain a +2 on all reactions and defenses for that exchange. You can declare that you're defending at the beginning of the exchange rather than waiting for your turn to come around. Similarly, if you haven't acted in the exchange at the time when you're first attacked, you may declare a full defense at that point; this means you'll skip your normal action for the exchange.

HOLD YOUR ACTION

You can opt not to act when your turn comes around. When you hold action, you have the option of taking your turn any time later in the exchange. You must explicitly take your turn *after* someone else has finished his turn and *before* the next person begins. You can't wait until someone declares what he's trying to do, then interrupt him by taking your turn.

BLOCK ACTIONS

When your character's action is preventative—trying to keep something from happening, rather than taking direct action to make something happen—you're performing a block action. Declare what you're trying to prevent and what skill you're using to do it.

You may declare a block against any sort of action or actions and may theoretically use any skill, but unless the block is simple and clear, the GM may assess penalties based on how difficult it would be, or how much of a stretch it would be. You should never be able to "cover all bases" with a single block.

When you're blocking, you can declare that you're protecting another character. Make this declaration on your turn and roll the skill you're using to block; the result is the block strength. When, later in that exchange, any enemy tries to attack the protected character, the protected character gets the benefit of your block or his own defense, whichever is better. The attacker rolls his attack as normal. The defender rolls his defense as normal. If that defense roll is higher than the block strength, he uses the defense result; otherwise he uses the block strength. The attacker then generates shifts as normal.

For other types of blocks, declare the block on your turn and roll the skill you're using to block, subject to any penalties imposed by the GM. The result is the block strength. Later in that exchange, every time another character tries to perform the blocked action, he enters into a contest with you. The character trying to get past the block rolls the skill he's using for the action (not necessarily a skill specifically appropriate to the block), and compares it to the block strength. If the attacker gets at least one shift, he successfully overcomes the block.

Trying to get past a block always takes an action, though the GM may grant latitude in deciding what skill is being used to get past it. Even if the action is normally a free action, getting past the block takes additional effort; thus the GM can declare that it takes up the player's action for the exchange. A variety of skills may be appropriate for getting past a block.

Example: The crew has been searching for this guy who bolts for the exit as soon as he catches sight of them. However, they had the presence of mind to send Brunda around to the back and she's standing in the door. Brunda puts up a block to stop the guy from running, using her Might skill. He has to push her out of the way to get clear. She gets a Fantastic (+6) result on her block, and he rolls a Mediocre (+0) on his Might. He bounces right off her and back into the room.

SUPPLEMENTAL ACTIONS

Sometimes you need to do something more complicated than just taking a single, basic action. Sometimes the complication is simple, like drawing a weapon and attacking; sometimes it's more complex, like composing a sonnet while fencing.

When your character performs a simple action while doing something else—like drawing a weapon and attacking, or firing off a signal flare while intimidating the snapping fang voles at the edge of the firelight—it's a supplemental action and imposes a –1 on your primary action roll (effectively spending one shift of effect in advance). When in doubt about which is the primary action and which is the supplemental one, the supplemental action is the one that normally wouldn't require a die roll.

Sometimes the GM may decide a supplemental action is particularly complicated or difficult, and may increase the penalty appropriately.

Example: The crew is under heavy fire at the delivery point. The tech who just signed the manifest got shot and went down, dropping the datapad with the signed manifest on the ground. Quinn's firing back at their attackers, but she needs that manifest, too. She uses a supplemental action to scoop up the datapad while shooting at the enemy at the same time. Her Guns roll will be at –1, but she'll have the manifest in hand.

MOVEMENT

Movement is one of the most common supplemental actions. When it's reasonably easy to move from one zone to the next, you can move one zone as a supplemental action (see "Framing the Scene," page 67, for an explanation of zones). If you want to move further than that, you need to perform a primary (not supplemental) sprint action, which entails rolling Athletics—you get to move an additional number of zones equal to the shifts generated.

Sometimes, it's more difficult to move from one zone to the next, such as when there's some sort of barrier (like a fence or some debris) or there's some other difficulty (like getting from a rooftop to the street below and vice versa). This movement complication is called a **border**. The difficulty of that border increases the penalty for a move action and subtracts shifts from a sprint action.

Example: Prbrawl is trying to move from his current position and regroup with the crew. He's one zone away, atop a roof, from where the rest of the crew has taken cover in the alleyway. The drop from the roof is a border, and the GM rules it's a border 2. Normally, moving one zone would be a supplemental action, but because of the border Prbrawl must make an Athletics roll. He needs to get at least two shifts to get from the roof to his friends.

SPRINTING

Your character may use his Athletics to move faster by taking a sprint action. Normally, characters may only move one zone on their turn by using one of their shifts as a supplemental action. If you spend your entire action moving, you're sprinting; rolling Athletics against a target difficulty of Mediocre (+0), you may cross a number of zones and borders equal to or less than the total shifts of effect. In the absence of borders, characters can always move a minimum of one zone.

Example: Quinn decides the opposition is too fierce to hold off on her own and makes a sprint for the ship. The ship is three zones away. She needs to make an Athletics roll of Good (+3) to make it there if she sprints.

Combining Skills

Sometimes the character needs to perform a task that really requires using two or more skills at once. You never know when a character is going to need to throw a knife (Weapons) while spinning in zero gravity (Athletics) or when he's going to need to explain fusion theory (Academics) to a Devalkamanchan Elite shock trooper (Resolve). In those situations, the GM calls for a roll based on the main skill being used (the primary thrust of the action), but modified by a second skill. If the second skill is of greater value than the first, it grants a +1 bonus to the roll; if the second skill is of a lesser value, it applies a –1 penalty to the roll.

When the second skill can only help the first—essentially, failing with the second skill won't detract from the success of the first—it complements the skill. A complementing skill never applies a –1, even if it's lower than the primary skill. This usually happens when the character has the option of using the secondary skill, but doesn't have to bring it to bear.

If the secondary skill comes into play only to hold the primary skill back, it restricts the skill—it can only provide a penalty or nothing at all. A restricting skill never applies a +1, even if it's higher than the primary skill. Often skills like Endurance or Resolve are restrictive skills—as you get more tired, you won't get better; but if you're resolute, you may not get worse.

In very rare circumstances, a primary skill may be affected by more than one secondary skill—say, a situation where a character needs to climb a wall (Athletics as primary), but is tired (Endurance restricts), but the wall's part of a building the character has been studying in order to burglarize (Burglary complements). In such cases, no matter the number of skills in play, the most the combination can produce is one +1 and one –1.

This is actually very quick to reason out:

First, look at all of the skills that complement; if any of them are higher than the primary skill, a +1 is applied.

Next, look at all of the skills that restrict; if any of them are lower than the primary skill, a –1 is applied. This may mean that multiple skills all affecting a roll results in no modification at all—the +1 and –1 cancel each other out.

It's important to note that combining skills can never be done to perform two full actions at once—if that's the goal, it should take two exchanges. When skills are used in combination, one skill almost always serves a passive role; it's the thing the character needs to do in order to be able to perform the other skill. If a character is trying to throw a knife while spinning in space, Weapons is the main skill rolled, but Athletics restricts the roll—without it, the character ends up facing the wrong direction and his throw is moot. Similarly, if the character is cowering in front of a dangerous Devalkamanchan soldier, his knowledge is simply not going to help him.

The difference between a supplemental action and an action that combines skills isn't always obvious. In general, if both components of the action are something you'd expect to roll for if they were done separately, then it's time to combine skills. If the lesser part of the action is something that normally doesn't require a roll, just handle it as a supplemental action.

Long Conflicts

When your character is in a position to control the pacing of a conflict (which generally requires the conflict be one on one, or ritualized in some way), you can stretch it out and try to wear down your opponent. When this happens, actions in the conflict start using both characters' Endurance skill to restrict the skill used on any of their actions. Similarly, actions may be restricted by Alertness if the conflict has a lot of distractions, or restricted by Resolve if the conflict has become mentally fatiguing.

Resolving Actions

Once a character takes his action, you need to determine the outcome.

Resolving Attacks

A successful attack inflicts stress on its target equal to the number of shifts on the attack—that is, the difference between the attacker's effort and the defender's effort. Stress represents non-specific difficulties a character can encounter in a conflict. In a fight, it's bruising, minor cuts, fatigue, and the like. In a social conflict, it's getting flustered or being put off your game. In a mental conflict, stress might mean losing focus or running in circles. Stress can usually be shaken off once a character has some time to gather himself, between scenes.

Stress

A character can only take so much stress before being unable to go on, represented by the stress track filling up. The stress track defaults to 3 boxes, but it can be increased by certain skills: Endurance and Resolve can both increase the stress track. See the skill descriptions of Endurance and Resolve on page 91 and page 101 for more details.

When your character suffers stress, mark off the appropriate box on your stress track. For instance, if your character takes a three-point physical hit, mark off the third box from the left on the stress track. Only one box is ever filled on a successful hit. So if your character hasn't yet been harmed in the conflict, the first and second boxes remain empty even as the third box is checked.

If the inflicted stress falls on a box that's already been filled in, the next higher empty box must be checked. This is called **rolling up** the stress. If you have no further boxes to fill, your character is **taken out** (described in more detail below). To avoid being taken out, you may take a **consequence**.

At the end of a scene, unless the GM says otherwise, a character's stress tracks clear out; minor scrapes and bruises, trivial gaffes and embarrassments, and momentary fears pass away. Deeper issues resulting from attacks—those consequences we just mentioned—may last beyond the end of the scene; they're discussed in more detail below.

Example: Prbrawl gets shot. His opponent does two stress. Prbrawl marks his stress track like so: □ ⊠ □

In the next exchange, he gets shot again, for two stress again. His two stress box is already full, so he rolls up and fills in the three stress box like so: □ ⊠ ⊠

He's in danger of being taken out. If he gets shot for two stress again, he can't take the damage since he doesn't have any empty stress boxes higher than two. If he takes one stress in an attack, he can still fill in the one box.

Consequences

Stress is a transitory thing, but sometimes conflicts have lasting consequences—injuries, embarrassments, phobias, and the like. These are collectively called **consequences**, and they're a special kind of aspect.

Any time your character takes stress, you can choose to take a consequence and reduce the amount of stress you're forced to mark off. If your character takes a hit you don't have a box for—either because it's higher than the number of boxes on his stress track or because it rolls up past his last box—your character *must* take a consequence or be taken out.

The exact nature of the consequence should depend upon the conflict—an injury might be appropriate for a physical struggle, an emotional state might be apt for a social one. Whatever the consequence, it's written down under the stress track. The first consequence a character takes is a mild consequence, the second is a moderate consequence, and the third additional consequence is severe. (To understand exactly what these mean, see "Removing Stress and Consequences," page 73.) A mild consequence reduces the stress suffered by the character by 2, a moderate consequence by 4, and a severe consequence by 6.

Characters normally take no more than a severe consequence, but there is a fourth type—extreme consequences. Taking an extreme consequence reduces stress by 8, but the character is permanently injured or scarred. An extreme consequence permanently replaces one of the character's existing aspects.

Normally, the player accepting the consequence gets to describe what it is, as long as it's compatible with the nature of the attack that inflicted the harm. The GM acts as an arbitrator on the appropriateness of a consequence, so there may be some back and forth conversation before a consequence is settled on. The GM is the final authority on whether a player's suggested consequence is reasonable for the circumstances and severity.

Characters may only carry one of each type of consequence at a time (barring certain stunts which allow more). If the character has already taken a severe (or extreme, if he has that option) consequence, then the only remaining option is to be taken out. We'll talk about that next.

But here's the thing about consequences being a special kind of aspect—as long as the consequences are on your character's sheet, they may be compelled or tagged (or invoked!) like any other aspect. This also means that opponents may start compelling those aspects pretty easily, since it's no secret that the consequence aspects are now on the character's sheet!

Example: Prbrawl's stress track is pretty full and he takes another hit for two stress. He would be taken out if he had to take the stress, so he takes a mild consequence to reduce the damage to nothing. He writes down BRUISED as his mild consequence.

On Prbrawl's opponent's next action, he tags BRUISED for a +2 on his attack roll.

Taken Out

If your character takes a hit that exceeds his highest stress box, he's **taken out**. He's decisively lost the conflict and, unlike the other levels of consequence, his fate is in the hands of his opponent, who gets to decide how the character loses. The outcome must remain within the realm of reason—very few people truly die from shame, so having someone die as a result of a duel of wits is unlikely, but having him embarrass himself and flee in disgrace isn't unreasonable.

The option to determine how a character loses is a very powerful ability, but there are a few limits on it. First, the effect is limited to the character who has been taken out. The victor may declare that the loser has made an ass of himself in front of the Council Premier, but he cannot decide how the Premier will respond (or even if the Premier is particularly bothered).

Second, the manner of the taken out result must be limited to the scope of the conflict. After the victor wins a debate with someone, he can't decide that the loser concedes his point and gives the victor all the money in his pockets—money was never part of the conflict, so it's not an appropriate part of the resolution.

Third, the effect must be reasonable for the target. People don't (normally) explode when killed, so that can't be part of taking someone out. Similarly, a diplomat at the negotiating table isn't going to give the victor the keys to the planetary system—that's probably beyond the scope of his authority, and even if it's not, it's unlikely to be something he'd give away under any circumstances. What he will do is make a deal that's very much in the victor's favor and possibly even thank him for it.

Lastly, players aren't always comfortable with being on the receiving end of this; they may, if they wish, spend all the fate points they have left (minimum one) and demand a different outcome, and the GM (or winning character) should then make every effort to allow them to lose in a fashion more to their liking. That said, if this is a real concern, the loser may want to concede before things reach this point (see "Concessions," on the next page).

Example: Prbrawl has been fighting for his life; he's now out of consequences and has no empty spots on his stress track. The pirate king then delivers a sword blow that he can't defend. Prbrawl has been taken out!

The GM, playing the part of the pirate king, gets to say what happens to Prbrawl now. Michael could say that Prbrawl is dead, stabbed through the heart with a pirate saber. However, dead is boring; also Nick has a fate point left and would most definitely spend it to avoid this. Instead, Michael says, "The pirates carry off your limp form. Your crew will find a big pool of blood and a note scrawled on the wall, 'We've got your pilot, so surrender now!'"

Concessions

Whenever a character takes a consequence, he also has the option of offering a concession. A concession is essentially equivalent to surrendering, and it's the best way to end a fight before someone is taken out (short of moving away and ending the conflict). It allows the player to offer of the terms under which the character is taken out. If the concession is accepted, the conceding character is immediately taken out, but he's defeated according to the terms of his concession rather than having the victor determine the manner of his defeat.

Many conflicts end with a concession when one party or the other simply doesn't want to risk taking moderate or severe consequences as a result of the conflict, or when neither party wants to risk a taken out result that might come at too high a price.

The character inflicting the damage can always opt to not take the concession, but doing so is a clear indication that the fight will be a bloody one (literally or metaphorically). If the concession is refused and the GM declares that the concession was a reasonable offer, then the character who offered it gains one fate point, and the character who refused it loses one.

Example: Prbrawl has a serious consequence slot left and one open stress box, the first one. The pirate king is moving in with his saber and Nick knows that he's got about two rounds at best before he loses this fight. He decides to make a concession instead. "I want to make a concession—the pirates take over our control room, but I manage to jump into the closet and lock it behind me. By the time they get it open I'll have slipped into the access ducts."

The GM agrees, and now Prbrawl has a couple of rolls ahead of him to crawl through the access ducts. Meanwhile, who knows what mischief the pirates will get up to in the cockpit?

Removing Stress and Consequences

Consequences fade with time—characters heal, rumors die down, and distance brings perspective. How long this takes depends upon the severity of the consequence, which in turn depends on how it was received.

Stress boxes are cleared any time the character has the opportunity to sit down and take a breather for a few minutes, usually at the end of the current scene. The only exception is if there's no break between scenes—if the character doesn't get a chance to take five, the stress boxes stay filled.

Mild consequences last a bit longer, but they're still transitory. Bruises and hurt feelings fade relatively quickly. Mild consequences remain for one additional

scene after they're suffered. After a subsequent scene, they're removed from the character's sheet. This is time-dependent, however. If there's an extended break between scenes during which the character has a chance to recuperate, the mild consequence is removed.

Moderate consequences require the character get a little more time and distance. A good night's sleep or other extended period of rest and relaxation is required. Moderate consequences remain in place until the character has had the opportunity to take several hours (at least six) of "downtime." This may mean getting sleep in a comfortable bed, spending time with a charming member of the opposite sex, reading by the fire, or anything else of that ilk, so long as it's appropriate to the consequence. An evening of drinking with a sympathetic buddy might be a great way to get past a HEARTBREAK consequence, but it's not a great choice for a BAD ANKLE.

Severe consequences require substantial downtime, measured in days or weeks. Generally this means that such a consequence lingers for the duration of a session, but will be cleared up before the next adventure begins.

A character gets a break if he's in back-to-back sessions where no in-game time passes between them, such as in a multi-part adventure—any consequences he begins the session with are treated as one level lower for how quickly they can be removed.

Example: Prbrawl has escaped the pirates, and his stress track looks like this: ☐ ☒ ☒. He's also got a mild (BRUISED) and a moderate (LONG CUT ON THE ARM) consequence.

He's escaped into the access tunnels and, rather than heading straight down to rendezvous with his crewmates, he takes a minute to rest in the tunnel before he continues. This lets him remove his stress, so his track now looks like this: ☐ ☐ ☐.

He regroups with the crew and they storm the control room. This is the first scene after his initial fight, so all of his consequences remain. The pirates are driven off from the control room, but they're still aboard ship and the crew needs to solve this issue. At this point, Prbrawl recovers from his mild consequence—his bruise isn't bothering him anymore. He now has only the moderate consequence to deal with.

It causes the crew a bit of trouble, but they eventually take back their ship and jump back into hyperspace. Prbrawl hands off the control to Quinn and retires to his quarters for some much needed rest. When he wakes in the morning, he's refreshed—stress and consequence free.

Healing Injuries

When a character has suffered physical stress, another character may use Medicine to attempt a quick healing in the middle of a fight. Both characters must take a full action to do this. Make a roll against a target of Mediocre (+0); if it succeeds with one shift, the medic may remove the checkmark from the injured character's first physical stress box. Every two shifts beyond the first improves the effect by one; for example, with five shifts, you can remove the checkmark in the patient's third stress box. Only one stress box can be cleared per roll. Success can also be used to "stabilize" a character who has taken a severe or lesser consequence that would appear to be catastrophic (e.g., a BLEEDING OUT aspect)—in game terms, this has the effect of limiting the extent to which the aspect can be compelled. A single character can't be the target of more than one emergency Medicine action in an exchange.

When using Medicine to address a patient's long-term damage—i.e., the patient's physical, long-term consequences—you must spend a scene assessing and attempting to repair the injuries. Such a scene needs to take place in a relatively safe and secure environment; a clinic or hospital is optimal, but sometimes just an empty room has to suffice. The GM should consider the circumstances when determining the difficulty of the roll. If the roll is successful, you can accelerate the normal healing process. The time it takes for the patient to remove the consequence may be reduced by one step on the time table (page 65, **Doing Things** chapter) for every two shifts by which the difficulty is exceeded. Multiple Medicine checks may not be made; the first roll stands.

Resolving Maneuvers

There are three types of maneuvers—uncontested maneuvers (without an opponent), scene-altering maneuvers, and maneuvers that target another character. If the maneuver is uncontested—for instance, the character is trying to grab a datapad from a table or leap across a gap—it's a simple action, resolved just like any other simple action. The GM sets a difficulty, and the character rolls his skill and applies the resulting shifts as normal.

A maneuver can also alter the scene in some way. This can range from trivially easy (setting a lighter to a puddle of fuel to add an ON FIRE! aspect to the scene) to virtually impossible (flapping one's arms very hard to try to remove the FOGGY aspect from a scene). Whatever the result, the GM decides whether or not the change the character makes merits adding or removing an aspect to the scene. The expenditure of a fate point can usually make a reasonable argument for making such a change—if the player's willing to spend the fate point, his character's actions to add or remove the aspect are invested with an unusual potency.

If the target is another character, the maneuvering character and the target make opposed rolls, using whatever skills the GM deems appropriate. Success is usually achieved if the maneuvering character generates at least one shift. A successful maneuver may add a temporary aspect to the targeted character; the target can either accept the temporary aspect or spend a fate point to avoid accepting it. An aspect that results from a maneuver is temporary and doesn't last very long—we'll get to the duration in a moment. The temporary aspect may then be tagged for a bonus on a subsequent roll. This first invocation usually doesn't cost the tagging player a fate point, but subsequent invocations usually do (page 59, **Aspects** chapter). If a character is simply trying to increase the difficulty of another target's action, this is considered a block action and should be resolved as such; see page 69.

Some Example Maneuvers

This isn't a comprehensive list of all possible maneuvers, but the examples provided below should cover a wide range of circumstances and provide the tools needed to quickly adapt them to cover unexpected situations.

BLINDING

Whether it's throwing sand in someone's eyes, spraying someone with a harsh chemical, or tossing a can of paint in someone's face, the goal is the same—keep that someone from being able to see. This likely involves the attacker rolling Weapons and the defender rolling Athletics, with the maneuver succeeding if the attacker gets at least one shift. A successful maneuver gives your target the aspect BLINDED. You could compel that to add to the defense of anyone he attacks or to cause him

to change the target or direction of an action. It can't force him to take an action he doesn't want to, so a blinded character can't be compelled to walk off a cliff if he isn't already moving around.

DISARMING

A successful disarm maneuver forces the target to drop his weapon or otherwise renders the weapon temporarily useless. The target must either spend an action to become re-armed or pick up the weapon as a supplemental action. A supplemental action is normally a –1 penalty to the main action, but when a disarm maneuver is used, the shifts on the maneuver increase the penalty. For example, if the disarm attempt succeeds with three shifts, when the target tries to recover his weapon, he'll be at –4 (–1 for the usual penalty, plus an additional –3) to his action that exchange—essentially, the disarm maneuver has resulted in a block. His defensive rolls aren't directly affected by this penalty, but they're indirectly affected; without a weapon in hand, he can't use the Weapons skill to defend (Athletics and Fists are still options).

INDIRECT ATTACKS

Sometimes you want to do something like push a stack of boxes down on your opponent, or scatter marbles across the floor to trip him up. While this can potentially be an attack, it's usually meant as an inconvenience. If it's an attack, it's treated like any other attack. If it's an inconvenience, you have two options. The first option is to make an opposed roll—such as Might to knock over the boxes versus Athletics to dodge—and generate at least one shift, allowing a temporary aspect—such as PINNED—to be placed on the target. The other option is to create a block—such as using Might to knock over the boxes, with the value of the roll representing the block strength created by the scattered contents, causing an opponent to have to roll Athletics in order to move through the mess.

CARRYING

When you carry something heavy, the penalty for a supplemental action is increased by the weight factor of what you're carrying for each zone you move. An object or person's weight factor is equal to 1 per 100 pounds of weight. Round to the nearest whole number when calculating.

PUSHING

Pushing a target requires a successful attack—usually Fists or Might—that generates a number of shifts equal to the weight of the target +1 for each zone the target will be pushed (the +1 is basically the usual −1 for moving). While a throw or knockback moves the target to a different zone, a push moves both the target and the acting character into the destination. Because of this, the "cost" in shifts for pushing remains flat, while the cost for body-throwing and knockback increases over distance (see below). Any applicable border conditions affect the roll to push.

THROW OR KNOCKBACK

It's possible to knock something or someone away from yourself, without moving. Knockback covers any maneuver that can accomplish this, including throws. To knock something back one zone requires the maneuver to generate a number of shifts equal to 1 plus the weight factor of the target (a normal person has a weight factor of 2, a small species has a weight factor of 1, a big species is 3, etc.). Each additional zone costs as much as the previous zone did plus one, so the cost increases dramatically over distance.

Other Common Situations

There are some common situations that we're going to look at more closely.

Environmental Hazards

Environmental hazards—fire, vacuum, poisonous atmospheric conditions—are rated by their intensity. The intensity rating is the amount of physical stress the environment inflicts on every person in the scene at the beginning of each exchange. Intensity basically means:

0: The area is hazardous, but the danger can be avoided.
1: Almost everything around you is hazardous, and the danger is pressing in.
2: Everything is deadly, and any action runs a risk of damage.
3: There may well be nowhere to run or hide, and you have only moments to live.

Exposure to the vacuum of space is always a risk in a game like **Bulldogs!** Space is dangerous, and the intensity depends entirely on what protection you have against it. A leaking space suit is a 0 or 1, a large tear would rate a 2, and exposure to the vacuum of space with no protection is definitely a 3.

Some environments are fatiguing rather than damaging, such as trying to operate out in the hot desert sun or on a planet with a hostile or toxic atmosphere. In those situations, it's more appropriate to have Endurance restrict other skills, rather than inflicting physical stress.

Zero Gravity

Ships and space stations in **Bulldogs!** use technology that creates an artificial gravity field, allowing long-term or even permanent living in space; it also enables ships to use massive acceleration without harming the crew inside. Outside the ship, or if the artificial gravity on board malfunctions, zero gravity conditions exist. For people unused to dealing with the conditions of zero or microgravity, activities are impaired.

Characters operating in zero gravity always suffer a −2 on all physical actions. This can be mitigated by certain aspects like VETERAN SPACER or ZERO-G COMBAT TRAINED. A character with an aspect like this can *spend a fate point* to be immune to the zero gravity penalty for the duration of a scene.

Explosions

Explosions and other area attacks have the potential to do damage against everyone within their radius. They're deadly and can quickly end a fight or alter a scenario significantly. Consider very carefully before allowing free and easy use of explosives in your game.

Explosives have three ratings—complexity, area, and damage. Here, we'll dig deeper into what these mean.

Complexity is the difficulty to disarm the bomb once the fuse has been lit or the pin has been pulled.

The **area** of an explosion determines how many zones the explosion will cover. An area of 1 means the explosion affects only one zone. An area of 2 means it affects one zone and every zone adjacent to it. An area of 3 expands it out to all zones adjacent to that. An area of 10 can pretty effectively cover a small town, and a 20 can cover a large city. This, of course, assumes that your zones are roughly the same size, that the explosion originates in the center of its zone, and so forth—feel free to tweak how things behave. There's nothing saying every area 2 explosion hits all of its adjacent zones, merely that it *could*.

The **damage** of an explosion is a measure of how dangerous it is when it finally detonates. When an explosive detonates in a zone that your character is in, you get a free action to roll your Athletics against the damage value to try to jump clear of the zone or to take cover behind something solid. If you succeed, your character can leap clear or duck under cover if it's available in the zone. If he fails, he takes stress from the damage value of the explosive. The exception is if the explosive is thrown into your zone. If you're unaware that a detonation is impending, your defense against the damage of the explosive is automatically Mediocre (+0).

The good news is that the damage of an explosion drops by one for each zone it crosses, so characters in an adjacent zone have to deal with a damage level that's 1 lower. If there's a border between the zones that would provide some cover—like a wall—it also reduces damage by the value of the border. The damage of an explosion drops to zero once it reaches its maximum radius indicated by the area.

Setting and using explosives can usually be done using the Engineering skill, but throwing a grenade is a Weapons roll. Explosives fired from a gun or mortar use the Artillery skill. Before a character throws, the GM should ask if the fuse is short, medium, or long (for some explosives this is fixed, and not the player's choice). This doesn't need to mean a literal physical fuse—it could just as easily be a timer or some other control. If the explosive is supposed to go off on impact, it needs a hair trigger.

Throwing an explosive as an attack works in two stages. When a character throws an explosive, it's an attack using Weapons against a difficulty of Mediocre (+0). If successful, the explosive lands in an appropriate zone—remember that thrown weapons have a range of one zone. If unsuccessful, it lands in the thrower's zone.

When the explosive lands, everyone in a zone covered by its area can roll Athletics against the attack result to get clear; if they succeed on this defense roll, they may move one zone, essentially "diving clear" as a free action. The thrower can choose to reduce everyone's difficulty to dive clear—after all, his allies also need to dive away!—as long as that difficulty isn't reduced below Mediocre (+0). If the thrower makes a bad throw—missing the Mediocre (+0) target—then, as noted, the explosive lands in the thrower's zone; the difficulty for the thrower to dive free is increased by one for each step below Mediocre (+0). The thrower doesn't have the option to reduce it, though in such a circumstance everyone else merely faces a Mediocre (+0) difficulty to dive clear.

After this initial "dive clear" check, the GM makes a quick check before each individual action to see if the bomb explodes, by rolling 2 dice:

On a fizzle result, make a mark on a piece of paper. The second time a fizzle result comes up, the bomb is a dud or otherwise unable to explode. If the GM allows, characters with appropriate aspects may invoke them to demand that the GM re-roll the dice after revealing the result.

Each time the turn comes back around to the person who lit the fuse, a full exchange has passed and the fuse's length drops by one step. So if a long fuse explosive is out there for a full exchange, it becomes a medium fuse explosive, and so on. If it's a short fuse explosive (pretty improbable that it lasted a full exchange), then it goes off right then and there.

Dice result	Short Fuse	Medium Fuse	Long Fuse
+2	Explode	Explode	Explode
+1	Explode	Explode	No explosion
+0	Explode	No explosion	No explosion
-1	No explosion	No explosion	No explosion
-2	Fizzle	Fizzle	Fizzle

Playing With Fire

When a character has an unexploded bomb in his zone and the opportunity to act, he can try a few things.

Pick It Up and Throw It

This uses the same rules for throwing the explosive that the original thrower used, but at a –1 penalty for taking the supplemental action of picking it up. This can turn into a deadly game of hot potato.

Pick It Up and Disarm It

A character may use Engineering to disarm a bomb. This action is at –1 for the supplemental action of picking it up and is at a difficulty equal to the complexity of the explosive. It's easy to pull the fuse out of a stick of dynamite, but somewhat harder to stop a grenade without the pin.

Leap on Top of It

Well, first off, this will pretty much kill the character dead. That said, it'll improve the chances of everyone around him by reducing the damage of the explosion by 3. If the character is armored in some way, then the value of the armor is also subtracted from the damage. Under particularly unusual circumstances, sets of stunts, or thick armor, the character might be able to walk away from this, but really, players should be discouraged from such actions unless they're looking to start a new character. Fate points could be brought to bear, of course, to force a fizzle once this is done, but the GM should feel quite free to charge the player every single fate point he has to pull it off.

Run Away

Usually the wisest course—using Athletics to sprint away from the bomb—isn't such a bad idea. The trick is that you need the chance to take a turn so you can exercise this option. Players often want to bring their friends along as they flee from the scene of a bomb, so GMs should make sure to review the rules on throwing, pushing, and carrying (page 75 and page 76). While an individual almost always gets away faster, the nature of a fuse—getting checked on every action—may make a player willing get less distance if he's helping a slower person get some distance, too.

Bombs Outside of Combat

When a character encounters a bomb in a situation other than having it thrown by a maniac, there are a few commonalities you can expect. The bomb is usually larger, heavier, and more powerful, and it usually has an explicit trigger, such as a timer on a countdown or an event that will trigger it, like a tripwire.

Such bombs are inevitably powerful enough that characters in close proximity to them when they detonate have very little chance of survival. Thankfully, the role of such bombs is not to blow up; rather, their role is to threaten to blow up. Usually such bombs are in important places so that, if they go off, there'll be serious consequences—even if the characters are unharmed.

Attempts to disarm one of these bombs require one or more Engineering rolls against its complexity. A failure on any roll shouldn't result in the bomb exploding immediately; instead, turn the bomb into one with a fuse that starts counting down! Roll a single die; minus means it's become a short fuse, blank means a medium, and plus means a long. Hopefully, this buys time enough for everyone to run like the dickens.

Minions

The term **minions** is used to refer to the large number of "faceless" followers of more important "named" characters in a scene. The named characters are the villains of the piece; the minions are the bodies of the faithful (or at least the hapless) that the heroes must climb over to take on the named characters.

Minions have two important statistics—quality and quantity. The GM may build the villains' minion mobs using stunts—see page 116—but should feel free to play a little loose with the rules when sizing the minions appropriately to the opposition.

Minions may be of Average (+1), Fair (+2), or Good (+3) quality. This quality denotes their base effectiveness in one kind of conflict (physical, social, or mental), as well as their capacity for stress. Average minions can take one box of stress, Fair can take two, and Good can take three.

The quantity of minions is simply the number of minions present; however, minions act in one or more groups, each of which is treated as a single character in a conflict. This allows the GM to minimize the number of die rolls she's making, even when her heroes are facing off against a group of twenty screaming pirates. This shorthand technique also makes it a touch easier for the heroes to eliminate several minions in a single action.

Minions who act together as a group are much more effective than individual minions. When there are two or three minions in a group, the group receives a +1 bonus to act and react. If there are four to six minions in a group, the bonus is +2; seven to nine minions get a +3 bonus, and any single group with ten or more members gets +4.

# of Minions	Bonus
1	+0
2-3	+1
4-6	+2
7-9	+3
10+	+4

As a rule of thumb, when a GM has a large number of minions, she should split them up into several smaller groups—preferably one group for each player character they face. These groups don't necessarily need to be equal in number; sometimes it makes sense to pit the largest group of minions against the most capable opponent.

When minions take stress, it's applied sequentially (i.e., filling all boxes instead of just a single one). Damage that overflows one minion is applied to the next minion. This means a solid enough effort can take out an entire swath of minions.

Mixed Groups

One of the main uses for minions, be they ninjas or yes-men, is to improve the effectiveness of their leader. Whenever a named character and a group of minions are attacking the same target, they're considered to be attached. This has two benefits for the leader—he receives a bonus based on the group size (including him), and damage is applied to minions before it's applied to him. It has no benefits for the minions, who give up their ability to act independently, but that's more or less their job (see the Leadership skill for more, page 96, *Skills* chapter). Leaving or attaching to a group is a free action, and a character may detach from a group automatically by moving away from it.

Companions

Companions are characters who are a little more important than minions but aren't quite full-fledged named characters in their own right. They're attached to named characters in the same way minion groups are, and they grant a +1 in appropriate conflicts due to group size. Companions don't have stress boxes, like minions do; instead, they give the named character the ability to withstand an additional consequence—specifically, the consequence that the companion is taken out, kidnapped, or otherwise removed from the conflict.

While characters aren't obliged to take their companion as an aspect, it's highly recommended. Companions are the first people villains choose as hostages and targets; by choosing to take an appropriate aspect, you ensure that you'll be rewarded for the inconvenience.

Companions are either granted as a short-term story element by the GM or are established by purchasing and using a number of stunts. By default, a companion is of Average (+1) quality and can assist in one type of conflict. The type of conflict that the companion can assist with determines his type.

Type	Conflicts
Sidekick	Physical
Aide	Social
Assistant	Mental

A companion can have a number of advances, with each advance making him more capable. Usually, when your character takes a stunt to gain a sidekick, aide, or assistant, the companion gets a number of advances to begin with, and you can buy more advances with additional stunts.

An advance can do one of the following:

Quality

Improve the quality of a companion by one step—from Average (+1) to Fair (+2), Fair (+2) to Good (+3), and so on. This advance may be taken several times up to the companion's maximum quality, one step lower than that of his partner. Characters usually top out at Superb (+5), so typically the highest a companion could be is Great (+4).

Scope

Improve the scope of a companion, allowing him to assist in an additional type of conflict (e.g., Physical and Mental, Physical and Social, Social and Mental). This may be taken twice, allowing the companion to be effective in all three scopes.

Independent

The companion can act independently of his partner, allowing the character to send the companion off to perform tasks. An independent companion is treated as a minion if he's caught out on his own (quality in this case indicates his capacity for stress), and isn't useful for much unless he's also skilled (see below).

Skilled

The companion may buy skills of his own. When your character and companion are together, you can roll the companion's skill rating instead of your character's skill rating. If the companion also has the Independent advance (above), the companion can use these skills even when he's not with your character. With one advance you can buy one skill at the companion's quality, two skills at quality −1, or three skills at quality −2. The Skilled advance can be bought multiple times, but a different skill or set of skills must be chosen each time.

Advancement

Characters change and improve over time. As you venture around the galaxy, your troubles and encounters teach you new things. Your character becomes more powerful and you take on greater threats. Change for a character is marked by **milestones**.

Milestones & Characters

Milestones mark important transitions for a character; they're opportunities for advancement and change. They happen mostly by GM discretion—how often milestones occur and for what reasons establish a lot about the tone of the game. GMs shouldn't be stingy with milestones, but you also don't want to have a major milestone every session. The more often milestones occur, the faster the characters will improve and the faster threats will escalate, compensating for the increase in player power.

There are three types of milestone—minor, significant, and major. Each is described below, along with what might prompt such a milestone and the effect on a character when one does occur.

Minor Milestone

Minor milestones usually occur at the end of a session of play or whenever a significant piece of a story is resolved. A minor milestone allows the characters to evolve in response to the story that's been unfolding before them.

When a minor milestone occurs, you may choose *one* of the following:

- Switch the rank values of any two skills, or replace one Average (+1) skill with one that isn't on your sheet.
- Change any single stunt for another stunt.
- Purchase new stunts, provided you have the refresh to do so.
- Rename one aspect.

Minor milestones are ideal when you want to switch the focus of your character's existing abilities or change something on the character sheet, like a skill or the wording of an aspect. Maybe something happens in the story that makes part of your character's sheet seem inappropriate, or you've simply discovered that your choice of skills, aspects, and stunts don't match your expectations in play.

Obviously, these changes should be justified as much as possible, either within the story ("My companion Bertie got killed, so I'm hiring a small gang to go after the guys who did it. I'm swapping out my companion for some minions.") or as a result of play ("So I thought I wanted this guy to have a Good (+3) Empathy, but I'm not really using it much—it'd be more fitting if he had a lower Empathy and a higher Rapport, so I'm going to switch it out with my Fair (+2) Rapport."). If the skill you're switching out is at Average (+1), you may change it for a skill that isn't on your sheet. Be careful when switching a character's highest skills, though—this can significantly change the character, which isn't the purpose of a minor milestone.

Keep it in character, so to speak.

Significant Milestone

A **significant milestone** usually occurs at the conclusion of a scenario or a major plotline—typically once every two or three sessions. Significant milestones are about advances of experience, as the characters have learned new things in dealing with problems and challenges.

When a significant milestone occurs, your character gets all of the following:

- One additional skill rank.
- Any of the benefits of a minor milestone.

Spending the additional skill rank on a new skill slot can be a little confusing. One skill rank buys an Average (+1) slot, which you can then fill with any skill you want. If you want a bigger slot, you have to bank a few significant milestones' worth of advancement first. When you're upgrading an existing skill, you only need to pay the difference in cost—if you have an Average (+1) slot, you can upgrade it to a Fair (+2) slot by paying one rank.

Important: You can't have more skills at any rank than you have at any lesser rank. For example, suppose you have a skill layout of one Great (+4), two Good (+3), three Fair (+2), and four Average (+1). Imagine that these are represented as building blocks stacked atop one another, each level representing a rank. Each block needs one below it to support it.

That would look like this:

☐   **Great (+4)**

☐☐   **Good (+3)**

☐☐☐   **Fair (+2)**

☐☐☐☐ **Average (+1)**

During a significant milestone, you decide you want to upgrade one of your Fair (+2) slots to a Good (+3) slot:

☐   **Great (+4)**

☐☐☐   **Good (+3)**

☐☐⊠   **Fair (+2)**

☐☐☐☐ **Average (+1)**

But the resulting gap in the Fair (+2) category means that you *can't* make that purchase at this time—you'd need an extra Fair (+2) skill in place to "hold up" the Good skill you want. You can buy a slot at Average now and upgrade it over the course of the next two milestones, or simply bank the points and buy a new Good slot directly when you have enough.

Major Milestone

A **major milestone** should only occur when something's happened in the campaign that shakes it up *a lot*—either when several scenarios have concluded or a long, large-scale plotline wraps up. When these happen, the characters jump up a step in power.

When a major milestone occurs, your character gets all of the following:

- You can "clear out" an extreme consequence slot, allowing it to be used again.
- An additional point of refresh.
- New stunts.
- Any of the benefits of a significant milestone.

Major milestones signify a *major change* in the power structure of your campaign—your characters will be dealing with a whole new tier of obstacles from here on out. You're basically moving your game one power level upwards. Even just the bump to a skill that a stunt provides can radically alter the nature of a character's effectiveness.

This is a *really* big deal; it means that the player characters are directly able to take on more powerful threats *and* have a wider variety of resources to draw on to face those threats. To use a boxing analogy, an advancement of power is like stepping up to the next weight class—you might be the most skilled boxer in the world, but if you're a featherweight, there's still only so much you can do against a less-skilled heavyweight.

Another option the GM has for a major milestone is to *increase the skill cap by one rank*. This allows the characters to raise their skills up into larger-than-life levels, transcending all previous expectations of human (or alien) capability. This can be combined with the normal refresh award as often as the GM wishes. By default, one skill cap increase should probably come every two or three major milestones, happening a few times per campaign. A campaign where the skill cap increases with every new refresh gain will get to Epic (literally) levels *very* quickly.

Skills

Skills are the way your character interacts with and changes the game world. Any time there's a question of whether or not your character can successfully do what you want her to, a skill roll is called for (page 65, **Doing Things** chapter).

The list of skills below should cover any action you choose to undertake. Each skill describes the circumstances where you can use it. Skills can generally be used in several ways:

1. Overcome Obstacles
2. Assessment
3. Declaration
4. Place Maneuver
5. Attack
6. Defend
7. Block

Not every skill can be used in all of these ways. Each skill description specifies how the skill can be used to achieve each of these goals. If one of these goals isn't mentioned in a skill description, the skill can't be used to achieve the goal.

Overcome Obstacles

Skills are tested when a character is presented with a problem or challenge and uses one of her skills to overcome it. This kind of challenge should be familiar to most players. If a character wants to use a grapple to swing across a deep chasm, she'll use her Athletics skill. If a character wishes to override an airlock's security mechanism to open both doors at once, she'll use her Burglary skill. If a character wishes to sweet-talk that good-looking docking bay administrator, she'll use her Rapport skill.

The skill description specifies what types of obstacles you can try to overcome with this skill. Some skills allow a character to create or repair items, and these uses count as obstacles to overcome—the main description of the skill covers these situations.

Assessment

Some skills let you assess a situation in advance of taking action, as part of putting together a plan or simply observing a target long enough to learn something that'll give a critical advantage. This approach is usually used with skills that have an element of perception— including Investigation, Empathy, even Burglary. With assessment, the skill isn't used to place a temporary aspect so much as discover an existing one. You can tag this aspect once for free (page 59, **Aspects** chapter).

All assessment efforts require the use of a significant chunk of time, usually indicated in the skill description. This lets you use skills that normally aren't particularly useful in more time pressured environments (like a fight), thanks to the time invested in advance.

Importantly, only one assessment can be made with a skill. A character can't use Investigation to make assessment after assessment about a spacecraft, for example. Once one skill is used to make an assessment about a target, it can't be reused. If you want to make a second assessment about the same target, you need to use a different skill.

Any aspects brought into play through assessment don't have to go away after they're used, if circumstances make it reasonable that they hang around or if the GM finds them useful or interesting. Any subsequent uses of such aspects, however, will cost (or grant!) a fate point, as usual. This does mean that occasionally assessments will backfire, leading to a compel. Since aspects are involved, such things are easily double-edged!

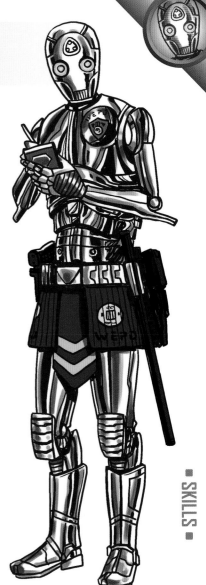

Declaration

Assessments only allow the discovery of what already exists. By contrast, some skills allow a declaration—in other words, using a skill successfully allows a player to introduce entirely new facts into play and then use those facts to his advantage. The new facts take the form of a temporary aspect. The GM is encouraged to use creativity as her primary guideline when judging the use of skills that allow declaration—creative and entertaining facts should be more likely to succeed than boring facts, since a success results in a temporary aspect. For example, a xenoanthropologist with a solid Academics skill might use the declaration ability to state new truths about an alien culture your crew has just encountered—if successful, suddenly the scene or the culture has an aspect on it that reflects the fact the player just invented. As with assessment, this aspect can be tagged once for free. Unlike assessment, declaration doesn't take any actual in-game time at all—just the knowledge skill to make use of it.

Like assessment, each skill may be used only once per scene to make a declaration. Also like assessment, the aspects created may persist depending on logic and the GM's discretion.

Place Maneuver

A maneuver is similar to assessment and declaration, but it usually occurs during an extended conflict and the aspects created are often fragile or transitory. A maneuver is an attempt to change the situation in some way, affecting the environment or other people, but without damaging or forcing the target—if force is used or damage is dealt, it's an attack and an attempt to cause stress. Trying to climb to higher ground, blast a hole in a steam pipe, distract someone with a clever lie, or negotiate a resolution to a standoff could all be maneuvers.

For more on maneuvers, see page 68, **Doing Things** chapter.

Skills List

Academics	Mental
Alertness	Mental
Artillery	Physical
Athletics	Physical
Burglary	Physical
Contacting	Social
Deceit	Social
Empathy	Social
Endurance	Physical
Engineering	Mental
Fists	Physical
Gambling	Social
Guns	Physical
Intimidation	Social
Investigation	Mental
Leadership	Social
Medicine	Mental
Might	Physical
Pilot	Physical
Psychic	Mental
Rapport	Social
Resolve	Social
Sleight of Hand	Physical
Stealth	Physical
Survival	Mental
Systems	Mental
Trading	Social
Weapons	Physical

Attack

When in conflict with another character, many skills can be used to attack an opponent and mark off boxes on the other character's stress track. More details on this are found in the **Doing Things** chapter (page 68). When a skill can be used to attack an opponent, this is noted in its description.

Defend

When one character attempts to use a skill on another, there's always a chance to defend. Certain skills are used to defend against specific attacks, and these uses are discussed in the skill description. Details on defending against attacks are found in the **Doing Things** chapter (page 68). A character can never use the same skill more than once in an exchange. That means a skill can't be used to both attack and defend in the same exchange.

Block

A character can use a skill to set up a blocking action. A block tries to prevent something from happening, rather than taking direct action to make something happen. Blocks can be declared against any sort of action or actions and may theoretically use any skill, although the GM may establish a difficulty based on the likelihood such a block would work.

For more on blocks, see page 69, **Doing Things** chapter.

Special

Some skills have other special uses that fall outside the ordinary. These are usually just automatic advantages conferred by the skill and rarely require a roll. Any such special uses will be noted in the skill description.

SKILLS

Academics

Academics measures a character's education, recall, and knowledge. Any knowledge that isn't specific to another skill falls under Academics, with some overlap to be expected. Characters with high Academics include information brokers, professors, scientists, Infocity acolytes, and know-it-alls.

Overcome Obstacles [Academics]

The main use of Academics is to answer a question. Questions covered by Academics include those of art, history, literature, sociology, or any of the sciences. You can ask the GM, "What do I know about this subject?" or "What does this mean?" Often, there'll be no need to roll, especially if the subject is within your character's specialty, but if the GM feels the information is something that should be hard to attain —such as a clue—then she may call for a roll against a difficulty she sets. If your character succeeds, he receives the information. If he fails, he doesn't, but he may still attempt to research the topic (see below)—or, perhaps more entertainingly, may stumble onto a false lead that gets him deeper into trouble.

Researching a topic is frequently a time-consuming and arduous task—exactly the sort of thing worth skimming over with a few quick dice rolls. It's treated as an extension of the knowledge your character has— some questions he can answer off the top of his head; others he can answer because he knows what data sources to search.

As such, research is something that can happen when a character *fails* an Academics check. Provided the researcher is willing to spend time researching—and that the answer *can* be found—the only question is how long it'll take and how good an information source he has access to.

Academic research requires a data source. The quality of the source of information determines the hardest possible question that can be answered within it—so a question of Good (+3) difficulty requires a Good (+3) data source or better. If a character is attempting to answer a question using a data source that's not equal to answering it, the GM should be up-front about its shortcomings.

Most ships, space stations, and private individuals have a Mediocre (+0), Average (+1), or Fair (+2) data bank. Small corporations or governments often have Good (+3) data sources while larger institutions may have Great (+4) ones. Superb (+5) and better data sources are few and far between. The Infocity satellite in Galactic Central Point has a Legendary (+8) collection of data. Some data banks are specialized and are considered one step higher in their area of specialty—for example, TransGalaxy's shipboard

data banks specialize in astrogation, so a typical TransGalaxy ship has an Average (+1) data source, which is treated as Fair (+2) for questions of navigation. Characters may own data of their own; see the *Gear* chapter (page 136) for more.

Academics can be used to perform scientific research as well, provided there's time and equipment. A scientist looking to solve a problem should figure out what question he's trying to answer, like "What killed this man?" or "What is this object composed of?" The GM calls for a roll to see if the character can answer the question. This requires a lab of some sort, and it's possible that some questions can't be answered without the right equipment. In the end, this functions the same as performing research (see above).

For the ten core species, the listed aspects should be considered common knowledge and available to a player after an Average (+1) Academics roll. If a new species is encountered, an Academics roll can reveal the aspects normally shared by that species. The rarity of the species determines the difficulty of such a roll; a good baseline starts at a difficulty of Fair (+2) for a species that isn't quite as common as the core species, and moves up the ladder from there for progressively more obscure species.

Assessment [Academics]

Research, as described above, is an excellent avenue for assessing a person, item, or location, provided your character has enough time and access to a data source with the proper information. You could look up blueprints, public records, legal history, or all manner of useful facts regarding your target. As always, these facts must be within the field of Academics and the GM has a right to veto them. The GM sets the difficulty for you to roll against. If successful, your character discovers some useful aspect; if not, the data is incorrect or outdated and your character is mistaken. Like most Academics rolls, the GM can decide not to share the difficulty, so your character may not know if he succeeded. If the academic is wrong, there's no penalty, but there may be complications—at her option, the GM can place a temporary MISTAKEN aspect on the academic, compelling it to represent the fall-out (and netting the mistaken academic a fate point!).

Declaration [Academics]

You can use your character's knowledge to declare facts, filling in minor details the GM hasn't mentioned. These facts must be within the field of Academics, and the GM has the right to veto them. You make a declaration and roll Academics against a difficulty the GM sets. If successful, the fact is true; if not, your character is mistaken. Consequences of a mistaken declaration are the same as failed assessment, above.

Attack [Academics]

Academics isn't an attack skill. It can rarely be used to cause stress to an opponent, unless the conflict is knowledge related, like a spelling bee or some other contest of knowledge. Academics could conceivably be used to attack in a legal trial by presenting facts contradicting the opposing counsel's theory, for example. In this case, your character is using Academics to marshal his knowledge to overwhelm or dismay his opponent.

Defend [Academics]

Academics can only be used as a defense if another character is using the Academics skill to attack. Your character could, in such a situation, use his own knowledge to present facts that refute his opponent and negate the attempted attack.

Special [Academics]

Your character may speak a number of additional languages based on his Academics score. Each step of Academics above Mediocre (+0) gives your character knowledge of one additional language—one at Average (+1), two at Fair (+2), and so on. You don't need to choose the languages when your character is created; instead, you can simply choose languages in the course of play, as is convenient.

Alertness

Alertness is a measure of your character's regular, *passive* level of awareness. Specifically, it's the perception skill to notice things the character isn't looking for. Characters with high Alertness include bodyguards, outdoorsmen, and criminals of a sneaky variety.

Overcome Obstacles [Alertness]

Players rarely *ask* to roll Alertness—if they're actively looking for something, Investigation is usually more appropriate. Alertness is more appropriate for things that players and characters don't expect or aren't looking for, such as a surprise or a hidden clue. In short, it's *reactive* perception. As such, it's a skill that, most often, the GM calls for players to roll.

Defend [Alertness]

Alertness can be used to defend against ambushes or attacks using the Stealth skill. When you're ambushed (see Stealth, page 102), you may make one final Alertness check against the Stealth of your attacker to see if you're surprised. If you fail this check, your defense skill is considered to be Mediocre (+0) for the first exchange.

Special [Alertness]

The initiative order in active, physical conflicts is determined by Alertness. The character with the highest Alertness acts first, followed by those with the next lowest Alertness, etc. Ties in initiative are resolved in favor of characters with a higher Resolve. Any remaining ties are in favor of the player closest to the GM's right.

Artillery

Artillery is the skill of using heavy weapons; these range from small portable types like mortars and grenade launchers all the way up to the massive cannon batteries equipped on military vessels. Any weapon larger than small arms is fired using the Artillery skill rather than the Guns skill. Characters with a high Artillery skill include ship gunners, soldiers, and bombardiers.

Assessment [Artillery]

The Artillery skill has limited use in assessment. You could use it to examine a battleground in advance of a conflict and determine the best places to put artillery pieces or to assess where an enemy might place their own. You might also assess the weak points in any defenses to determine the best place to strike them with an artillery shot. Characters with the Artillery skill can also identify weapons by the gunports on a ship or identify what sort of heavy weapons caused burn scars or holes.

Declaration [Artillery]

As with assessment, Artillery can only be used in very specific circumstances to make a declaration. Artillerists can keep their weapons in good firing order and know about storage and care of munitions. The skill can be used to make declarations about where munitions might be stored in a new environment, the condition of an enemy's weapons, the suitability of a particular piece of ordnance in a given environment, or other facts specific to heavy weapons.

Place Maneuver [Artillery]

In the heat of combat, Artillery can be used to place maneuvers on an opponent. In this case, the gunner is firing or aiming for effect, rather than trying to attack an opponent. Covering an opponent or getting him in your sights are appropriate maneuvers. Artillery can also be used in ship combat to force an opponent off course or to force him to make defensive maneuvers.

Attack [Artillery]

This is the main use of the Artillery skill. These weapons are designed to cause stress to large groups of people or big pieces of equipment. The Artillery skill is primarily used in ship-to-ship combat, and these guns are among the few things that can damage the opposing ship.

Many artillery pieces aren't really designed to fire at personnel. Ship's guns especially are designed to blast through ship armor, not fire at tiny individuals on the ground. Ship targeting systems won't even register a single person as a target, making firing these weapons at people relatively difficult. More details on weapon scale are in the *Ships* chapter, page 151.

Block [Artillery]

An expert artillerist can use the Artillery skill to set up a block by laying down suppressive fire—concentrating heavy fire in a single area and forcing an opponent to avoid it or take cover. This can be used to bombard a particular area and prevent people from moving through; in the context of a dogfight, you could prevent an opponent from moving in a direction you choose to block.

Athletics

This is a measure of the character's general physical capability; the exception is raw power, which is a function of Might. Athletics covers running, jumping, climbing, and other broadly physical activities you might find in a track and field event. Characters with high Athletics include athletes, soldiers, and outdoorsmen.

Overcome Obstacles [Athletics]

Athletics is often the "when in doubt" physical skill, and it gets a lot of use. If you're confused about when to use Athletics and when to use Might, here's a rule of thumb—Athletics is used to move yourself, while Might is used to move other things and people. When an action calls for both, they may modify one another. If there's no clear indication which should be primary, default to Athletics as primary and Might as secondary.

Athletics is used for things like sprinting, jumping, or climbing. Generally, the GM sets a fixed difficulty to be met or exceeded. Often, there's a set amount of time, also set by the GM, that's required to run a distance or climb over an obstacle. A chase on foot or a race between two characters also uses the Athletics skill. Extra shifts can be used to reduce the time required. If a character is competing against another, the skill results are directly compared to determine who completes the task more quickly.

Declaration [Athletics]

Athletics can only be used to make declarations in very specific situations. You might be able to make declarations about conditions likely to affect an attempt to use the skill—a cliff face is made of a particularly crumbly material, not immediately obvious to the untrained; the landing spot of a jump is uneven; or an enemy minion didn't stretch out before a run, risking a cramp, etc.

Place Maneuver [Athletics]

If you wish to move to place a maneuver on an opponent in a conflict, Athletics is an appropriate skill to use. Your character can move behind an opponent, move behind cover, or climb over an obstacle. You must describe how his actions give your character an advantage, and the GM sets the difficulty for the roll. Athletics-based maneuvers are usually quite fragile, often negated by some simple movement or action on the part of the enemy.

Defend [Athletics]

Athletics is used as a defensive skill against attacks in physical combat; it works very well in conjunction with taking a full defense action (yielding a +2 to the roll; see page 68). Athletics can be used as a dodge to counter attacks by Artillery, Fists, Guns, or Weapons. It's important to note that taking a full defense action means that you can't use Athletics for other things, like movement between zones in combat.

Block [Athletics]

By maneuvering your character between an opponent and a place that opponent wishes to go, you can use Athletics to set up a block. This is strictly putting your character's body as an obstacle between an opponent and something he wishes to reach, and it can be countered in a lot of different ways. An Athletics block doesn't include grappling or otherwise physically restraining another character—that would fall under Might.

Burglary

The ability to overcome security systems, from alarms to locks, falls under the auspices of this skill. This also includes knowledge of those systems and the ability to assess them. Characters with a high Burglary include burglars, private eyes, and even some security officers.

Overcome Obstacles [Burglary]

Burglary is really used for a single thing—to disable alarms and locks. Any time you wish to override a lock on a door or compartment, you use Burglary to make the attempt. Burglary gives your character the skill to override electronic locks and other security devices, as well as locks and bars of a more physical nature. Burglary is also used for safecracking. The difficulty of any Burglary attempt is determined by the rating of the device you're trying to get past. An ordinary footlocker is likely to have an Average (+1) or Fair (+2) lock, while a vault in a G'n'vese bank will have a Superb (+5) or better security system.

Assessment [Burglary]

Burglary can be used as a very specialized perception skill, specifically to assess the weaknesses and strengths of a potential target. Here, you're trying to determine the existence of unobvious or hidden aspects, using assessment. Casing a target with Burglary is limited to security facts, including potential escape routes.

Declaration [Burglary]

Burglary can also be used to make a declaration during the course of a burglary. Again, this utility is limited to security facts. You can identify the brand of ID pad used at a facility and declare the manufacturer's particular security weakness, for example.

Contacting

Contacting is the ability to find things out from people or to find the people you're looking for. Your character may know a guy who knows a guy, or maybe he just knows the right questions to ask. Whatever his methods, he knows how to find things out by asking around. Characters with high Contacting include reporters, private eyes, fences, and spies.

Overcome Obstacles [Contacting]

A character with a high Contacting skill knows a wide variety of people and has at least a minor connection with virtually any organization. There are Contacting stunts which give a character deep ties to a specific field like crime or business, and those allow a deeper level of contact within that field (page 110, *Stunts* chapter).

Contacting doesn't work in a vacuum. The character needs to be able to get out and talk to people for it to be useful; when that isn't possible, neither is Contacting. Contacting is also limited by familiarity—if your character finds himself in an entirely unfamiliar environment such as a planet he's never visited before, he may encounter difficulties increased by as much as +4. Thankfully, Contacting also covers the skill for building new social networks, so if your character stays in an area for any amount of time, he can diminish the difficulty by one for each week he spends there.

Contacting also keeps the character apprised of the general state of things—it acts as a sort of social Alertness, keeping the character abreast of things that might be coming his way. It's far from foolproof and, like Alertness, the GM is usually the one to call for a roll—a player can't go out looking for a tip off, though he can tell the GM he's going out talking to his contacts just to check on what's up, which is a good hint that he'd like a tip off.

Assessment [Contacting]

Contacting may be used for assessment by canvassing locals and gathering information about a situation, place, or person. Your character must go out and talk to people, trying to find the answer to a question like, "Who's trying to kill me?" You describe where your character is going to talk to folks (usually "the street"). If your character is being "shut out" for one reason or another, no amount of dogged persistence and time investment is going to help. When that happens, it usually means there's another problem you need to solve first.

One important warning about authenticity—being the most informed guy and knowing all the latest gossip aren't necessarily the same thing. Contacting finds out what people know, and people always have their own biases. Information is only as good as the sources it comes from. Contacting rarely tests the veracity of the information provided—unless you discover that contradictory answers are coming from different sources. If you want to determine the truthfulness of the information you're finding, that's a more in-depth conversation that may involve Empathy, Rapport, Deceit, and more.

Declaration [Contacting]

Characters can use Contacting for declarations as well as assessment. By going through your network and gathering information, you can use Contacting to create a new aspect that applies to the target, based on the rumors and inside information you're able to unearth through your contacts.

Contacting is also useful for planting rumors, not just for ferreting them out. Make a declaration that represents the rumor you want to plant. It's worth noting that your roll is also the target for someone else's Contacting roll to find out who's been *spreading* rumors, so be careful!

Deceit

Deceit is the ability to lie, simple as that. Whether through word or deed, it's the ability to convey falsehoods convincingly. Characters with high Deceit include grifters, spies, and politicians.

Overcome Obstacles [Deceit]

For simple deceptions, a contest between Deceit and an appropriate skill (usually Empathy, Alertness, or Investigation) is all that's necessary. Sometimes, Deceit is the undercurrent rather than the forefront of an action; as such, the skill may be used secondarily to modify, restrict, or complement another skill's use.

Deceit also covers disguises, using the disguised character's Deceit skill against any attempts to penetrate the disguise. Such disguises are dependent on what props are available and won't hold up to intense scrutiny (specifically, an Investigation roll) without the use of stunts, but they're fine for casual inspection (Alertness rolls).

Place Maneuver [Deceit]

In a conflict, Deceit can be used to give your opponent a false impression, setting him up for a later attack. In social conflict, this can be the weaving of a web of lies or false impressions. Deceit can also be used in physical conflict by making a feint or executing a fake-out. Deceit maneuvers are only good until something occurs to reveal the deception; in the case of feints or other quick deceptions, they last only until the deceiver's next action. However, a well-placed lie that's difficult to refute can create an aspect that lingers for a long while.

Attack [Deceit]

For deeper deceptions—like convincing someone of a lie or selling someone Job Tower—a social conflict is appropriate, complete with Deceit attacks and stress being dealt. Stress caused by Deceit is almost always some sort of social anguish or emotional manipulation.

Defend [Deceit]

You may opt to use Deceit instead of Rapport to defend against someone using Empathy to get a read on your character. This roll is modified by Rapport. If you fail your defense roll, then the Empathy reader proceeds as usual—in attempting to hide something, you've blundered and revealed a truth. If you succeed, however, you may provide a false aspect to the reader, sending her off with an utterly fabricated notion of your character (page 62, **Aspects** chapter). When she tries to take advantage of the aspect that she falsely thinks is there, it can end up being a waste of a fate point or worse!

Block [Deceit]

A particularly clever lie can be used to block an opponent by giving the impression that an option is closed off when it in fact remains open. This is a difficult feat to pull off, but a character truly skilled in Deceit can often make an opponent abandon a course of action under false pretenses.

Empathy

This is the ability to understand what other people are thinking and feeling. This can be handy if your character is trying to spot a liar or you want to tell someone what he wants to hear. Characters with a high Empathy include gamblers, reporters, and socialites.

Assessment [Empathy]

Empathy can be used to gauge emotion and subtle tells. If information can be gleaned from the body language or verbal stress of another character, you can perform an Empathy roll to attempt to detect it. This can lead to discovering deception or detecting nervousness or repressed emotion. This counts as assessment—the emotional state of a character can be revealed by the GM if your Empathy roll is high enough.

The most powerful use of Empathy is to figure out what makes another character tick. Given at least a half hour of intense, personal interaction, you may make an Empathy roll against the target's Rapport roll. If you gain one or more shifts on the roll, you discover one of the target's aspects that you didn't already know. It might not reveal the aspect in precise detail, but it should paint a good general picture; for instance, you might not learn the name of the character's brother, but you will learn that the character has a brother. This process may be repeated, taking longer each time; ultimately you can learn a number of aspects equal to your Empathy skill's value (minimum one)—so, a Fair (+2) skill would allow two aspects revealed through at least two different rolls.

Defend [Empathy]

Empathy is used as a defense against Deceit. An Empathy roll determines the difficulty the opponent using Deceit must overcome.

Special [Empathy]

Empathy is the basis for initiative in a social conflict. The character with the highest Empathy acts first, followed by those with the next lowest Empathy, etc. Ties in initiative are resolved in favor of characters with a higher Resolve. Any remaining ties are in favor of the player closest to the GM's right.

Endurance

Endurance is the ability to keep performing physical activity despite fatigue or injury. It's a measure of the body's resistance to shock and effort. Endurance also measures how well a character shrugs off poisons and disease. Characters with a high Endurance include explorers, athletes, and cargo loaders.

Overcome Obstacles [Endurance]

Endurance is a passive skill. Players very rarely ask to roll Endurance; instead, the GM calls for rolls when appropriate. Endurance particularly comes into play in long-term actions as a secondary, restricting skill, where the character's ability to keep performing at peak is limited by how able he's to overcome fatigue and pain; this is why top athletes have their Endurance skill on par with—or better than!—their Athletics skill. Someone without a solid Endurance skill may be a good sprinter, but he'll find himself winded and falling behind in a marathon.

Sometimes, a direct Endurance test arises. This only applies in long-term conflicts, such as tests of a character's ability to keep going after a long effort. It applies most often in travel, when a character is attempting to push on after his body wishes to rest, or in attempts to endure harsh environments. An Endurance roll could be used to resist cold conditions or to determine how long a character can hold his breath.

Place Maneuver [Endurance]

It's difficult to use Endurance to place a maneuver on an opponent, but a character with a high Endurance can sometimes play defensively in a physical conflict and attempt to draw it out. By making the conflict last longer and require more vigorous effort, it's possible to place a maneuver such as TIRED on an opponent. This should be allowed only judiciously, since not all conflicts lend themselves to the tactic.

Special [Endurance]

Endurance also determines a character's stress capacity (the length of a character's stress track), since stress in part represents physical wounds and fatigue. By default, players have 3 boxes for their stress track. Better-than-Mediocre (+0) Endurance increases the number of boxes as shown here. Resolve also increases stress capacity. Any additional stress boxes from Resolve and Endurance are added together to determine a character's stress capacity.

Endurance	Stress
Average-Fair	+1
Good-Great	+2
Superb-Fantastic	+3

Engineering

Engineering is the understanding of how machinery and complex technology works, both for purposes of building it and taking it apart. While it's complemented by an understanding of Academics, Engineering can just as easily be the result of getting your hands dirty and having a natural feel for how things work. Characters with a high Engineering include ship engineers, mechanics, and, frequently, pilots.

Overcome Obstacles [Engineering]

Engineers are essential aboard ship because a skilled engineer can modify and repair vital parts of the ship. Engineering covers all mechanical and electrical engineering, including the ship power plant and life support. Engineering covers all hardware. Repairs and modifications to software require the Systems skill. Engineering tasks require the right tools, the neessary parts, and enough time. On-the-fly repairs and system rerouting can take place during ship combat. More details on this topic are found in the **Ships** chapter (page 150).

An engineer with time, tools, and materials can also build custom items. For details on how to do this, check out the **Gear** chapter (page 138).

Assessment [Engineering]

Engineers can use their knowledge of physics and material to make detailed assessments of objects. Engineers can often assess value, spot materials that can be used to jury rig temporary repairs or machinery, or spot flaws in buildings, ships, or smaller items. An engineer who can gain access to plans or design documents can also determine any anomalies or secret weaknesses in an object or building's design. This is especially useful for finding overlooked access points or structural flaws.

Declaration [Engineering]

As with assessment, Engineering declarations typically involve pointing out details about physical items or buildings. Typical Engineering declarations cover structural weaknesses that are about give way, warning indicators, or other such declarations about problems with an item.

Place Maneuver [Engineering]

Engineering is also the skill for unmaking things. Given time and tools, an engineer can topple virtually any building or structure. In those circumstances, Engineering works like a very peculiar combat skill, possibly resulting in maneuvers or weirdly indirect attacks, like setting up a bridge to collapse when someone walks across it. Again, the right tools are required, as is enough time to work on a given item in order to break it. Materials are less important, unless the engineer is using explosives.

Fists

This is the ability to hold your own in a fistfight, with no weapons available but your own natural assets. With specialized training, this may include the practice of more disciplined fighting styles, such as formal martial arts. Characters with high Fists include soldiers, thugs, and martial artists.

Assessment [Fists]

Fist fighters are also well-versed in a variety of fighting styles from all over the galaxy and may use this skill as a limited sort of knowledge skill covering those areas. A fist fighter can analyze another character's stance and technique to determine where she was trained and perhaps to know any weaknesses in her particular technique.

Place Maneuver [Fists]

In combat, you might use Fists to place a maneuver on an opponent. Feints, setup moves, big windups, and causing an opponent to be off balance or overextended are all possible maneuvers from Fists. When using Fists, your character must be in the same zone as your opponent in order to place a maneuver on him.

Attack [Fists]

Most of the time, you use Fists to deliver stress directly to an opponent. Striking an opponent, throws, and stress holds all fall under fists. As with maneuvers, Fists can only be used when in the same zone as an opponent.

Defend [Fists]

As a combat skill, Fists allows your character to defend himself as well as attack. You can use Fists to block blows from another character using Fists, Weapons, or Might to attack in combat. The GM may assess a penalty for an unarmed character using Fists to defend himself against an armed opponent, however. Like attacking, defense with Fists is only effective when you're in the same zone as an opponent.

Gambling

Some games of chance are pure luck, but a good gambler doesn't play those. Gambling is the knowledge of how to gamble and, moreover, how to *win* when gambling. It also includes knowledge of secondary things like bookmaking. Characters with a high Gambling include gamblers, casino owners, and dapper secret agents.

Overcome Obstacles [Gambling]

The most common use of the Gambling skill is playing games of chance, whether it's at cards or Don Jon cubes. At the table, your Gambling skill roll determines if you win or lose. The size of the pot indicates what you stand to win or lose. To raise the level of your Resources, the pot must be larger than your current Resources value. The higher the game's stakes, the more difficult it is for you to win big enough to increase your Resources. The difficulty of the Gambling roll increases equal to the Resources at stake, combined with the Gambling skill of the highest ranked opponent. If you fail your Gambling roll, you stand to lose one rank of Resources.

Example: Sparkle Twist is in game with some high rollers. She's aiming to increase her Resources, currently a Fair (+2). The stake must be at least Good (+3) if she wants her Resources to go up. The best gambler at the table has a Gambling skill of Good (+3). This means Twist needs to beat the highest Gambling skill plus the stake, a Fantastic (+6) difficulty, in order to both win and increase her Resources to Good (+3).

You can usually find a game when you're short on cash—or just in the mood for sport. Finding a game, or obtaining an invitation to one, requires a Contacting roll complemented by Gambling, with a difficulty equal to the Resources value of the game. A high stakes game is a game at least one level above your current Resources. A high stakes game also includes the potential for complications, like sore losers or strange table stakes. Winning a game without raising Resources gives you a Resources aspect, like Took Home a Big Pot. For more on Resources, see the *Gear* chapter, page 123.

Assessment [Gambling]

A gambler learns how to examine a gambling area for potential cheats or tricks. You can also determine information about your opponents by observing how they set up a game, whether they have confederates at the table, and if they're attempting trickery before a game begins. You can determine the best place to sit at the table, identify less skilled opponents, or find less risky games by using Gambling to assess.

Declaration [Gambling]

During the course of a game, you can learn your opponent's tells in order to better read his actions during a game and place strategic bets against him. Positioning, cheating, and spotting confederates within a game can all be declared during a game as well.

Defend [Gambling]

Sometimes, you aren't trying to win big. Sometimes you just want to preserve your own stake rather than trying to increase it. If you finds yourself in this situation, you can use your Gambling skill defensively. This reduces the risks of a game considerably, reducing the difficulty by two. If you succeed with your Gambling roll, you can't increase your Resources. You merely prevent them from being reduced.

Special [Gambling]

A high Gambling skill can change your starting Resources. You must choose to use Gambling instead of Trading for this purpose. By default, players begin with Average (+1) Resources. Better-than-Good (+3) Gambling gives you starting Resources in the amounts listed.

Gambling	Starting Resources
Great	Fair (+2)
Superb	Good (+3)

Guns

Often, characters just need to shoot things. Thankfully, there's a skill for that. Guns users are well-versed in a variety of small arms and ammunitions. Guns can also be used to cover non-gun weapons that shoot at a distance, such as bows and gravity guns. Characters with high Guns include soldiers, killers, and hunters.

Overcome Obstacles [Guns]

Any sort of sharpshooting your character performs outside of combat is resolved with a simple skill roll. When your character is firing his weapon at an inanimate object—to cut a rope, knock something off the top of a wall, or some other similar feat of marksmanship—a general Guns roll is all that's required. Particularly tricky shots have a higher difficulty, of course.

Assessment [Guns]

You can use this skill as a limited sort of knowledge skill covering the identification and care of firearms. If you want to identify a particular make or model of weapon based on observation or from the spent ammunition packs or burn marks left by weapon fire, Guns is used for assessment. This application of the Guns skill should be very narrow and should only be allowed judiciously. Guns is really for in-the-moment firing of weapons and little else.

Place Maneuver [Guns]

The most common maneuver of the Guns skill is aiming. An aspect called IN MY SIGHTS is a very useful setup for a subsequent Guns roll. Skilled gunmen can also perform more difficult feats, such as shooting things out of an enemy's hands and the like.

Attack [Guns]

The Guns skill is primarily used to deliver stress to an opponent. With a gun, you can shoot at an enemy up to two zones away—three if it's a rifle or other long-distance firearm. Unfortunately, without a gun in hand, or at least close at hand, the skill isn't much use.

The Guns skill doesn't allow you to defend yourself as well as attack; it trades the defense component for the ability to act over greater range. A character who's both a good shot and good at getting out of the way needs to also invest in either Athletics or Fists (or both!).

Block [Guns]

Guns can be used to block movement or force other characters to remain under cover. Heavy fire on an area or just squeezing off a shot every time someone pokes out his head can make a very effective block.

Intimidation

There are more graceful social skills for convincing people to do what you want, but those skills tend not to have the pure efficiency of communicating the idea that failing to comply may well result in some manner of harm. Nothing personal. Characters with high Intimidation include mob enforcers, bouncers, and "bad" cops.

Overcome Obstacles [Intimidation]

Once things get to the point of a face off, your opponent has a lot of other options besides standing there and being intimidated—such as disengaging or pulling out a weapon. However, one of the real strengths of Intimidation is that first flash of contact, when people instinctively get out of the way of someone intimidating. Intimidation can establish a powerful, menacing first impression. If your character is actively doing something intimidating, you can roll a quick contest of Intimidation against the opponent's Resolve. If successful, the target is taken aback for a moment, generally long enough to brush past him. This can't be done in a fight or against any target who's already prepared to fight, but in those "first contact" situations, Intimidation is gold for control.

Place Maneuver [Intimidation]

Intimidation can easily be thrown in as an action during the heat of conflict. Within a conflict, Intimidation can make an opponent flinch, hesitate, or become shaken. Sudden shouts, terrifying glares, or even just a cool demeanor can be used to place a maneuver on an opponent.

Attack [Intimidation]

Using Intimidation is a blatant social attack, which someone can defend against with his Resolve. This is the skill for interrogation (as opposed to interviewing) as well as scaring the bejeezus out of someone. Even without a basis for fear, Intimidation can occasionally be used to provoke a strong burst of negative emotion—such as provoking someone into a fight, or at least to anger. Regardless, it's never pretty.

If there's a reason for your target to believe that you're capable of harming him when he can't do anything about it—such as if the target's unarmed and you're wielding a weapon—it's worth a +1 bonus, +2 if the target's completely helpless. Conversely, if the target is the armed one, his defense roll is likely at +1, possibly at +2 or more if the target's very secure in his position—such as being behind something solid or having lots of backup. If these circumstances suddenly change, it's certainly call for another Intimidation roll! The lesson here is simple—Intimidation works best from a position of power. Achieve that position first, then apply the skill.

Block [Intimidation]

Intimidation can also be used to stop another character dead in his tracks. When you use Intimidation to block, you're just making yourself look so scary that another character doesn't have the will to even try to confront you or force his way past. This is the bread and butter of a bodyguard or bouncer. Just stand there and look intimidating and the threats never even materialize.

Investigation

Investigation is the ability to look for things and, hopefully, find them. You use this skill when you're actively looking for something, such as searching a crime scene or trying to spot a hidden enemy. Characters with a high Investigation include private investigators, bounty hunters, and planetary security officers.

Overcome Obstacles [Investigation]

Investigation is the skill most commonly called for when you want to look for something like clues. It's also useful for eavesdropping or any other activity where you're trying to observe something over a period of time. The more obscure or trivial the clue, the higher the difficulty. A character trained in Investigation also knows all the latest tricks in evidence gathering—infrared trace analysis, genetic marker flagging, etc.

Assessment [Investigation]

When looking for deep patterns and hidden flaws, Investigation may be used as an assessment action. This makes Investigation the flipside of Alertness; it's mindful, deliberate perception, in contrast to Alertness's passive mode of operation. This also means that an equivalent Investigation effort is nearly always going to yield better, more in-depth information than an Alertness effort would; the downside is that Investigation is far more time consuming.

Declaration [Investigation]

In a clutch, a skilled investigator often notices things that others overlook—ripped clothing, a hidden panel, or a dusting of powder—that offer valuable clues. A truly great investigator can deduce a lot of information from seemingly trivial details that a more casual observer would overlook.

Leadership

Leadership is a multi-faceted skill. A good leader knows how to direct and inspire people, but he also understands how to run an organization. As such, the Leadership skill covers acts of both types. Characters with a high Leadership include military officers, ship captains, politicians, bureaucrats, and lawyers.

Overcome Obstacles [Leadership]

A good leader has knowledge of organizations and the rules that govern them, including knowledge of laws, bribery, and other means of dealing with red tape; this is why Leadership is a key skill for lawyers. Leadership serves as an all-purpose knowledge skill for knowing how to act in a given organization, including important things like how much to bribe.

Command is another key component of Leadership, and the skill can be used to direct troops, workers, or any other group activity. Any time your character is in a position to give orders to a group of minions, you can apply your Leadership as a modifying secondary skill on the minions' skill roll. In a conflict, offering this assistance is your action for the exchange.

Assessment [Leadership]

With Leadership, you can research to find legal loopholes. When facing a bureaucratic challenge or obstacle, you can analyze the organization causing the difficulty, look for exceptions and weak points, and use red tape to your advantage. You can discover bribable officials or which key official must be contacted in order to actually get something accomplished when lower level individuals are stonewalling.

Declaration [Leadership]

In more tense situations, you can use a Leadership roll to analyze the hierarchy of a group. You can observe how the group interacts and determine which individuals are in charge or are key middlemen. This is often helpful when you need to know just where to apply an attack or a bribe.

Special [Leadership]

Any organization a player character is in charge of uses his Leadership as its default value for any question of how organized it is. This establishes the difficulty for things like bribery or theft, and also gives a general sense of how quickly and efficiently the organization acts.

Medicine

Medicine indicates training in the use of medical technology; knowledge of injury, disease, and anatomy; and general health training. Characters with Medicine can apply high-tech treatments, stop bleeding, and sometimes even revive the dead. Characters with high Medicine are doctors, surgeons, medics, nurses, and medical researchers.

Overcome Obstacles [Medicine]

A great deal of what characters deal with in the course of an adventure is damage inflicted in combat. Immediately after—or even during—combat, a character with the Medicine skill can patch up other characters. See page 74, **Doing Things** chapter, for information on adjudicating healing.

More detailed and complex medical procedures are dealt with by surgery. This requires a full medical setup, with a sterile environment and lots of high-tech equipment. Longer term healing—like removing consequences or narrative surgical procedures—needs a stable environment and a skilled practitioner.

A character skilled in Medicine can also improvise cures in a situation where the necessary drugs and equipment are unavailable. Medicine also allows for the creation of medical supplies, given enough materials and a lab to prevent contamination. See the **Gear** chapter for more (page 138).

Assessment [Medicine]

Physical damage isn't the only area covered by Medicine. Characters skilled in Medicine can deal with disease, as well as poison. A Medicine roll can be used to identify illnesses or toxins, as well as pharmaceuticals, either by observing the symptoms or effects in a living creature or through directly examining the material in question.

Declaration [Medicine]

Medicine can also be used to glean important information in the heat of the moment. Noticing that someone is afflicted by a particular illness, impaired by an old injury, or under the influence of drugs or toxins can lead to interesting and fruitful declarations.

Might

This is a measure of pure physical power—either raw strength or simply the knowledge of how to use the strength you have. For lifting, moving, and breaking things, Might is the skill of choice. Might may be used indirectly as well, to modify, complement, or limit some skill uses. Characters with a high Might include wrestlers and laborers.

Overcome Obstacles [Might]

Might is the skill of choice for applying brute force to break things in halves or smaller pieces; it includes breaking boards, knocking down doors, and the like. Using Might, items can be damaged over time or broken with a single dramatic blow.

Might also controls how much the character can lift or move. The weight of the thing being moved sets the difficulty for the roll.

Assessment [Might]

Might can be used for assessment in only very proscribed circumstances. Might counts as a knowledge skill if you're attempting to determine how difficult it would be to break something or move a heavy object. It can also be applied if you're attempting to assess the strength of another person. A successful Might roll can determine what rank of Might the target possesses.

Place Maneuver [Might]

Might can be used to place maneuvers related to lifting, moving, or holding things with brute strength. Pinning someone against the wall, knocking over a massive column of crates, hefting and hurling a barrel of volatile chemicals, or holding open a closing blast gate are all examples of Might maneuvers.

Attack [Might]

In combat, Might can help with particular applications of Fists and Weapons—if force is a very significant element at play, Might modifies the primary skill. Furthermore, someone successfully engaging an opponent in a one-on-one exchange can potentially switch from Fists to Might when executing a hold or other wrestling move where it's less about hitting someone and more about overwhelming him with physical force. Such a switch would result from a maneuver of some sort.

Defend [Might]

You can use Might to defend against another character in special situations. When an opponent has engaged in grappling with your character, Might is an effective defense. Might is also used to defend when an opponent is attempting to disarm your character, or if an opponent tries to wrest away some other object your character is holding.

Block [Might]

Might can be used as a block if you can get a hold on an opponent or if you're trying to block another character from moving something. Might can only be applied if you have a grip on whatever you mean to block, or if you're physically blocking the path of another character so he'll have to move you to reach what he's trying to get.

Pilot

This skill measures a character's ability to control and drive any sort of vehicle, from a ground bike to an interstellar freighter. Pilots are familiar with the controls of most standard vehicles and can guide the vehicle in stressful situations and straight courses alike. Characters with a high Pilot include chauffeurs, starship pilots, and sailors.

Overcome Obstacles [Pilot]

In most cases, the Pilot skill is rolled when attempting to guide a vehicle in a time-sensitive or stressful situation. Performing a general move in such a situation, or a dangerous or risky move in normal circumstances, requires a Pilot roll against a difficulty set by the GM.

Piloting can also be used to attempt to shorten the time required for a journey. If the pilot can plot a new course and fly it, he can attempt to make a Pilot roll to reduce the time on the time scale required for the trip. Note that going faster puts more wear and tear on a ship and consumes more fuel. More rules on this are found in the **Ships** chapter, page 143.

When engaged in a chase, a character's Pilot skill is used to close the distance between him and the vehicle he's chasing (or increase the distance if he's the one being chased!). It's also used to bring quick resolution to the issues brought up by terrain and other obstacles. For an extensive treatment of chase rules, see the **Ships** chapter on page 147.

Assessment [Pilot]

Pilots can use their knowledge of vehicles to assess the capabilities of their own vessel or to compare and contrast the abilities of two different vehicles in a specific situation. For example, a pilot might look at an opponent's ship and assess its abilities relative to his own and determine who has the advantage in a race requiring tight maneuvering. A pilot can also guess travel time based on his Pilot skill with a great deal of accuracy.

Declaration [Pilot]

When using Pilot for declaration, you might identify design flaws in a particular model of vehicle, or discover hidden tricks or abilities that a ship or ground vehicle might possess. A pilot can also identify any special enhancements that have been made to a vessel.

Place Maneuver [Pilot]

In a dogfight, a pilot can use his maneuvering ability to place a temporary aspect on another ship. Most often, this is used to get an enemy in optimal firing range for a gunner or to ensure that a friendly ship or some obstacle is between the pilot's own ship and an enemy vessel. A good dogfighter knows lots of tricks to give his own ship any edge he can manage.

Defend [Pilot]

When in ship-to-ship combat, Pilot is used primarily to defend. Corkscrew rolls, sharp turns, dips, and banking are all used to make your ship harder to hit. This does have an effect on a gunner's ability to fire back at an opponent, but other than relying on ship shields and hull armor, Pilot is the best defense. See the **Ships** chapter for more details (page 149).

Psychic

Some species or individuals possess mental powers beyond the norm. These abilities are represented by the Psychic skill. Characters who don't possess this skill have no abilities in this area and can't perform any psychic feats, even at Mediocre (+0) ability. Characters with this skill must clarify and specify their specific mental abilities with the GM before play and can't exceed these limits using the Psychic skill. Possible powers include emotion projection, telepathy, telekinesis, clairvoyance, illusion projection, precognition, or other mental powers that the GM deems plausible. Characters with a high Psychic skill are mentalists, telepaths, or other mental savants.

Overcome Obstacles [Psychic]

A psychic's chief talent is the ability to read minds. The most rudimentary form of this ability is detecting or projecting emotions. Some psychics can also move objects with their mind, but this isn't always the case with this skill.

Any attempt to use a paranormal mental power of any sort is covered by the Psychic skill. The GM sets the difficulty for any such use. Obviously, the more powerful the effect or the more outlandish the psychic ability in question, the higher the difficulty. Surface thoughts and emotions are easy to read. Hidden thoughts or plumbing the depths of another character's psyche are much more difficult. Also, mental powers decrease with range. The farther away a target is, the more difficult it is to use mental powers. Most powers work only within conflict ranges. A character outside Zone 3 is particularly difficult to affect.

Assessment [Psychic]

Many Psychic powers are useful for assessment. A character with precognitive ability can spend time exploring the future in order to determine aspects that apply to a situation. Clairvoyance is also obviously useful for this purpose. The ability to examine an area or situation from a distance is quite valuable. Telepathy and emotion detection can also be used if a psychic can position herself to use them before any action needs to be taken.

Declaration [Psychic]

Within a situation, a psychic often receives flashes of insight from her ability which can be used to make declarations. Telepathy is especially useful when you learn of an opponent's intent seconds before he acts, for example. Precognition is again appropriate, as the ability to see even a few seconds into the future becomes useful once characters are in motion.

Place Maneuver [Psychic]

A Psychic ability can place a maneuver on an opponent through an outright mental assault. Using telepathy or emotion projection to push thoughts and emotions onto an opponent as he tries to act can be distracting, and a character with the ability to create mental illusions in other people can place all sorts of disadvantageous maneuvers in a conflict.

Attack [Psychic]

A psychic with telepathic abilities can also mount a direct psychic blitz on another character. This is just a matter of projecting strongly enough to cause actual mental harm to the other character. Most psychics aren't powerful enough to do this, and it's generally more difficult than passive psychic powers; however, it's a very effective attack against an area where most beings have hardly any defenses. Psychic attacks target the mind and therefore are resisted with Resolve.

Defend [Psychic]

If you choose not to actively use your Psychic abilities in an exchange, you can use Psychic instead of Resolve to defend youself. The Psychic skill can also be used to defend against social attacks such as Rapport, Trading, or Intimidation if you have telepathic or emotion detection powers. In this case, you're detecting the opponent's true intents and can react accordingly.

Block [Psychic]

If a character has the ability to project thoughts, emotions, or illusions, she can sometimes set up an effective block directly in a target's mind. In the case of telepathic blocking, the target just won't think of a possible option. Emotion projection can be used to create a very strong negative emotional reaction to some particular course of action, effectively blocking it. Illusion projection is a bit more of a blunt instrument. Doors, switches, or even opponents can just be erased from the target's mind.

Rapport

The flipside of Intimidation, this is the ability to talk with people in a friendly fashion, make a good impression, and perhaps convince them to see your side of things. Any time you want to communicate *without* an implicit threat—such as during an interview—this is the skill to use. Characters with high Rapport include grifters, reporters, and good cops.

Overcome Obstacles [Rapport]

Any time a character is involved in casual conversation and a skill roll is required, Rapport is generally the appropriate skill. Rapport is far more subtle than most social skills, and targets of Rapport generally don't realize that a character is digging for information or has an ulterior motive. Rapport is used to conceal these motives and project a friendly and likeable demeanor. A character with Rapport is charming and witty. Any attempt to charm another character and change his attitude toward the character uses Rapport.

The first time your character meets someone, the GM may call for a quick Rapport roll to determine the impression your character makes.

Place Maneuver [Rapport]

Rapport can be used to weave a rhetorical web. When engaged in a social conflict with another character, you can use Rapport to set traps farther along in the conversation. Seemingly innocuous comments can later force another character to concede a point or reveal more information than intended.

Attack [Rapport]

Rapport can be used as a direct attack in a social conflict. This is definitely the velvet glove, as an opponent can be forced off balance or embarrassed without even realizing your malicious intent. When engaging the enemy in witty banter to enrage him—or even in apparently casual conversation—you can use Rapport to get the verbal better of your opponent.

Defend [Rapport]

Rapport controls the face your character shows to the world, and that includes what you choose *not* to show. As such, when a character tries to use Empathy to get a read on your character, it's opposed by Rapport. If you wish to simply reveal nothing, you can use Rapport and take the equivalent of a defensive action, gaining a +2 on your roll. This is over and above the "default" of a Rapport defense because it's is openly obvious—your character is wiping all emotions off of his face. It also requires that you're consciously aware that someone's trying to get a read on you. If your character's trying not to look like he's actively warding off the read, or he isn't really aware he's being read, then he isn't taking a full defensive action and doesn't get the +2.

In the reverse, characters skilled in Rapport are able to control which side of their personality is shown to others—they seem to open up while actually guarding their deepest secrets. Since *true things* are still revealed about the character, this isn't an inherently deceptive action. When your character opens up, he defends against an Empathy read with Rapport, as usual. If your opponent succeeds and generates at least one shift, he finds something out, as usual. If your opponent fails, he still discovers an aspect—but you get to choose which one. This can effectively be used to stonewall someone without the obvious poker face. On top of it all, you can always choose to reveal something that the other character already knows about.

Resolve

Resolve is a measure of a character's self-mastery, as expressed through things like courage and willpower. It's an indicator of coolness under fire and also represents the drive not to quit. It plays a key part in efforts to resist torture or psychic attack. Characters with high Resolve include insurgents, leaders, spies, and obsessives.

Overcome Obstacles [Resolve]

Like Endurance, Resolve is a passive skill. Players very rarely ask to roll Resolve; instead, the GM calls for rolls when appropriate. Resolve comes into play whenever a character is attempting to overcome some mental obstacle. Extreme pain, illness, or crippling mental blows can impair a character, but he can roll Resolve to overcome these hardships. Any time your character reaches a point where a lesser person would just give up, you can ask for a Resolve test to have your character overcome the situation and keep going.

Defend [Resolve]

Resolve is almost always rolled in response to something, rather than on its own. Its primary role is as defense against most kinds of social manipulation or distraction. Resolve also shines in situations that have spun very much out of control. A character with a high Resolve has a distinct advantage in continuing to keep his head about him and respond calmly. Similarly, when all seems lost, a character with a strong Resolve is often capable of soldiering on. Resolve is the mental or social parallel to physical Endurance.

Special [Resolve]

Resolve also determines a character's stress capacity (the length of a character's stress track), since stress in part represents the character's resilience in the face of mental, emotional, and social stress. By default, players have 3 boxes for their stress track. Better-than-Mediocre (+0) Resolve increases the number of boxes as shown here. Endurance also increases stress capacity and combines with Resolve to increase a character's stress track.

Resolve	Stress
Average-Fair	+1
Good-Great	+2
Superb-Fantastic	+3

Sleight of Hand

The hand can certainly be quicker than the eye. This skill covers fine, dexterous activities like stage magic, pickpocketing, and quickly concealing a weapon in your clothing. While Athletics is appropriate for gross physical activities, most things requiring manual speed and precision fall under this skill (that said, if you're picking a lock, use Burglary). Characters with a high Sleight of Hand include pickpockets, spies, and entertainers.

Overcome Obstacles [Sleight of Hand]

Picking a pocket is a quick contest between Sleight of Hand and the target's Alertness—which may be complemented by the target's own Sleight of Hand. Due to the difficulty of this sort of work, the target usually receives a +2 bonus, as if he were performing a full defense against the action. If the target is distracted by something else, he loses the +2 bonus. If anyone else is in a position to observe the attempt, they also may make Alertness rolls to spot the attempt (though they don't gain the +2).

Characters may use Sleight of Hand to try to hide things in plain sight; the Sleight of Hand roll opposes any perception check for something that the character tries to hide, misplace, or distract attention from. When a character uses this skill to hide something, his skill roll indicates the difficulty of any Investigation rolls to find it.

Place Maneuver [Sleight of Hand]

During a conflict, Sleight of Hand can be useful to set up an opponent with a trick. Hiding a weapon from view, flipping clothing to distract an enemy, or flashing light in an opponent's face are all examples of how Sleight of Hand can be used to trick or mislead an opponent and thus gain a temporary advantage in a conflict.

Stealth

This is the ability to remain unseen and unheard. Directly opposed by Alertness or Investigation, this ability covers everything from skulking in the shadows to hiding under the bed. Characters with a high Stealth include burglars, assassins, and sneaky children.

Overcome Obstacles [Stealth]

When your character is hiding, he's remaining perfectly still and—hopefully—out of sight. Lighting, obstacles and other environmental factors can affect your roll, and the result of your Stealth roll is the basis for any contest with a searcher's Alertness or Investigation. Skulking is the art of *moving* while trying to remain unnoticed; it's somewhat more difficult for obvious reasons.

Stealth is also used to set up ambushes. When an attack is made from ambush, the target gets one last Alertness check to see if he notices something at the last moment. On a success, the target(s) can defend normally. If that Alertness roll fails, the attack is made with the target's first defense roll at Mediocre (+0).

Place Maneuver [Stealth]

If a character can get out sight, she can hide herself and gain the advantage of Stealth in a future action. This isn't as effective as striking from ambush, as the opponent is already alerted and therefore somewhat more ready for a stealthy attack. It's possible to place a maneuver on the opponent and strike from hiding, gaining the normal advantage a temporary aspect confers.

Survival

This is the skill of outdoorsmen. It covers hunting, trapping, tracking, building fires, and lots of other wilderness skills that spacefarers rarely have a use for, unless they happen to crash-land on a hostile planet. Characters with a high Survival include explorers, hunters, and scouts.

Overcome Obstacles [Survival]

Survival also covers the breadth of interaction with animals, from training them to communicating with them, albeit in a limited fashion. This includes handling beasts of burden or carriage animals, as well as common pets. Survival serves as a stand-in for all social skills when dealing with animals. Not to say animals are great conversationalists, but when you're trying to soothe or stare down an animal, Survival is the skill to roll.

The Survival skill covers the basics of riding animals and should operate much as Pilot does when it comes to chases.

Survival can be used to construct blinds and devise other ways to help remain hidden outdoors. On a Mediocre (+0) roll, a character can build a blind or otherwise create a place to hide, which lets Survival modify Stealth rolls. Such a construction takes a few hours to build and lasts a day, plus one extra day per shift.

If characters need to scrounge up something from the wilderness—sticks, bones, sharp rocks, vines that can serve as rope and so on—they can roll Survival to find these things.

Assessment [Survival]

When attempting any action in a wild area, you can use Survival to make an assessment of the terrain, weather, and natural resources available. This can be exceptionally useful in advance of any complicated action in a wilderness area. You can make a basic assessment using data available about a wild site, but the most effective use of the skill is to actually scout the area beforehand.

Declaration [Survival]

Survival can be used during an action to declare that there are hazards or valuable resources. A Survival expert can identify blinds set up by other characters, spot hazardous terrain, or identify useful or dangerous animals and plants as he moves through the wilderness.

Place Maneuver [Survival]

When a conflict breaks out in a natural area, a character with the Survival skill is at a distinct advantage. He may use Survival to place maneuvers using the plants, animals, or terrain in the area. Getting an opponent to step in a tangling vine or disturb the nest of stinging insects can be quite effective in combat.

Systems

Systems gives a character the ability to use the high-tech computer systems that are ubiquitous in the galaxy. These are used to gather or block information, as well as to operate the sensors aboard ships; used this way, Systems serves as a perception skill. Characters with high Systems are technicians, engineers, and hackers.

Overcome Obstacles [Systems]

Any general use of a data system or complex computer console requires a basic Systems roll. Operating a communications console is one of the main ways a character makes use of the Systems skill. Most of the time, use of these systems is routine.

Communication normally doesn't require a Systems check unless there's some kind of difficulty or interference. Communication over extremely long ranges can also be problematic. In these situations, a Systems check can be required to enable successful communications. Systems can also be used to intercept and eavesdrop on communications traffic. If the communication is encrypted, the communications operator has to spend time decrypting it, probably requiring another roll.

Systems can also be used to program robots or change a robot's programming. See more rules on robotics in the ***Alien Species*** chapter (page 28).

You'll need to roll Systems when attempting to hack into protected data files or overcome security programs. Almost all data systems have some sort of basic password or encryption, so unauthorized use always requires a Systems roll. The greater the security, the higher the difficulty. When using an electronic interface to override locks or other physical barriers, use the Burglary skill rather than Systems.

Assessment [Systems]

Systems can be used to assess any area that can be scanned by sensors, whether in a fixed location or from shipboard systems. Ships possess both short and long range sensors. Short range sensors detect fine detail better than long range, and both can be used in either passive or active mode. In passive mode, only the most obvious details can be gleaned, but the sensors don't call attention to their operation. Sensors in active mode can automatically be detected by another sensor operator.

When using Systems as a sensor operator, Systems operates just like a perception skill. Sensors can be used to detect life forms, chemical compositions, atmospheric conditions, or any other information that the GM thinks can logically be gleaned from a sensor sweep.

Declaration [Systems]

Systems can be used to detect sudden changes during the action, and this is when declaration comes into play. For example, Systems can be used to detect when a weapon or defensive system comes on line, whether a communication has been sent, or if enemies are advancing outside of physical sight lines. Systems can be quite useful in ship-to-ship battles, since combat in space generally takes place over distances great enough that regular visual perception is useless.

Place Maneuver [Systems]

When in a conflict where Systems is in play—such as ship-to-ship combat—Systems can be used to jam communications, disable enemy targeting systems, or fool sensors. These maneuvers are often quite difficult, but they're very useful if they can be brought into play.

Attack [Systems]

A skilled operator can actually attack other Systems in an effort to disable them. A Systems attack can't deal stress to a regular opponent, but vehicles or robots are vulnerable to direct Systems attacks. This is an on-the-fly malware assault, where the Systems operator is creating malicious programs and sending them against an opponent during a conflict. Generally, the Systems user needs to somehow gain access to his enemy's data systems for this to work, either actually aboard the ship he's attacking or through some sort of remote access. Most systems used in combat are closed for precisely this reason.

Defend [Systems]

When another Systems user is attempting an attack or maneuver, you can use Systems to create encryption to defend against hacking. Systems can be used to throw up an active defense and try to block incursions in real time. This is often most useful in combat when another Systems user is trying to place maneuvers on you.

Block [Systems]

To protect a system, a Systems user can set up defenses that act as a block against any future incursions. This is typically the obstacle a hacker is trying to overcome, unless the other Systems user is working in real time to stop the hacker's incursion.

Trading

Trading is a measure of the ability to find and broker deals. This involves some portion of charm, deceit, and on-the-fly mental calculation. The character can identify good deals or opportunities, negotiate contracts and agreements, and generally try to get the most out of any trade of goods or services. Characters with high Trading include lawyers, itinerant traders, shop owners, and corporate sharks.

Overcome Obstacles [Trading]

Trading is typically pitted against another character's Trading skill. A Trading roll is always a negotiation, and it's implied that the character is trading something he has for something another character possesses. Trading isn't a something-for-nothing proposition—there's always a give-and-take in a Trading roll. If a character is skilled in Trading, though, he can often get a great deal for very little in return.

A bribe is just another kind of transaction. You give something and get a service in return. You can use your Trading skill to assess who's receptive to a bribe and how much to give. Judicious use of Trading allows you to avoid being too obvious or trying to bribe the wrong person. Just like a regular negotiation, something of value must be given in exchange.

Assessment [Trading]

In some situations, a business opportunity exists that isn't obvious to the untrained eye. Trading can be used as a perception skill with the specific goal of finding some situation or individual that's open to lucrative trade. Not all Trading uses are strictly legal. Trading can be used to identify where contraband is available—whether it's banned substances, weapons, or other items that may be useful to a group of intrepid starfarers. If you find yourself in possession of contraband, Trading can also help you find a fence to unload the items. This use is of course riskier than legitimate trade, and failure can indicate law enforcement entanglements.

Declaration [Trading]

Trading can be used to make declarations about valuable items available for trade or to discover other characters that may be on the lookout for an opportunity to make deals. You can also make a declaration about an item that's under- or overvalued.

Special [Trading]

Trading has a special relationship with a character's Resources score—Trading determines a character's starting Resources. By default, players begin with Average (+1) Resources. Better-than-Average (+1) Trading confers starting Resources in the amounts listed.

Trading	Starting Resources
Fair to Good	Fair (+2)
Great	Good (+3)
Superb	Great (+4)

Weapons

This is the skill for fighting with weapons—from swords to knives to axes to clubs to whips. The exact weapon is more a choice of style than anything else, as this skill covers everything from military saber training to spacers using knives and clubs on the docks. Characters with high Weapons include thugs, pirates, and some athletes and circus performers.

Overcome Obstacles [Weapons]

Weapons is usually used in combat, but any non-combat use of a weapon—using a sword to cut a rope or throwing a knife at a target outside of combat, for example—can be simulated with a simple Weapons roll.

Assessment [Weapons]

Weapons users are also well-versed in a variety of fighting styles and weapons; they may use this skill as a limited sort of knowledge skill covering those areas. A Weapons user might be able to tell you the strengths and weaknesses of Saldrallan military saber training, for example, or assess the combat value of a particular knife.

Declaration [Weapons]

To make a declaration using Weapons, you can do things like identify an opponent's training by observing him in action, or determine the manufacturer of a particular blade once it's drawn. Again, this use of Weapons is very specific and not of a great deal of use outside the narrow area of expertise.

Place Maneuver [Weapons]

A Weapons roll can be used to place a maneuver rather than deal stress in combat. You could pin an opponent's clothes to the wall with a knife, for example, or cut someone's belt loose, entangling his legs in his pants.

Attack [Weapons]

The most common use of the Weapons skill is to deal stress in combat. Obviously, to use Weapons, you need a weapon to hand. This is a slight disadvantage over Fists, but the Weapons skill also covers the ability to throw small handheld weapons up to one zone away, or to use weapons with unusually long reach—like a whip—to attack adjacent zones. This is the skill for a good knife fighter and knife thrower.

Defend [Weapons]

As a combat skill, Weapons inherently carries the ability to defend yourself in a fight and, as such, may be rolled for defense. This involves parrying with the weapon. Weapons can be used as a defense against Weapons or Fists attacks. Weapons can't be used to defend against attacks with Guns.

Block [Weapons]

Weapons can also be used as a block. This generally means using the threat of attack to prevent someone from performing some action. Placing a blade in front of a door or resting it across a person's hand communicates the threat.

Stunts

What Stunts Do

Stunts provide guaranteed situational benefits, special abilities, or minor powers under particular circumstances.

A stunt may grant a character the ability to use a skill under unusual circumstances, such as using it in a broader array of situations, substituting it for another skill, or using it in a complementary fashion to another skill. A stunt might allow a character to gain an effect roughly equal to two shifts when using a skill in a specific way, or otherwise grant other small effects. Put more simply, stunts allow the usual rules about skills to be broken—or at least bent.

Some notes about stunts:

- Some stunts require the use of a fate point in order to activate.
- In general, you want to take stunts tied to skills you have at Average or higher.
- You can purchase stunts when creating a character for one refresh per stunt (page 52, **Crew Creation** chapter).
- Characters can gain additional stunts as the game progresses (page 81, **Advancement** chapter).

The stunts in this chapter are presented skill by skill. This isn't a comprehensive list of stunts. In fact, we encourage GMs—and players with GM supervision—to create their own stunts to fit their game.

If you're building a character quickly, take a look at the stunts listed here—it may be easiest to simply take all the stunts within a skill group, as they're all thematically similar and can quickly establish what your character's niche is.

Creating Stunts

It's often best to build your own stunts for your character, although you can also pick from the list of pre-created stunts split up by skill. Creating stunts is relatively easy. Each stunt gives a character some type of advantage or additional use for a skill. The guidelines here help you build your own stunt. Pick one of these suggestions and pair it with a skill to create your own stunt.

Give a +2 to a specific application of a non-attack or defense effect.

The specific application can be a maneuver (page 68, **Doing Things** chapter), because a maneuver isn't an attack since it doesn't inflict stress. The bonus may be reduced to +1 for a broader application or increased to +3 or even +4 for very, very narrowly defined situations.

Stellar Cartographer: Gain a +1 to Academics rolls whenever researching star positions or attempting to recall information about nearby systems. Specify a deeper sub-field of knowledge (Templari border worlds), and you gain an additional +1 when the research is relevant to the sub-field.

Give a +1 to an attack, improving its accuracy under a specific circumstance.

Target-Rich Environment: Gain a +1 to attacks with Guns when you're personally outnumbered in a firefight.

Give a +2 to an attack's result under particular conditions, applied only if the attack was successful.

The Slow Knife Kills: You know a technique to exploit a universal weakness of personal shields. When using Weapons to attack an opponent wearing a shield, your weapon gains Damage +2.

Give one or two expendable 2-shift effects or a persistent 1-shift effect.

An expendable 2-shift effect could be an additional mild consequence, for example. A persistent 1-shift could be Armor: 1 against certain types of things.

Never Give Up: You just don't know when to quit. You may take one additional mild consequence (page 71, *Doing Things* chapter).

Reduce the amount of time necessary to complete a particular task by two steps.

Capable Researcher: You have an ability to find obscure connections between data. Any scholarly research you do is completed two time increments (page 65, *Doing Things* chapter) faster than usual.

Reduce the difficulties faced by a skill under a particular sub-set of circumstances by two.

Lock Spoofing Maestro: Poor tools are no trouble when picking locks. Any increase to difficulty due to poor tools (such as having only a screwdriver and an expired ID card) is reduced by up to two.

Combine any two of the 2-shift effects from above at half value.

Scene of the Crime: You have a practiced eye when combing over a crime scene. In such a circumstance, you gain +1 to your Investigation roll and arrive at your findings one step faster than usual on the time table (page 65, *Doing Things* chapter).

Get a more powerful effect, but only when you spend a fate point.

Usually only allowed once per scene.

Killer Blow: Add 3 to the damage of a Fists attack on a successful hit, once per scene, for a fate point. This stacks with any other damage-increasing stunts for Fists.

Sample Stunts

Here are some pre-made stunts for each of the skills available in **Bulldogs!**

Academics

Been There, Done That
Your research has taken you all over the galaxy and there aren't many places you know nothing about. Gain a +2 on any Academics roll to know about the local culture of any planet in the galaxy.

Capable Researcher
You have an ability to find obscure connections between data. Any scholarly research you do is completed two time increments (page 65, *Doing Things* chapter) faster than usual.

Extensive Education
Your extensive studies allow you to recall obscure facts about a specific topic. Gain a +2 to Academics rolls when attempting to recall a fact in your field of expertise.

Linguist
You have a natural affinity for languages. You speak five additional languages beyond Galactic and the native tongue of your species. You don't need to specify which languages you speak at character creation— you can add a language to one of your slots as needed during play. You can take this stunt multiple times for additional languages.

Scientific Expert
You're one of the true experts in your field of study and you recognize connections a lesser expert would miss. If you *spend a fate point*, you can use this ability to attempt a declaration on an Academics roll relating to your field. You declare an aspect as usual on a successful roll, but for each additional two shifts you may declare another aspect. You can only do this once per scene for a particular topic.

Stellar Cartographer
Gain a +1 to Academics rolls when researching star positions or attempting to recall information about nearby systems. Specify a deeper sub-field of knowledge (Templari border worlds), and you gain an additional +1 when the research is relevant to the sub-field.

Alertness

Danger Sense

You have a quick and easy awareness of ambushes and other nasty surprises. When you're ambushed (page 102, *Skills* chapter), you're able to take a full defensive action, gaining a +2 on your defense roll, regardless of whether or not you're surprised.

Danger Is My Middle Name

You're never surprised. You may *spend a fate point* to take a full, regular action even when ambushed.

On Top of It

You may *spend a fate point* to go first in an exchange, regardless of your initiative. If multiple people with this stunt decide to use it, they go in turn of their normal initiative; after that, those without the stunt get a chance to act.

One Step Ahead

You're an expert at anticipating your opponent's plan in a physical fight. You gain a +1 to your defense when an opponent attempts a block or maneuver against you in a melee or firefight.

Ready for Anything

Your quick reflexes mean you're always ready for a fight. Gain a +2 to your Alertness for the purposes of determining initiative order.

Sharp Eyes

You're always laying a keen eye on your environment. You gain a +2 on Alertness checks to notice important clues or situations that others have overlooked.

Artillery

Covering Fire

You know how to place fire for the best screening effect. Gain a +2 bonus when performing blocks with Artillery.

Devastating Barrage

You can lay down a massive barrage of fire in a short time frame. If you hit your opponent, you gain +1 to damage on the Artillery attack.

Gunner's Eye

You're an expert at calculating arcs and parabola. Gain a +2 on your Artillery roll with any artillery piece that uses indirect fire.

Nuke the Site from Orbit

You're a methodical and relentless bomber. When bombarding targets on a planet's surface, gain +2 to damage.

Precision Targeting

You're an expert at precise targeting. Gain a +2 bonus when attempting to hit targets man-sized or smaller.

Target Their Systems

You know how to inflict purposeful and specific damage to an enemy ship to take out a particular subsystem. If you *spend a fate point* when you hit your opponent's ship, you can choose to cause an immediate consequence of your choice to the enemy ship rather than have the ship check off a stress box. You may only do this once per dogfight.

Athletics

Acrobat

You're able to perform any number of impressive acrobatic feats. Gain a +2 to Athletics rolls for complex maneuvers while simultaneously balancing or hanging from something.

Safe Fall

You know how to slow yourself and reduce damage when falling. Gain a +2 to Athletics rolls to defend against falls.

Marathon Training

You know how to conserve your energy when undergoing lengthy athletic activity. You may use Athletics instead of Endurance when making tests against fatigue; in most other cases, you may complement any Endurance rolls with your Athletics.

Fast Runner

You're incredibly fast on your feet. When sprinting (page 70, *Doing Things* chapter), you may move one additional zone with no increased difficulty.

Expert Climber

You're an excellent climber. You receive a +2 bonus on any climb.

Mighty Leap

Your leaping ability is prodigious. You may reduce any height related borders (page 70, *Doing Things* chapter) by up to three.

Burglary

Cat Burglar

You're an expert second-story man. Use Burglary instead of Athletics to make difficult climbs or acrobatic feats in order to break in to some place.

Criminal Mind

You have an acute understanding of what it takes to burglarize a place and can investigate such crimes from the perspective of the criminal instead of the cop. You may use your Burglary skill instead of Investigation when investigating a crime committed by someone using the Burglary skill.

Hidden Weakness

You have a talent for spotting flaws in a location's security protocols. Gain a +2 when using Burglary to pass a security checkpoint without arousing suspicion.

Lock Spoofing Maestro

Poor tools are no trouble for you when picking locks. Any increase to difficulty due to poor tools (such as having only a screwdriver and an expired ID card) is reduced by up to two.

Mental Blueprint

You're highly skilled at visualizing the whole of a target based on just a part of it. When casing a location, you gain a +2 on your Burglary roll.

Tripwire Sensibilities

You've run into enough traps that you've developed an instinct for avoiding them. You may roll Burglary instead of Alertness or Investigation to uncover or otherwise avoid stumbling onto a trap.

Contacting

Ear to the Ground

You're well-known and well-liked among the spaceport community. People watch for trouble and give you the tip-off early. Gain a +2 on Contacting rolls to hear in advance about some threat to you or your crew.

Grease the Wheels

You know just when to apply a bit of a bribe to the situation. A successful Resources roll (page 123, *Gear* chapter) against the difficulty set by the GM reduces the difficulty of your Contacting roll by three.

I Know a Guy

You're so well-connected and well-traveled that you can find someone you know on almost any planet. Gain a +2 to make a contact in a place where you haven't already established a connection.

Insider

You're able to navigate the intricacies of corporate and government bureaucracies easily—not because you understand them, but because you know people within the bureaucracy who can provide you shortcuts. You may roll Contacting instead of Leadership to deal with any sort of bureaucratic entanglement.

Talk the Talk

You know how to ingratiate yourself with people. Use your Contacting instead of Rapport when making a first impression on someone.

Well-Known

You're well-known in a specific community—Criminal, Business, Politics, Espionage, and Spacers are the most common. You gain a +2 on any Contacting rolls made within the chosen community. This stunt may be taken multiple times, each time for a different field.

Deceit

Clever Disguise

You're an expert at creating disguises. Gain a +2 when using your Deceit skill to disguise yourself, even if you're attempting to pass as another species.

Con Man

You're a bona fide confidence man, which lets you size people up, easy. You may use your Deceit instead of Empathy to get a read on someone. You may only discover aspects that are character weaknesses—never strengths or other advantages.

The Fix Is In

You're an inveterate cheater. You may use your Deceit skill instead of Gambling in a game of chance, but doing so means that you're cheating to win. If you fail, you're caught, and the game's loss is treated like a high stakes game, even if it wasn't. Gamblers don't take kindly to cheaters, either, so you're likely in for a mess of trouble.

The Honest Lie

The best lies are the ones that contain a healthy dose of truth. Whenever you incorporate a hefty portion of the truth into a lie, you gain a +2 on your Deceit roll. The truth must be relevant, not unimportant, and significant, not trivial—it must be on par with (or bigger than) the lie, or at least in the ballpark.

Masterful Feint

You're a tricky fighter; you like to convince an opponent he has you on the run when you are, in fact, still in control of the situation. You gain a +2 to your Deceit when making a maneuver in a conflict to place an aspect like OVEREXTENDED on your opponent. This aspect is particularly fragile—it must be used before your opponent's next action or it goes away.

Takes One to Know One

As an accomplished liar yourself, it's particularly hard for someone to pull one over on you. You may use your Deceit skill instead of your Empathy skill when trying to figure out if someone is lying. This isn't the same thing as getting a read on someone, as with the Con Man stunt, above; instead, it's a quick check: Is this guy lying? Is it a big lie or a small one? Is he mixing in the truth or is it all fabrication?

Empathy

Cold Read

You can size people up in a glance. Normally, using Empathy to get a read on someone requires at least a few minutes of conversation, if not more. You only need a few moments.

Heart's Secret

You have an instinct for going right to the heart of a person and finding out what matters most to him. Whenever you make a successful Empathy read on someone, the GM must select one of the aspects that's of utmost importance to the character—normally, the GM has a freer rein in her selection.

Hit Them Where It Hurts

Your skill at reading people makes you adept at provoking a strong emotional response if you're trying to get them angry, depressed, or something similar. Normally, the Intimidation skill is used for such efforts; however, if you've succeeded at any Empathy roll against the target previously, you may use Empathy to wage such psychological warfare instead.

Preemptive Grace

You're so attuned to social situations that you can act quickly and decisively to shape the situation to your liking. With this stunt, you gain a +2 to Empathy for the purposes of initiative in a social conflict. If you're tied for initiative with someone without this stunt, this stunt breaks the tie.

The Skeptic's Ear

The world is full of lies and liars, and you're always looking out for them. You can tell when someone uses Deceit on you and may take full defensive actions (getting a +2) with your Empathy if appropriate—normally, the use of deception isn't easy to spot in advance, so justifying full defensive actions is difficult. Successfully determining that something is trying to deceive you isn't the same as revealing the truth, however, no matter how well you do.

Track the Soul

Your understanding of people you've met is sufficiently strong that it gives you an easy sense of how to find them. You can anticipate their moves based on your knowledge of their personality. In any situation where you're tracking down or otherwise trying to find someone you've met before, you may roll Empathy instead of Investigation.

Endurance

Bounce Back

You heal quickly. Reduce the required healing time by two steps on the time chart (page 65, **Doing Things** chapter) when determining your recovery time from physical injuries.

Feel the Burn

You can push through incredible pain. You can take one extra mild physical consequence, allowing you a total of four consequences in a physical conflict.

Last Leg

No matter what comes at you, you keep standing. Use this stunt when you'd be taken out by or otherwise suffer a consequence from a physical hit. If you *spend a fate point* to remain standing or otherwise defer a consequence or concession for one more exchange or until you're hit again, whatever comes first. You may keep spending fate points this way until you run out. Once the extra time you've bought is up, all your deferred effects come to bear at once.

Now You've Made Me Mad

Once per scene, you may turn a wound you've taken into pure motivation. After you take physical stress, in the next exchange you can *spend a fate point* and add the value of the wound to an action against the person who inflicted the stress (the original value, not the box it was recorded in if it rolled to a different box).

Thick Skinned

You just don't feel pain and can take more punishment than a lesser being. You get one additional physical stress box.

Tireless

You can survive on considerably less rest than the average person. Normally, someone who hasn't gotten a regular night's sleep takes a consequence indicating his lack of rest. You may roll Endurance against a difficulty of Mediocre (+0) to stay up without sleep. The difficulty increases one step per night without sleep. Once you fail a roll, you begin to suffer consequences normally and can't make a roll again until you've made up the lost sleep.

Engineering

Demolitions

You're an expert with explosives. When you can take the time to properly set up charges—placing the bombs at the exact weak points of the targeted structure—the resulting explosion's force rating is increased by three. This benefit doesn't apply without preparation, a specific target structure, and a chance to study the target. Thus, it doesn't apply in situations such as setting charges hastily or lobbing explosive devices at Saldrallan shock troopers.

Grease Monkey

If it's a vehicle of any sort, you "get" it, intuitively and completely. When making an Engineering roll involving a vehicle—repairing, building, upgrading, etc.—you gain a +1 on your roll; additionally, the time to get the work done is reduced by one step on the time table (page 65, **Doing Things** chapter).

Jury-Rigger

You can make the best of makeshift materials. When you lack the proper tools or materials, you can still affect repairs or build temporary machinery or systems. Difficulties assessed because of lack of parts or tools are reduced by two, but your jury-rigged solution will only last through one task or scene.

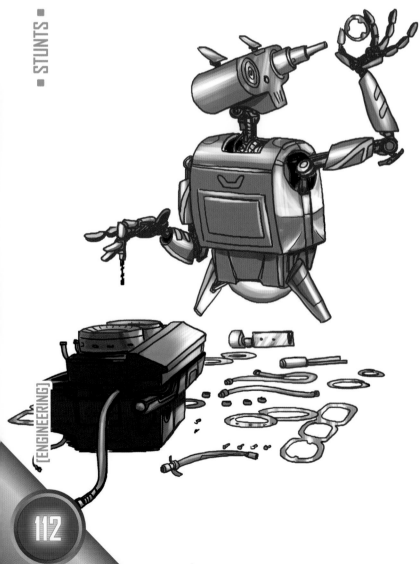

Mister Fix-It

You have a talent for getting things repaired under time-critical circumstances. The time it takes for you to fix something is reduced by two steps. If the situation is already operating on the fastest possible amount of time, the difficulty of the repair effort is reduced by one. These bonuses stack with Grease Monkey.

Reroute the Systems

You're an expert at damage control. When your ship's been damaged and suffered a consequence, you may make an Engineering roll against a target of Mediocre (+0) for a mild consequence, Fair (+2) for a moderate, or Great (+4) for a severe consequence. If successful, you may deny the free tag against the consequence. The consequence must be compelled at the cost a fate point.

Thump of Restoration

Sometimes all it takes to get something going again is a good swift thump. You must *spend a fate point* to activate this ability and roll Engineering against a target of Mediocre (+0). Then you hit the device that isn't working, and it starts working immediately, regardless of the difficulty rating to repair it under time pressure. It'll continue to work for a number of exchanges equal to the shifts gained on the Engineering roll. Once the time is up, the device stops working again, and any efforts to repair it are at a one step higher difficulty (since, after all, you hit the thing). If you wish to thump again, you may do so at the cost of another fate point, but the difficulty for the Engineering roll increases by one for each subsequent thump.

Fists

Army of One

You're a one-man army; the odds don't matter to you. When you're attacked, you may *spend a fate point* and, for the rest of the conflict, ignore the bonus your opponents have to their attacks due to their advantage of numbers. You must defend with Fists to gain this advantage.

Brawler

You're at home in any big old burly brawl, especially with multiple opponents and ideally some beer in you. When you're personally outnumbered in a fight, your defense rolls with Fists are at +1. When fighting two or more opponents, you deal one additional stress on a successful hit.

Crippling Blow

When you injure an opponent with your Fists, you may *spend a fate point* to force the target to take a consequence rather than check off a stress box. This can only be done once per opponent in a given fight scene. The target may choose to concede rather than take the consequence.

Demoralizing Stance

As a trained fighter, you can adopt a stance that makes it unequivocally clear how capable you are of handing someone his ass. Whenever displaying your fighting stance or techniques, you may roll Fists instead of Intimidation.

Dirty Fighter

You have a talent for fighting dirty and are experienced in pulling all manner of tricks in order to get the upper hand on your opponents. By exploiting an opponent's weakness, you can strike deep and true. Any time you tag or compel an opponent's aspect in a fight, you get an additional +1 on the roll.

Rope-a-Dope

When you get your guard up, it's very difficult for an opponent to land a blow. When you mount a full defense, you gain an additional +1 to your Fists rolls for a potent total defense bonus of +3.

Gambling

Double or Nothing

When it comes to head-to-head conflict, your skill at gambling and taking risks is paramount. Once per scene, after you've lost a Gambling roll, you have the option to declare "Double or Nothing!" This is a call for both sides to reroll and, as such, doesn't involve fate points. If you win the next roll, the initial exchange is treated as a scratch (no loss to any participants), but if you lose by whatever amount, you take a hit equal to double the value of the initial loss. Regardless, such a move often elevates the stakes of a game. This can turn a regular stakes game into a high stakes one, and a high stakes game into a matter of life and death.

Gambling Man

As a gambling man, you're rarely able to turn down a bet or an opportunity to take a risk; you have one or more gambling aspects to prove it. Compels involving your gambling aspects automatically start out at a point of escalation—you gain two fate points if you accept them, but you must spend two fate points to avoid them.

Know When to Fold 'Em

You're an expert at reading your opponents in a game of chance. When gambling with a non-player character, you may ask the GM to roll her Gambling in advance. The roll is secret—she doesn't have to show it to anyone. However, she does need to indicate to you whether the non-player character's roll is above or below your Gambling skill—just not by how much. With this knowledge, you then choose whether to participate or excuse yourself from the Gambling contest. If you do participate, the GM reveals the value of the roll and may still spend fate points on behalf of her non-player character as usual once the contest starts in earnest.

Never Bluff a Bluffer

Your experience with Gambling gives you an occasional insight into other parts of life. When dealing with a bluff of some kind, you may use Gambling instead of Deceit (to run a bluff) or instead of Empathy (to see through one). Whenever you're the target of something that might be a bluff, you should remind the GM that you have this stunt so she knows to call for the correct skill to be rolled.

Players' Club

You've played in so many games in so many places, it's rare that you can't find someone who knows you. You may use your Gambling skill instead of Contacting whenever making a Contacting roll—though doing so invariably colors the results with the nature of Gambling.

There's Always a Game

No matter the planet or port, you've played in so many places you know how to find a game. When looking for a game, you gain a +2 to your Gambling roll for identifying games of chance that are relatively safe and fair.

Guns

Long Shot

For whatever reason, you're able to take shots at a greater distance than you should be. You can use pistols up to three zones away (instead of two); rifles and other such weaponry also reach an additional zone (or two, if the GM feels generous).

Quick Draw

You can bring your gun to hand so fast it's as if by magic. You take no penalty for drawing a gun as a supplemental action; if someone is actively blocking such an action, treat that block as if its value is two steps lower.

Rain of Lead

You're skilled at laying down a scathing hail of suppressive fire. When using Guns to perform a block, you can ignore up to two points of penalties imposed by the GM due to the complexity of the block.

Shot on the Run

You're light on your feet with a gun in your hand, able to keep the gunplay going while evading attempts to harm you. You may use Guns as a defense skill against physical attacks; normally, Guns can't be used defensively.

Stay on Target

You're a deliberate shooter. Taking slow and careful aim can be done as a maneuver, placing an aspect on your target—such as IN MY SIGHTS. When performing an aiming maneuver against a target, you may roll your Guns at +1 to place the aspect, +2 if you've brought along a targeting scope or similar aiming device—this is in addition to whatever bonuses the scope itself provides.

Two Fisted Shooter

In combat, you fight with a gun in each hand. Normally, shooting with two guns just looks cool without providing a bonus. With this stunt, when you fire two weapons you have a decisive advantage. When you use two guns and hit a target for at least one stress, you gain +1 to damage on the attack.

Intimidation

Aura of Menace

You are the terror of all those who oppose you. Others are often at a loss to describe what exactly about you is so unsettling; regardless, it has the effect of rooting them to the spot and believing the threats you make. Once per scene per target, you may *spend a fate point* to intimidate your target as a free action, no matter what the circumstances; this happens immediately if you're between actions, or immediately after the current action underway. This free action is in addition to any other action you might take during the exchange.

Infuriate

You have a real talent for making people very angry. When deliberately trying to get someone angry at you, you receive a +2 bonus. If this results in an attack or other action against you by your target, you may use Intimidation to complement the skill you use on the first exchange, no matter the circumstance—after all, you made it happen, so you were ready for it.

The Promise of Pain

You make a promise—really, a threat—to a target, and make an attack using Intimidation. If you successfully hit for one or more mental stress, you may *spend a fate point* to immediately force a mild psychological consequence instead. The consequence must represent an appropriate response to the threat—such as FOLDING UP IN FEAR or A BROKEN SPIRIT. The target may choose to concede rather than take the consequence.

Scary

You're just someone people don't want to cross, and that's clear even to other intimidating folks. Normally, Intimidation attempts are resisted by Resolve; you can counter Intimidation attempts with your own Intimidation.

Subtle Menace

You exude menace far in excess of your capability to act. Even bound and behind prison bars, you're so ripe with the promise of the awful things you could do that you're still scary. You may use Intimidation no matter what the power imbalance in the situation is, and your target's bonuses for acting from a superior position are reduced by 2 (to a minimum of +0).

Unapproachable

Opponents have trouble trying to manipulate you when they're constantly reminded of how scary you are. You may use Intimidation in lieu of Resolve to defend against Rapport, Deceit, and Empathy.

Investigation

Focused Senses

You can concentrate on one of your senses to the exclusion of all others. The sense must be specified when you take this stunt. With a few moments of concentration, you enter a focused state. For as long as you use nothing but Investigation, all Investigation actions you take using the specified sense gain a +3.

Impossible Detail

When you're paying attention, your senses operate at a profound level of focus; you pick up on details that others just won't notice. Reduce difficulties due to a physical detail being too small or subtle by two.

Location Awareness

You have a strong visual memory; when you revisit a place where you've used Investigation before, you may make an immediate Investigation check to determine what's changed since you were last there, as if it were an unusually detailed Alertness check.

Pin the Tail

You're tough to shake once you're on someone's trail. Gain a +2 to your Investigation rolls when trying to keep track of a target using surveillance. When shadowing someone using Stealth, you may use your Investigation skill as a complement.

Quick Eye

You can investigate a location quite quickly while still being very thorough. All Investigation efforts you make happen one to two time increments faster than normal; you can either make one or two additional rolls in the same amount of time, or simply conclude your investigation faster than you would otherwise.

Scene of the Crime

You have a practiced eye when combing over a crime scene. In such a circumstance, you gain +1 to your Investigation roll and arrive at your findings one step faster than usual on the time table (page 65, ***Doing Things*** chapter).

Leadership

Chain of Command

When you give an order, people hop to it. If you *spend a fate point* and command another character to perform a certain action, he gains a +3 on his roll if he complies. The command must be a specific use of one of the character's skills, such as "Fly behind the asteroid to lose them." You may do this once per scene.

Companion

You have a companion—a close confederate or lieutenant who is willing and able to accompany you on your adventures. Give your companion a name and write a brief sentence describing his personality and his relationship to you. Your companion has three advances for you to spend as you wish (page 80, ***Doing Things*** chapter). This stunt may be taken multiple times, defining a different companion each time.

Cut the Red Tape

You're familiar with how bureaucracy works—or rather, doesn't work. When dealing with complex paperwork or organizational hierarchy, you can speed things up by two time increments just by knowing who to talk to and what's truly important and what isn't.

Grease the Wheels

You know just how much to use for a bribe and when to do it. When using Leadership to determine the amount to offer for a bribe, gain a +2 to your roll.

Legal Eagle

You're very well acquainted with the law and are skilled at exploiting loopholes in it. You gain a +2 when using Leadership to deal with legal matters.

Minions

You have minions. As the default, you may have the bare minimum of minions easily on hand in a scene—two or three of Average (+1) quality (page 78, ***Doing Things*** chapter). You may make three upgrades to improve your minions, spent at the point you bring them into the scene. Each upgrade either adds three more to their number or boosts the quality of three of them by one step—no minion can be more than Good (+3) quality. You must spend all of your upgrades at once when you bring in your minions.

You can take this stunt multiple times to increase the starting number of minions (taking it twice means you start out with five or six of Average quality) and the number of upgrades (taking it twice also means you have six upgrades).

Medicine

The Best of Care

With a proper facility, you can greatly assist another character's healing process. If you get the other character to rest and can tend to him regularly, you reduce the amount of time it takes to recover from a consequence by two steps on the time chart (page 65, ***Doing Things*** chapter). The character must rest and be immobile for the duration of the time required. If the patient doesn't rest during care, the effects of this stunt don't apply.

Booster

You can use modern drugs to get someone going in combat. Until the encounter is over, the character can spend fate points to avoid being taken out, as described in the Last Leg stunt (page 112). Once the encounter ends, however, the character takes the mild consequence EXHAUSTED in addition to any other consequences taken during the conflict.

Field Medic

You have a talent for delivering medical care in the field. Normally, someone providing first aid can remove a stress mark for every two shifts gained on the roll (page 74, ***Doing Things*** chapter). With this stunt, every shift past the first one improves the level of stress that may be removed—so three shifts removes a checkmark up to the three-stress mark, rather than the two-stress mark. If you roll well enough to remove a stress mark that's higher than the subject's physical stress capacity (e.g., six or more shifts for a character who has Mediocre (+0) Endurance), you can remove a mild physical consequence.

Miracle Worker

You aren't just a doctor; you're a miracle worker. You can bring back those that others think are beyond hope. If you treat someone who's been taken out, you can revive him if you *spend a fate point*. All his injuries remain, but he's no longer taken out. This ability can even be used to revive people who are apparently dead, so long as most of their vital parts are relatively intact.

Not as Bad as It Looks

You're an expert at getting the injured back in action. If you *spend a fate point*, you can move a physical consequence one step down on a character's sheet. A Medicine check is required, but you can change a moderate consequence to a mild one, or even make a severe consequence only moderate. You can only do this once per character per session.

Patch 'Em Up

You can get the injured back on their feet in no time. If you *spend a fate point*, you can erase a mild consequence from a character's sheet in the middle of the action with a quick Medicine roll.

Might

Hammerlock

When you perform a block (page 69, ***Doing Things*** chapter) by personally grabbing hold of someone, you do so at +1. Any time that person tries to break through the block and fails, you may inflict a single point of stress.

Herculean Strength

You're incredibly strong, capable of lifting great weights. All weight-based difficulties that don't involve combat are reduced by two steps.

Piledriver

Your powerful blows land with hammer-like force. At their best, these blows can rip apart steel cages and knock down walls. You add +4 to your attacks with Might against inanimate targets.

Unbound

If you're physically restrained in some fashion—such as by chains or a mob of people—you gain +2 to your Might in your efforts to break out of those bonds. Combined with Piledriver, you simply can't be held in place by most mundane methods.

Unstoppable

Once in motion, you're very difficult to stop due to your sheer muscular force. All blocks to your movement, including borders that can be smashed through, are considered to be two lower.

Wrestler

As a trained wrestler, you may use your Might skill instead of Fists to attack in combat.

Pilot

Daredevil

You can squeeze a vehicle through places where it has no business fitting. Normally, you'd have to spend a fate point to declare that the vehicle has enough clearance space to fit through. You never need to spend a fate point—if it *could* fit, it does. What's more, if you do spend a fate point, you can fit the vehicle into places it absolutely should not be able to go. This stunt also helps when landing vehicles in improbably tight quarters.

Defensive Flying

You're good at keeping your vehicle in one piece. When attempting a Pilot maneuver in a chase (page 147, ***Ships*** chapter), you may treat the difficulty as if it were one lower. The difficulty of the maneuver itself isn't affected, however, for any vehicles that might be chasing you.

Hard Target

You're hard to keep in the gun sights. You gain a +2 to defensive uses of Piloting in dogfights.

One Hand on the Stick

You're good at handling distractions. Piloting while performing another action—such as firing the ship's weapons—normally results in a –1 penalty. You don't suffer that penalty, regardless of whether you're rolling Pilot (piloting is your primary action and the supplemental action is something minor) or rolling some other skill (some other action is primary, but keeping the vehicle steady isn't all that challenging, so piloting is a supplemental action). Furthermore, if your Pilot skill would restrict or modify a primary skill, your Pilot skill has no negative effect, even if it's lower than the primary skill you're using.

Stick to Their Six

Once you're tailing someone, you're practically impossible to shake. When chasing another vehicle, gain a +1 against any maneuvers your target attempts.

Walk Away From It

You have a great instinct for crash-landing vehicles and can walk away from even the most catastrophic-seeming landings. When you pilot a vehicle into its crash landing, you and your passengers survive. The crash is described, without any reference to harm to you or your passengers, and you all stagger out after the landing with all of your physical stress cleared and a single mild consequence to reflect the dangers survived. Every survivor must spend half of their remaining fate points, rounded up. They must have at least one to do this. If a character has no fate points, she's taken out.

Psychic

Flash Forward

You often receive brief visions of the near future, almost unbidden. When you *spend a fate point*, you can describe something that's about to happen. No roll is necessary. The GM must make sure that what you described occurs in the scene. As with all premonitions, things may not turn out exactly as you expect. You can't describe an enemy or another player character being taken out, but you can describe new threats or hazards suddenly appearing.

Fortress of the Mind

You're particularly good at defending your mind from psychic attack. Gain the equivalent of Armor: 1 when someone attempts to use psychic powers to harm you.

Just Not There

You can create excellent distractions in a person's mind. You can conceal objects, including people, from someone's gaze just using your psychic powers, keeping the person from noticing something that's right in front of him. Gain a +2 on your Psychic roll when attempting this.

Mind Knife

You're particularly skilled at using your psychic powers in a direct assault on someone's mind. When you make a successful mental attack using your psychic powers, you gain +2 to damage on the result.

Powerful Empath

You're a specialist in calling up a particular emotion in your target. Choose an emotion—rage, fear, love, etc. When you're attempting to increase this emotion in your target you gain a +2 to your Psychic roll.

Telepathic Link

You can establish a strong mental connection with someone, enabling you to send and receive mental images. This allows for instantaneous communication over long distances. You can't communicate words, but you can show what you see or send mental images of situations or objects to the other person. This is two way, and the other person can do the same even if he doesn't have this stunt or even if he has no psychic powers of his own. The link works over thousands of miles. If the two people are on the same planet, or even in orbit around a planet, it works fine. This link isn't powerful enough for interplanetary communication within a system, much less across space between two star systems.

Rapport

The Art of Conversation

You're good at drawing people out, getting them to talk about themselves. If you're engaged in a long conversation with someone, you can use your Rapport instead of Empathy to get a read on her (page 91, *Skills* chapter) as you get her to hint at or flat out reveal secrets about herself and her past.

Center of Attention

You're used to focusing people's attention on you and keeping it. Any time you use your Rapport to attract attention and distract someone you gain a +2 bonus to your roll.

Five Minute Friends

You're a naturally friendly person and seem to find friends quickly even if you've never visited a place before. If you *spend a fate point*, you can make a steadfast friend in a place you've never been, given a chance for five minutes of conversation. With this stunt, nearly impossible opportunities to make friends become merely improbable, improbable opportunities probable, and probable opportunities outright certain.

Smooth Operator

You're adept at catching the eye of the opposite sex and keeping it once you've got it. Any seduction attempts you make with Rapport receive a +2 bonus provided the target is someone who could be receptive to it (this isn't always a simple case of gender and preference).

Smooth Over

You're adept at stepping into a bad situation and dialing it down to something more reasonable. As long as you aren't the direct reason someone's upset, your attempts to calm him down using your Rapport receive a +2 bonus.

Starfarer

Your mastery of etiquette leaves you comfortable, even glib, in any situation. You never suffer any penalties or increased difficulty from unfamiliarity with your setting, making it easy to maneuver through local customs you haven't encountered before and to cover up any gaffes with a laugh and a sparkle in your eye.

Resolve

Inner Strength

When someone's trying to get inside your head—whether through psychic means or through extensive torture—you receive a +2 to your Resolve defense even without resorting to a full defense action. You may go for a full defense, but it only nets you a +3 in total.

Iron Will

You can push through pain and injury and just keep on going. You get one additional stress box.

Right Place, Right Time

You always seem to be in a safe spot, without moving in any obvious way. When you're engaged in physical combat, you may use Resolve as your combat skill when defending, moving, or taking cover as long as you merely saunter—no sprints allowed. To the outside world, it appears that you're simply staying put, unfazed as gunfire and other attacks miss you by scant inches.

Smooth Recovery

Most people with Resolve can keep things together under stress, but for you it's second nature; you can regain your footing in the face of even the direst of outcomes outside of physical conflict. You may take an additional mild social or mental consequence, allowing up to four total consequences of that variety.

Still Standing

You simply don't know when to quit. If you *spend a fate point*, you may take one additional moderate consequence of any type.

Unflappable

You simply aren't prone to fear. While Intimidation efforts against you might provoke other emotions, they rarely scare you; gain a +2 to your Resolve when defending against a purely fear-based Intimidation action.

Sleight of Hand

Bump and Grab

You're exceptionally skilled at taking advantage of distractions in order to make a quick grab. You may *spend a fate point* to make a simple Sleight of Hand attempt to do something—pick a pocket, palm an object—as a free action.

Cool Hand

A steady hand can be critical when things get hairy. Your hands never shake and never waver. You may ignore any difficulty increases from the environment when performing any fine manual work. This holds true even if that fine manual work doesn't involve the Sleight of Hand skill, such as Burglary for lock picking, or Medicine for surgical work.

Dizzying Distraction

Your bag of tricks in a physical conflict is inexhaustible. You're constantly moving, tossing, distracting, and otherwise confusing your opponent with clothing, items in your pockets, or other light objects. Gain a +2 when attempting to place a distracting maneuver on an opponent in combat.

Light Touch

As a pickpocket, you're a particularly light touch. The target of your pickpocket attempt doesn't get the normal +2 bonus to detect your work.

Sucker Punch

If you're initiating an attack on someone who isn't expecting it, you may use your Sleight of Hand skill as your attack skill on the first exchange, provided you can directly interact with your target and narrate a reasonable distraction.

Vanish in Thin Air

You can quickly and easily hide an object from someone, even when she's looking right at you. You can make it appear you passed it to someone else or set it down when in fact you kept it on your person, or vice versa. Gain a +2 to your Sleight of Hand roll when attempting to conceal the movement of an object in your hand.

Stealth

Hush

Your talent with stealth may be extended to others close by you, provided that you travel as a group. As long as the whole group stays with you and follows your hushed orders, you may make a single Stealth roll for the whole group, using your skill alone. If someone breaks from the group, he immediately loses this benefit and may risk revealing the rest of you if he doesn't manage to pull off a little Stealth of his own.

In Plain Sight

You suffer no environment-based difficulty increases when using Stealth. Even when you're out in the open and wouldn't normally be able to justify using Stealth, you may. Also, once you're hidden, even people actively searching for you don't get a +2 to their Alertness or Investigation rolls. This ability only functions as long as you don't move or do anything other than hide. The moment you do something else, you break cover and are immediately visible.

Lightfoot

It's difficult to track you when you take care to walk lightly. Traps and devices that depend on pressure or some other weight-based trigger are two steps easier for you to circumvent; any attempts to trace the physical evidence of your steps—such as with Investigation or Survival—face a difficulty two higher than you rolled.

Like the Wind

When you move while using Stealth, the bonus to notice you (page 102, *Skills* chapter) is cut in half. This means that out of conflict, observers are at +1 for a slow creep, +2 for walking pace, +3 for jogging, and +4 for a full-out run; in a conflict, observers are only at +1 per zone moved.

Quick Exit

A momentary distraction is all you need to vanish from the scene. Provided you aren't in the midst of a conflict, you may roll a quick contest between your Stealth and the highest Alertness in the room. If you succeed, the next time someone turns to look at or talk to you, you're not there.

Shadowed Strike

You strike from out of the darkness, leaving your foes bewildered and in pain. When hidden, you can launch an attack while remaining hidden, using your Stealth for any defense rolls for the duration of that exchange. Once you strike, you must find another hiding place before you can strike using this stunt again.

Survival

Animal Companion

You've cultivated a close companion from the animal kingdom. Design this companion with the companion rules (page 80, **Doing Things** chapter) with a few changes and limitations. Animal companions have four advances. Your companion operates only with a "physical" scope and must spend at least two of its advances on "Skilled" or "Quality." Any "Skilled" advances must be taken from a short list: Athletics, Fists, Might, Stealth, and Survival. You may take only one skill outside of that list, within reason, based on the animal type. If the animal is an appropriate size, it may be ridden as a mount, at +1 to Survival.

Due North

Your natural talent for navigation is such that you rarely get lost. You have an unerring sense of direction—even underground or on a space station—without any devices to guide you. You get a +2 to Survival when trying to find your way out of a place and you face no familiarity penalties to your efforts to navigate.

Experienced Survivor

You've lived rough on a wide variety of alien worlds. Any penalties assessed for being unfamiliar with the local environment are reduced by two.

One with the Wilderness

You move silently and almost imperceptibly through wild areas. You can conceal your movements and hide easily in a natural environment. When attempting to hide or sneak in the wild, you may substitute your Survival skill for Stealth.

Scavenger

You always seem to be able to come up with whatever you need in a natural environment. Whether searching for firewood, material for a fishhook, or any other item you wish to scrounge from the local environment, you gain a +2 to your Survival roll to find just the thing you need.

Tracker

You're skilled at tracking and can infer a great deal of information from a trail. When studying tracks, you may roll Survival. For each shift from this roll, you can get one piece of information about the person or creature being tracked—weight, how they were moving, and so on. Normally, Survival can't be used to track something, leaving such attempts at a Mediocre (+0) default.

Systems

Black Hat

You're a top-tier hacker, capable of launching devastating assaults. When direct assaulting a system and attempting to deliver stress, your malware gains +2 to damage on a successful assault.

Decrypting

You're an expert at hacking encrypted signals and listening in on protected conversations. When attempting to crack an encrypted communiqué, you gain a +2 on your Systems roll.

Deep Scan

You're a maestro on the sensor console. If you *spend a fate point*, you can make a quick active scan without risking detection, just as if you'd used the passive scanners. The GM gives you results as if you'd performed a full active scan, but your activity is no more detectable than the typical passive sensors.

Master Jammer

You know how to disrupt enemy sensors and jam weapon lock-on attempts. When an enemy attempts lock-on, you gain a +2 on your Systems roll to break the lock.

Roboticist

You're very familiar with robotic programming systems. You can reprogram a robot's skill tree very quickly. When adjusting a robot's skill tree, you can complete the reprogramming two time steps faster on the time scale than normal (page 65, **Doing Things** chapter).

Security Expert

You have an instinctive feel for system security, both how to put it in place and how to overcome it. When setting up security on your own systems and files, your Systems block gains a +1 against attempts to hack it. In addition, when attempting to crack someone else's security you can usually figure out a way more quickly than the average user. You can move the time required for each attempt two steps down the time scale (page 65, *Doing Things* chapter).

Trading

Cool Customer

You're cool and controlled while in negotiations. You use Trading rather than Resolve to defend against Intimidation when attempting to make a deal. Outside of negotiations, this stunt can't be used.

Ear for Bull

You can tell when someone's trying to fool you. Instead of Empathy, you can use Trading to detect a falsehood. This isn't the same as getting a read on someone; it's just a quick check to determine if someone is lying.

Long Term Investment

You've had your money for a while now, and you've had a chance to make several strategic investments that you can cash in when pressed for money. Once per session, you may sell one of these investments to get a +2 to any one Resources roll, as if you'd spent a fate point to invoke a Resources aspect.

Merchant Prince

You know how to ferret out a good deal and you know how to get the goods you need in order to make a trade. When attempting to find trade goods to sell, or when searching for a buyer once you have the material, you gain +2 to your Trading roll.

Ready Cash

Sometimes a deal requires more cash than you have on hand, but that's no barrier to a skilled dealmaker. You can tap friends, family, and business partners to raise some ready capital. You may use your Trading skill as if it were Resources for a single transaction. Of course, the money's on loan, so you need to turn enough profit to pay everyone back. You can only have one such loan at a time. The value of the loan is equal to the difference between your Trading skill and your Resources score. For more on loans, see page 124, *Gear* chapter.

Smell Fear

You can sniff out weaknesses in your negotiating opponent. You may use Trading to get a read on someone (page 104, *Skills* chapter) over the course of negotiating with her. The aspect revealed must be directly relevant to the negotiation at hand.

Weapons

Anything Goes

You suffer no complications for an awkward or improvised weapon—virtually anything can be a lethal weapon in your hands, as long as you can comfortably and casually lift it. The key here is that the weapon must be improvised—a chair, a priceless urn, a beer bottle. There's also a catch—most improvised weaponry doesn't survive more than a few uses. However, you should never need to spend a fate point in order to declare that an improvised weapon is close at hand, unless your surroundings have been deliberately prepared against this, such as a prison cell.

Close at Hand

You can bring your weapon to hand faster than the eye can track. You never take a supplemental action penalty when drawing your weapon if you have it nearby or on your person. If someone is actively blocking such an action (page 69, *Doing Things*), treat that block as if its value is two steps lower.

Flawless Parry

You're skilled at defending yourself when holding a weapon. When you take a full defense action using Weapons, gain a +3 bonus rather than the usual +2.

Good Arm

You have an amazing throwing arm and can throw weapons with great force, allowing you to be effective at a much longer range than usual. You may make an attack using a thrown weapon up to two zones away instead of the usual one.

Riposte

You can reverse an enemy's attack on you into a dangerous reply. When you're physically attacked by an opponent within the same zone as you, and you successfully defend yourself using Weapons well enough to gain spin (page 66, *Doing Things* chapter), you may use that spin to inflict a single point of physical stress on your attacker, immediately, as a free action.

Strike to the Heart

You can deliver a deadly accurate blow that few opponents can resist. Once per scene on a successful hit, *spend a fate point* to add 3 to the damage of your Weapons attack. This stacks with any other damage-increasing stunts for Weapons.

Gear

While a player character in **Bulldogs!** is likely to rely more on natural ability and learned skills than gear, gear is still important. Gear gets you from place to place. Gear allows you to shoot the other guy before he shoots you—with his gear. Depending on the equipment in question, a particular piece of gear may be every bit as important as your natural abilities, given the situation.

Buying Things

You'll end up buying most of your gear, and to do that you need to know how much money you have. Wealth in **Bulldogs!** is an abstract concept. Specific numbers of galactic credits aren't important and—thanks to things like a purely credit-based economy, huge amounts of property ownership, and other such complications—keeping track of specific credits would likely be a game in and of itself, and not a very fun one. As such, wealth in **Bulldogs!** is measured using your character's **Resources** score. Resources works a lot like a skill in play, but there are some significant differences.

Resources

Resources represents the cash and credit a character has on hand and can muster to make purchases. All characters begin with Average (+1) Resources. A high Trading or Gambling skill can increase starting Resources (page 94 and page 105, **Skills** chapter). Use whichever skill confers the greater Resources level—the starting Resources indicated by the skills isn't cumulative.

Making a Purchase

All items have a cost rating—you'll find tables with costs later on, where gear is listed. When you want to buy an item, its cost sets the difficulty for a Resources roll. A Resources roll is slightly different than a skill roll. You can't invoke any regular aspects. There's a special kind of aspect called a Resources aspect; if you have any of these, you may invoke them. Resources aspects are always fragile—they disappear once they're used. Resources aspects are the only modifier you can use on a Resources roll.

If your roll succeeds, you acquire the item, either through spending liquid cash, liquidating other assets, barter, or any combination.

If your roll fails, you're faced with a choice. You may still purchase the item by reducing your Resources by one step for every shift the roll failed by. This means you liquidated assets, emptied your bank account, and permanently reduced your available cash in order to get the item. If you don't want to reduce Resources based on the failed roll, the GM can offer you the following options:

- You can't find the item at a price you can pay. You may not try to purchase it again until you've gone to a completely new region or planet.
- You can't gather your credit and cash quickly enough to purchase it; by the time you do, it's no longer for sale.
- The item is of inferior quality. It has negative aspects that the GM can tag for free once per session. The item has one of these aspects for each shift by which your roll failed.
- You can get a less valuable item of comparable purpose. This item is valued at your actual Resources roll result. If you rolled Average (+1), you can get an Average (+1) value item, etc.

If you settle for one of these conditions, your Resources isn't reduced by the purchase.

Multiple characters can't pool their Resources. Even one step of Resources represents a big difference in available cash. Poorer characters really can't help wealthier ones.

Example: Prbrawl wants to buy an item that has a Fair (+2) cost. His Resources is Average (+1). He rolls a ■□+□■; adding his Resources gives him a total of Average (+1). This fails the roll by one shift. Prbrawl can acquire the item and reduce his Resources to Mediocre (+0), but Nick doesn't want to do this. The GM offers to give him the item, along with the aspect CUT-RATE KNOCKOFF. Nick thinks this sounds like fun and takes the item along with the attendant aspect.

Resources Aspects

When you successfully complete an unusually big job, or come across some loot or treasure, you can gain a Resources aspect. Resources aspects are things like A BIG SCORE, FLUSH WITH CASH, or SALVAGED PARTS. The GM awards these based on the situation. Resources aspects are always fragile—they disappear when you use them. These are the only aspects that can be used to help a Resources roll.

Getting in Debt

When you're attempting to purchase items that cost significantly more than your current Resources, things get a bit more interesting. To buy an item that costs more than your current Resources score, loans or other agreements must be made. The value of the loan is equal to the value of the item being purchased less one—you need a Good (+3) loan to buy a Great (+4) item. This assumes you're covering part of the cost yourself from your own Resources. If your Resources is Mediocre (+0) or less, no one will give you a loan.

The value of the loan—Great (+4), Superb (+5), Legendary (+6), etc.—is noted on your sheet below Resources. The GM can compel a loan just like an aspect, so the person or organization that gave you the loan must be noted. Until the loan is paid off, it acts just like a regular aspect.

Make a Resources check using the loan instead of your regular Resources. You gain a free shift (+1) on this roll. If successful, the loan can buy the item. If the roll fails, refer to the failed Resources check rules above, but you still owe the money on the loan. Yes, it's possible to fail the purchase roll after securing the loan!

You pay back your debt by making a Resources roll against the loan as if it's an item with a value equal to the loan amount. Such a payment reduces the value of the loan by one step—Good (+3) to Fair (+2), for example. It's considered paid off when its value is Mediocre (+0). You may not make more than one repayment attempt per session.

Failed repayment rolls either reduce your Resources by one step or increase the value of the loan by one step (interest!).

Example: Quinn wants to buy a sniper rifle. Don't ask why. You don't want to know. She has Average (+1) Resources. The sniper rifle has a Great (+4) cost. She's pretty certain she won't be able to buy it without a loan. She goes to a shady character she knows and asks for the money. Her loan shark gives her a loan with a value of Good (+3), and she makes a Resources check with a free +1 using the loan value instead of her Resources. It's enough to buy the rifle, and she notes the loan down on her sheet: SLICK FRONTED THE CASH (+3).

After a couple of missions, the GM decides to tag the loan. Quinn's loan shark wants a payment now, or she can do him the favor of roughing up another debtor. Quinn would rather just pay her loan down, so she makes a Resources roll. She's rolling her Average (+1) Resources against the loan value of Good (+3). This will be tough, but luckily Quinn and the crew just made a big score and she has the Resources aspect FLUSH WITH CASH. She rolls, getting a Fair (+2) result—not quite good enough. She invokes FLUSH WITH CASH, bumping her result to Great (+4). She makes the payment to Slick and reduces her loan to a Fair (+2) value.

Raising Resources

How do you get more Resources? An Average (+1) Resources is barely enough to buy anything, and obviously it's not too hard to end up with a Resources of Mediocre (+0). To increase Resources, you need an available Resources aspect, which represents a one-time score or infusion of liquid cash. You can turn this into permanent Resources by investing it, purchasing property, or something along those lines.

To raise your Resources, make a test against the new Resources score and invoke a Resources aspect you've acquired. This aspect gives you a +2 on the roll, just like a regular aspect. If successful, adjust your Resources up one level. If you fail, you make some bad investments and it goes down one level. You can invoke other Resources aspects if you're failing the roll. Like always, Resources aspects are lost once you invoke them.

Example: Brunda is also FLUSH WITH CASH after the last mission, but she doesn't owe some scumbag for a loan. She decides to bump up her Resources. Her Resources are currently Average (+1), so she needs to make a roll against a Fair (+2) difficulty to raise it one step. She makes her roll, burning her FLUSH WITH CASH aspect. She gets a Great (+4) result, more than enough to increase her Resources to Fair (+2).

Trading

Trading is riskier. To trade, you need to first acquire the goods you wish to sell. This is a standard Resources roll, with the difficulty equal to the value of the goods. You can take out loans for this, and you can get inferior goods if you fail the roll.

Once you have the goods, take them to a market where they can be sold. Usually, this means flying them to another planet. To negotiate a sale, you make a Trading skill roll against the person to whom you're selling the goods. If you succeed, you earn a Resources aspect. If the roll fails, you take a negative Resources aspect like TAPPED OUT or BAD CREDIT.

When buying items to trade, you can buy items from the lists below. However, it's generally easier to buy a generic "trade goods" item and work with your GM to determine its value based on what you can afford and the kinds of profits you hope to gain. You can give these trade goods a name—such as "two dozen cases of Ryjyllian brandy"—to make the galaxy come to life a bit.

Example: Prbrawl wants to make a little extra cash on his delivery missions. He's not a good trader—his Trading skill is Mediocre (+0)—but he decides to risk it anyway. He buys some cheap trade goods of Average (+1) value. He manages to make this roll, barely, with an Average (+1) result. He notes down "Cheap Knock-Off Jewelry" as his trade goods.

At the next planet, Prbrawl tries to unload them. He makes another Trading roll, but this time he's testing it against a local merchant. This guy has a Trading of Fair (+2) and gets a Good (+3) result. This is Prbrawl's new difficulty, and he doesn't do so well, rolling only Mediocre (+0). This means he made a very bad deal. He has to take a negative Resources aspect, TAKEN TO THE CLEANERS. He won't be doing any more trading any time soon.

Starting Gear

Every character begins with some starting gear. You can choose an item of Average (+1) value or make a Resources roll for an item of higher value, with all of the attendant downsides. You may have one weapon for each of your combat skills—a hand-to-hand weapon for Weapons, a firearm for Guns, etc., one set of armor or a personal shield, and a tool kit if you have a skill such as Engineering or Medicine which requires such things. Each player gets only one roll per item and must accept the results. Failing the roll doesn't reduce Resources, but it can't be re-rolled.

Example: Quinn is buying her starting gear. She has Average (+1) Resources. Quinn has two combat skills, Guns and Weapons. The GM gives her a roll for each skill. She wants a sidearm for her Guns skill, but she doesn't want a big heavy weapon. She opts not to roll and chooses a blast pistol with a Mediocre (+0) cost, well within her means.

For the Weapons skill, she decides to try for a disruptor sword with a cost of Fair (+2). She rolls against her Resources and gets an Average (+1) result. She could take the item and reduce her Resources or accept one of the choices for an inferior item. Rather than take a disruptor sword with a negative aspect, she picks out a knife for herself instead.

Moving on, she decides that she wants a personal shield instead of armor. It's more concealable and pretty effective. After her previous failed roll, she decides to just take a defense screen, an Average (+1) cost that's within her means.

Lastly, she has the Burglary skill, and a lock spoofing kit is a tool available for this skill. It also has an Average (+1) cost, luckily for her. She adds that to her sheet.

Lifestyle Maintenance

Of course, if all transactions were merely sales and purchases, life would be simple. People, and especially ships, require maintenance. Feeding and clothing yourself costs money. For every GCP standard month that goes by, you need to pay for food, lodging, and incidentals. If your Resources is equal to or above the lifestyle you're trying to maintain, no roll is necessary. You're able to maintain this level of comfort.

If you're trying to live at a level above your current Resources, you must make a roll every month. If you succeed, you manage to maintain your lifestyle. If you fail, your Resources is reduced by one level.

Some jobs, like TransGalaxy Freight, provide food and a place to sleep. This is equal to a Mediocre (+0) lifestyle—these standard resources are provided, but they pretty much suck. If you're willing to accept this lifestyle you don't need to make a Resources check, even if you have a lower Resources than the lifestyle requires.

Ships also require maintenance, and they're far more expensive to maintain than a person. See the **Ships** chapter (page 143) for more details.

See the table below for a list of lifestyles and the kinds of things that are included within those lifestyles.

Lifestyle	Benefits and/or Effects
Terrible (–2)	You're effectively homeless. This lifestyle covers nothing whatsoever, and one item of your gear gains a new negative aspect every week.
Poor (–1)	A Poor lifestyle covers food and not much else. Life is hand-to-mouth. One item of your gear gains a new negative aspect every month.
Mediocre (+0)	At Mediocre, you're getting by on the basics. You have a (not very nice) place to sleep, and you have food. You don't have a lot else.
Average (+1)	Most citizens of the galaxy live at Average. You can afford a place to stay and decent food.
Fair (+2)	This is the equivalent of middle class. You live in a nice house or large apartment, and you have a well-stocked larder. You probably have some sort of personal vehicle, too, or can at least afford local transportation.
Good (+3)	You're starting to live well. Your residence is large and well-furnished, you eat good food, and you can afford the occasional splurge on off-world transportation. You probably have at least one vehicle and a small personal staff, too.
Great (+4)	You may own multiple residences and you probably have several vehicles of a variety of types. Your personal staff is larger and includes people whose job is to manage other staff members.
Superb (+5)	You're among the very, very rich. You have multiple large residences and a large staff attending to your every need. Regular chartered flights off-world are routine.
Fantastic (+6)	You're counted among the wealthiest in the galaxy. Very few live at this level, and those who do often have their own personal security force that rivals most mercenary companies and paramilitary organizations. Some even have their own fleets of ships.
Epic (+7)	Your wealth is practically unparalleled in the galaxy. You are likely a ruler or head of state; your every need is attended to without any involvement from you.

Weaponry

Weaponry in the **Bulldogs!** galaxy comes in a wide variety of forms and is disturbingly commonplace. While it's true that ordinary citizens on highly developed, highly policed worlds are unlikely to carry weapons, roughly 85% of the population outside of these civilized planets does carry some form of sidearm. In most cases, this is for simple self-defense, but there are quite a few mercenaries and bounty hunters out there, and any freighter worth its salt has at least one or two armed guards among its crew. Weapons have the following attributes:

- All weapons have a **damage** attribute. Damage measures how deadly a weapon is; the higher the damage, the more you want to avoid being hit by it. A weapon's damage is the minimum amount of stress it causes with a successful hit. If you hit someone with a weapon with a Damage: 2 and generate no shifts on your attack roll, it still deals 2 stress. In order to deal more stress, you have to generate shifts above and beyond the weapon's damage attribute. So, in the example above, you'd have to generate at least 3 shifts to deal extra stress (which would, in this case, be a total of 3 stress). Note that a weapon's damage can be reduced to the point that it's a negative number. In this case, the weapon's damage applies as a penalty to any shifts generated by the attack roll. For example, a sword that is Damage: –1 against armor would require you to generate at least 2 shifts to deal 1 stress; the first shift is effectively wasted.

- All weapons have an **accuracy** attribute. Accuracy is a representation of how easy it is to successfully land a hit with a weapon. Laser guns, for example, are more precise than blast guns; a small knife is likely much easier to hit someone with than a large, cumbersome chainaxe. A weapon's accuracy is a flat bonus to your attack roll with that weapon. For example, if you're attacking with a gun that has Accuracy: 1, you roll your Guns skill and add 1 to the result. If a weapon's accuracy is negative, then it applies as a penalty to your roll.

- All weapons have a **range**. Range indicates the number of zones you can attack someone with the weapon. A weapon with Range: 0 can be used only in melee range, while Range: 1 indicates that you can use the weapon against anyone in the same zone that you're in. Range: 2 means that you can attack someone in a zone adjacent to the one you're in, Range: 3 extends your attack one zone beyond that, and so on and so forth.

- All weapons have a **type**. This indicates the nature of the weapon and often carries with it certain modifiers to damage against certain kinds of defenses, as well as limitations on which improvements can be applied to your weapon; it also usually determines base damage and utility of a weapon. The most common types are ballistic, laser, blast, explosive, and physical, but other types exist—such as fire and electricity, for example; these types are, in general, left up to the individual gaming group to define. Types of common weapons are discussed in more detail later in this chapter.

- All weapons have a **form**. Form indicates the general shape and size of a weapon. Like type, it carries with it modifiers—usually to accuracy—and limitations on improvements. It also determines a weapon's base accuracy and range. Forms are specific to the kind of weapon being created—that is, there are particular forms of guns, which are different from forms of archaic weapons, which are different from forms of explosives—and are discussed below in more detail.

- Some weapons—notably explosives—have an **area**. The specific rules for explosions are covered elsewhere (page 76, ***Doing Things*** chapter); suffice it to say that the larger an explosive's area is, the more zones the explosion will affect.

Guns

For the most part, people rely on energy-based firearms; the blast pistol is easily the most common sidearm in the galaxy and is powered by a universal power pac—a sort of battery that powers the majority of energy-based firearms. Ballistic weapons—that is, guns that fire old-fashioned bullets—are significantly less common, having been made obsolete by the much easier (and cheaper) to produce blast weapons, though such guns can still be found in many places. Backwater worlds often rely on old-fashioned bullet technology, as energy weapons are often in short supply there, as are the people with the necessary skills to maintain them. More than a few collectors display ballistic weapons.

When you're creating a gun, you choose a type and a form; this gives you your basic attributes (damage, accuracy, and range). So, if all you want is a basic blast pistol, you add the blast type to the sidearm form, and you wind up with a gun with Damage: 2, Accuracy: 0, and Range: 2. A basic weapon has a cost of Mediocre (+0), modified by form, type, and improvements. Your basic, no frills blast pistol falls into this category. Anything fancier will have improvements added to it.

[GEAR]

In general, guns come in the following types:

- **Ballistic** guns fire physical projectiles. Widely viewed as very low-tech, these weapons have fallen into disfavor for a variety of reasons. They're louder, smellier, dirtier, and far more dangerous to use inside a spaceship or space station, due to the dangers of ricochet and hull breach—while this problem still exists with energy weapons, it's often mitigated by ray-coating on the inside of ships. They're still used by some mercenaries and pirates, though, because modern personal energy shields are pretty ineffective against ballistic attacks. A ballistic gun has a starting Damage: 3; however, they're only Damage: 1 against armor.

- **Blast** guns are the best of both worlds, really. They incorporate mass-driver technology, firing a tiny physical projectile, but they surround the projectile with plasma energy, creating a devastating effect that's equally effective against armor, shields, and flesh. Best of all, blast guns are cheap to produce and easy to find, making them the preferred weapon of gunfighters all over the galaxy. They're somewhat less accurate than laser guns, but they're extremely reliable. A blast gun has a starting Damage: 2 and is equally effective against all types of armor.

- **Explosive** guns fire projectiles that detonate on impact. Missile launchers and grenade launchers are good examples of explosive guns. They're typically large, expensive, dangerous, and extremely potent when used correctly. Their ammunition tends to be somewhat more limited than that of other types of guns. An explosive gun has a starting Damage: 4. In addition, explosive guns often—but not always—follow the rules for explosive devices (page 76); this can be modeled using the High Explosive improvement. **Cost +2.**

- **Laser** guns use a concentrated beam of light to cause severe burns to a target. They're excellent at cutting through physical armor and are extremely accurate at range, but their cost is somewhat high. Laser sidearms are uncommon, but longarms—which need accuracy at range—often incorporate laser technology. The primary weakness of laser technology is that it's weak against personal energy shields, making laser guns somewhat ineffective when used against enemies who are prepared for them. A laser gun has a starting Damage: 3 and Accuracy: 1. Laser guns are only Damage: 1 against energy shields. **Cost +1.**

- **Unconventional** guns are the catch-all category for everything that doesn't fit into one of the above categories. A rifle that fires a bolt of electricity or a pistol that emits concussive sound waves are good examples of unconventional weapons. Unconventional weapons are typically designed for a specific purpose, such as setting things on fire, disabling shields, and so forth. They're basically set up to put maneuvers on targets.

In addition to the types of guns, firearms generally fall into one of the three following forms:

- **Sidearms** are designed to be wielded in one hand, but they can typically be wielded in two hands for greater accuracy and recoil compensation. They're small, portable, and typically easy to conceal, but they're somewhat less accurate and deadly than longarms. A sidearm has a starting Accuracy: 0 and a starting Range: 2.

- **Longarms** are larger and harder to conceal than sidearms, but they tend to pack more of a punch. Many longarms also allow for much greater accuracy at range than sidearms do, making them ideal for snipers and soldiers. A longarm can't be used at hand-to-hand range. A longarm has a starting Accuracy: 1 and a starting Range: 3. **Cost +1.**

- **Heavy Weapons** are truly huge guns—much too large to simply carry with you all the time. They're typically specialized weapons, designed to be used against vehicles or designed to be mounted for greater accuracy. Rocket launchers, machine guns, and artillery pieces are all good examples of heavy weapons. A heavy weapon can't be used within the same zone as the wielder. Heavy weapons have a starting Accuracy: 0 and a starting Range: 3, but gain +1 to damage. **Cost +1.**

Type and form give you the basics. However, a basic blast pistol isn't very exciting and is rarely enough for enterprising player characters. For those who want a little bit more, there are improvements. When designing a weapon, you can choose any number of improvements to apply to it. Each improvement increases its cost by 1.

It's possible to buy many improvements multiple times, getting the same increase each time. However, doing so gets very expensive very quickly.

Accurate: Whether because of gyroscopic stabilizers or enhanced targeting scopes, you tend to hit with this weapon more often than not. Accuracy: +1. This improvement may be taken more than once.

Additional Capability: This gun can be used to fire different types of ammunition or can be reconfigured into a completely different gun. When you choose this improvement, choose an additional type or form; you can use a supplemental action to switch between types or forms. The gun uses the Damage and Accuracy attributes for whatever form or type it's currently using, and any other improvements apply to all forms and types that this gun possesses.

Aspect: You can add an aspect to a weapon. This aspect can be invoked and compelled just like any aspect. This improvement may be taken more than once.

Autofire: With a weapon capable of autofire, you can focus fire on a single enemy or attack multiple enemies in the same zone. You can either add Damage: +1 or attack one additional target within a single zone; however, it's a supplemental action and you suffer Accuracy: −1. Taking this improvement again increases the damage bonus and the number of targets you can attack by one, but it also causes an additional Accuracy: −1 penalty; it doesn't add to the number of supplemental actions you need to take.

Concealable: Sometimes it's important to be able to hide a gun on your person. Maybe your gun is just smaller than normal, or it's collapsible, or it can be reconfigured to look like something non-threatening. You gain a +2 bonus to any Deceit rolls made to hide this weapon.

High Explosive (Explosive guns only): This gun fires an explosive projectile with a large blast area. The gun gains an area of 1; each time you choose this improvement, the area increases by 1. Any gun with this improvement is considered to fire hair-trigger explosives (page 77, ***Doing Things*** chapter).

Indirect Fire: This weapon is capable of firing shots over walls, around corners, or otherwise past obstacles that pose difficulties for direct-fire weapons. When you use Artillery instead of Guns to fire this weapon, you can ignore 1 point of borders. This improvement makes the most sense with explosive and unconventional guns, though it could be applied to others with sufficient justification.

Long Range: Some guns have sniper scopes, while others have advanced targeting systems. When you fire this gun, you can attack things that are further away; you gain Range: +1. This improvement may be taken more than once for guns.

Non-Lethal: This gun, though it deals stress normally, can't be used to kill someone. Whenever someone gets a consequence or is taken out as a result of an attack from this gun, its non-lethality must be taken into account. This improvement has a **Cost +0.**

Persistent Effect: Whether it's a flamethrower that lights things on fire, a laser gun that stuns enemies in addition to causing stress, or some other effect that persists, this improvement lets you apply an aspect to the target each time you attack successfully. The aspect is chosen when you choose this improvement. Once you've applied the aspect to a target, it lasts until the end of your next turn; you or one of your allies can tag the aspect once for free. **Cost +2.**

Powerful: The weapon is simply more damaging than others of its kind; it has Damage: +1. This improvement may be taken more than once.

Scattershot: This gun fires a spread of projectiles, a wide cone of laser light, a scattering blast shot, or something similar. This grants the weapon Accuracy: +1, but if your fire at a target outside your zone, you get Damage: −1 for each zone it crosses.

Specialized: Some weapons are really good against armor while others are extremely effective against synthetic targets, such as robots. Some guns are designed to disrupt shields or fire extremely well in low-gravity. When you choose this improvement, the weapon gains Damage: +2 or Accuracy: +2 under specific circumstances or against specific targets. The GM is the final arbiter of what circumstances or targets are too general or too specific; in general, you should get the benefit of the specialization at least a couple of times per session, but probably not much more than that. This improvement may be taken more than once, but not for the same circumstance.

Weapon	Damage	Accuracy	Range	Improvements	Cost
Blast Pistol	2	0	2	None	Mediocre (+0)
Heavy Blast Pistol	3	0	2	Powerful, Aspect: Big and Intimidating	Fair (+2)
Blast Rifle	2	1	3	Longarm	Average (+1)
Heavy Blast Rifle	3	1	3	Longarm, Powerful	Fair (+2)
Repeating Blast Rifle	2	1	3	Longarm, Autofire	Fair (+2)
Blast Sniper Rifle	3	2	4	Longarm, Powerful, Accurate, Long Range	Great (+4)
Scatterblaster	3	1	2	Powerful, Scattershot	Fair (+2)
Ballistic Pistol	3 (1 vs. armor)	0	2	None	Mediocre (+0)
Heavy Ballistic Pistol	4 (2 vs. armor)	0	2	Powerful	Average (+1)
Automatic Ballistic Pistol	3 (1 vs. armor)	0	2	Autofire	Average (+1)
Ballistic Rifle	3 (1 vs. armor)	1	3	Longarm	Average (+1)
Ballistic Assault Rifle	3 (1 vs. armor)	1	3	Longarm, Autofire	Fair (+2)
Ballistic Shotgun	3 (1 vs. armor)	2	3	Longarm, Scattershot	Fair (+2)
Flechette Pistol	3 (1 vs. armor)	1	2	Scattershot, Specialized (Damage: +2 vs. unarmored organics), Aspect: Scary as Hell	Good (+3)
Ballistic Sniper Rifle	4 (2 vs. armor)	2	4	Longarm, Powerful, Accurate, Long Range	Great (+4)
Mag Rifle	5 (3 vs. armor)	2	4	Longarm, Powerful (x2), Accurate, Long Range	Superb (+5)
Laser Pistol	3 (1 vs. shields)	1	2	Aspect: Elegant Looking	Fair (+2)
Laser Holdout	3 (1 vs. shields)	1	2	Concealable	Fair (+2)
Laser Rifle	3 (1 vs. shields)	2	3	Longarm, Autofire, Accurate	Great (+4)
Laser Sniper Rifle	4 (2 vs. shields)	3	5	Powerful, Accurate, Long Range (x2)	Superb (+5)
Grenade Launcher	4	0	2	Indirect Fire, High Explosive	Great (+4)
Gyrojet Pistol	4	0	2	None	Fair (+2)
Mini-Missile Launcher	4	1	4	Longarm, Long Range, Specialized (Damage: +2 vs. vehicles)	Superb (+5)
Inferno Launcher	4	0	3	Heavy Weapon, High Explosive, Persistent Effect: On Fire!	Fantastic (+6)
Stunner	2	0	2	Non-Lethal, Persistent Effect: Dazed	Fair (+2)
Proton Rifle	4	1	3	Longarm, Powerful (x2), Specialized (Damage: +2 vs. armor), Aspect: Knocks Holes through Barriers	Superb (+5)
Sonic Shotgun	2	1	2	Specialized (Damage: +2 vs. targets in the same zone), Scattershot, Persistent Effect: Prone	Great (+4)
Disruptor Pistol	4	0	2	Powerful (x2), Specialized (Damage: +2 vs. unarmored organic targets)	Good (+3)
Gravgun	2	0	2	Non-Lethal, Persistent Effect: choose either Low Gravity or High Gravity	Fair (+2)

Archaic Weapons

Guns are, far and away, the most common weaponry in the galaxy. When you meet a Hackragorkan who's looking to board your ship, he'll probably have a gun. However, there are instances where alternatives to guns are preferable, and on some worlds guns are hard to come by. In addition, archaic weaponry—by which we mean pretty much any melee weapon, as well as things like bows and throwing knives—is often used in combat sports, both the bloody, gladiatorial variety and the more civilized variety such as shooting arrows at non-living targets.

Similar to guns, all archaic weapons have both a type and a form. Basic, common weapons, like a simple knife, sword, or axe, have a starting cost of Mediocre (+0). To make a weapon even slightly better requires improvements, which increases cost. Archaic weapons have the following types:

- **Physical** weapons are by far the most common type of archaic weapon, largely because they're easy and cheap to produce. Physical weapons are archaic weapons at their most basic—a simple knife, sword, or axe, a bow that fires a standard arrow. Modern armor has rendered most physical weapons obsolete, though people who rely solely on energy shields are still at significant risk from these weapons. Physical weapons have a starting Damage: 1. They receive a Damage: +1 bonus against shields, but suffer a Damage: –2 penalty against armor.

- **Vibro** weapons are less common but more effective. Only bladed weapons—both melee and thrown—can be outfitted with this technology, which causes the blade of a weapon to vibrate at a high frequency when activated. This allows the weapon to cut through armor much more effectively. Vibro weapons start at Damage: 3, but they suffer an Accuracy: –1. Note that all vibro weapons can be used as physical weapons, too, simply by turning them off. In this case, they use the statistics for physical weapons rather than vibro weapons.

- **Unconventional** weapons are strange and unusual, typically incorporating some form of energy into a weapon inspired by archaic designs. Whips made of electricity, swords with blades made of focused light, or knives with blades of sonic energy are good examples. Unconventional weapons are typically designed for a specific purpose, such as setting things on fire, disabling shields, and so forth.

In addition, archaic weapons have the following forms:

- **Melee** weapons are designed to be used in close combat. Swords, axes, bludgeons, even more exotic things like whips or pole-arms fall into this category. A melee weapon has an Accuracy: 0 and a Range: 0.

- **Projectile** weapons fire physical—or, sometimes, non-physical—projectiles at much lower speeds than guns. Bows and crossbows are the most common examples of projectile weapons. Projectile weapons have a starting Accuracy: 0 and a starting Range: 2.

- **Thrown** weapons tend to be smaller and lighter than most melee weapons, but they can be used as melee weapons in a pinch. They're designed for short-range combat and are typically concealable, though this isn't always the case. Daggers and axes are the most common thrown weapons, though more exotic varieties do exist. Thrown weapons have one serious disadvantage—once you throw one of them, you have to retrieve it if you want to throw it again. Thrown weapons have a starting Accuracy: 0 and a starting Range: 1.

Just as with guns, once you combine a type and a form for your archaic weapon, you can add improvements to it. Most of the improvements are the same as those listed for guns, and the rules for adding them are the same. The following improvements can be added to archaic weapons:

Accurate: Some weapons have superior balance and craftsmanship, while others—bows and crossbows, in particular—add targeting scopes for greater accuracy. The weapon gains Accuracy: +1. This improvement may be taken more than once.

Aspect: You can add an aspect to a weapon. This aspect can be invoked and compelled just like any aspect. This improvement may be taken more than once.

Concealable: Some weapons are designed to be hidden, such as collapsible bows or swords that disguise their sheath in a cane. These weapons are typically used by assassins. You gain a +2 bonus to any Deceit rolls made to hide this weapon.

High Explosive (Projectile and Thrown weapons only): This weapon explodes on impact or fires ammunition that does the same. The weapon gains an area of 1; each time you choose this improvement, the area increases by 1. Any weapon with this improvement is considered to fire hair-trigger explosives. This improvement may be taken more than once.

Indirect Fire (Projectile weapons only): This weapon is capable of firing shots over walls, around corners, or otherwise past obstacles that pose difficulties for direct-fire weapons. When you use Artillery instead of Weapons to fire this weapon, you can ignore 1 point of borders.

Long Range (Projectile and Thrown weapons only): Many modern bows and crossbows use high-tech alloys for their bodies and incorporate pulley systems that allow for increased tension and force. In addition, some thrown weapons incorporate propulsion systems to improve range. When you fire this weapon, you can attack things that are further away. The weapon gains Range: +1.

Non-Lethal: This weapon, though it deals stress normally, can't be used to kill someone. Whenever someone gets a consequence or is taken out as a result of an attack from this weapon, its non-lethality must be taken into account. This improvement has a **Cost +0.**

Persistent Effect: Whether you're talking about a staff that stuns its target with an electrical discharge, a sword that lights things on fire, or some other effect that persists, this improvement allows you to apply an aspect to the target each time you successfully attack it. The aspect is chosen when you choose this improvement. Once you've applied the aspect to a target, it lasts until the end of your next turn. When you apply this aspect to someone, you or one of your allies can tag it once for free. **Cost +2.**

Powerful: The weapon is simply more damaging than others of its kind and gains Damage: +1. This improvement may be taken more than once.

Specialized: Some weapons are really good against armor, while others are extremely effective against synthetic targets, such as robots. Some weapons are designed to disrupt shields or to secrete poison that's effective against a specific species. When you choose this improvement, the weapon gains Damage: +2 or Accuracy: +2 under specific circumstances or against specific targets. The GM is the final arbiter of what circumstances or targets are too general or too specific; in general, you should get the benefit of the specialization at least a couple of times per session, but probably not much more than that. This improvement may be taken more than once, but not for the same circumstance.

Weapon	Damage	Accuracy	Range	Improvements	Cost
Knife	1 (2 vs. shields/ −1 vs. armor)	0	0	None	Mediocre (+0)
Heavy Cutlass	2 (3 vs. shields/ 0 vs. armor)	0	0	Powerful	Average (+1)
Spiked Axe	2 (3 vs. shields)	0	0	Powerful, Specialized (Damage: +2 vs. armor)	Fair (+2)
Vibrodagger	3	−1	0	None	Mediocre (+0)
Vibrosword	4	−1	0	Powerful	Average (+1)
Chainaxe	5	−1	0	Powerful (x2), Aspect: Really Damn Scary	Good (+3)
Stunstick	1	0	0	Non-Lethal, Persistent Effect: Stunned	Fair (+2)
Disruptor Sword	2	0	0	Powerful, Specialized (Damage: +2 vs. unarmored organics)	Fair (+2)
Neutron Scrambler	3	0	0	Powerful (x2), Specialized (Damage: +2 vs. organic tissue), Persistent Effect: Grievous Wound, Aspect: "Shit, he's got a neutron scrambler!"	Fantastic (+6)
Bow	1 (2 vs. shields/ −1 vs. armor)	0	2	None	Mediocre (+0)
Crossbow	2 (3 vs. shields/ 0 vs. armor)	0	2	Powerful	Average (+1)
Bolt Gun	2 (3 vs. shields/ 0 vs. armor)	0	2	Powerful, Persistent Effect: Burning Wound	Good (+3)
Throwing Knife	1 (2 vs. shields/ −1 vs. armor)	0	1	None	Mediocre (+0)
Vibro-Shuriken	3	0	1	Concealable, Accurate	Fair (+2)
Energy Bola	1	0	1	Non-Lethal, Persistent Effect: Tripped	Fair (+2)
Razorang	2 (3 vs. shields/ 0 vs. armor)	0	1	Powerful, Aspect: Return to Sender	Fair (+2)

Weapon	Damage	Improvements	Cost
Fragmentation Grenade	5	Powerful	Fair (+2)
Concussion Grenade	4	Non-Lethal, Persistent Effect: OFF YOUR FEET	Good (+3)
Energy Grenade	4	Recharge and Reuse	Fair (+2)
EMP Grenade	4	EMP, Recharge and Reuse	Good (+3)
Land Mine	5	Powerful, Fuse	Good (+3)
Energy Bomb	4	Tamper-Proof, Remote Detonator, Recharge and Reuse	Great (+4)

Explosives

Not to be confused with explosive-firing guns or archaic weapons that explode on impact or fire explosive arrows, the explosives category covers two different kinds of things that explode: explosives that you throw—such as grenades—and explosives that you set ahead of time and trigger later—such as land mines or shaped charges. While other types of weapons can be explosives, it's generally assumed that these weapons have a fairly small blast radius—unless, of course, they have the High Explosive improvement. By contrast, explosives in this category all start with an area of at least 1, meaning that they affect an entire zone at minimum. They are, therefore, somewhat dangerous to use, especially on a starship where collateral damage can spell disaster for everyone aboard.

When creating an explosive, things work a little bit differently. You don't choose a type for an explosive, and you only choose from two different forms. Afterward, you can feel free to add improvements and aspects, as normal. The two explosive forms:

- **Grenades** are small, hand-held explosive devices designed to be thrown. Compared to other explosives, they do relatively low damage to a relatively small area, but they're still devastating in comparison to other kinds of weapons. A grenade has the following starting attributes:
  - Damage: 4
  - Area: 1
  - Accuracy: 0
  - Range: 1
  - A hair-trigger fuse
  - Cost +1

- **Charges** are explosives that are set in place and detonated at a later time, whether through a remote detonator, a timer, a pressure sensor, or some other method. Charges tend to be larger than grenades and considerably harder to use in the midst of combat, but they're considerably more dangerous, too. They require some planning

to utilize effectively, as well as some skill in Engineering. When creating a charge, you start with your base stats, then use improvements to increase damage, area, and complexity, and to apply different types of fuses. Use the following rules to create charges:
- Damage: 4
- Complexity: 4
- Area: 1
- No range or accuracy attribute; charges follow different rules from other weapons
- A hair-trigger fuse
- Cost +1

Once you've gotten a basic explosive put together, you can add improvements just like with other weapons. These improvements follow the same rules as for other weapons:

Aspect: You can add an aspect to an explosive. This aspect can be invoked or compelled like any aspect. This improvement may be taken more than once.

Concealable: Some explosives are smaller than normal, or designed to be assembled on-site, or made to look non-threatening. You gain a +2 bonus to any Deceit rolls made to hide this weapon.

EMP: Unusual and specialized, but no less potentially dangerous than other explosives, an EMP explosive disables any electronics within the blast radius—including personal shields, but not including robot characters—until they can be repaired. Against robot characters, these explosives deal Damage: 4. However, EMPs deal no damage against organic targets.

Fuse: Rather than detonating on impact, the explosive detonates after a short, medium, or long period of time (page 77, **_Doing Things_** chapter).

Non-Lethal: This explosive, though it deals stress normally, can't be used to kill someone. Whenever someone gets a consequence or is taken out as a result of an attack from this explosive, its non-lethality must be taken into account. This improvement has a **Cost +0.**

Persistent Effect: Whether it's incendiary charges or grenades that snap-freeze their targets, some explosives are designed to do interesting things; this improvement allows you to apply an aspect to a target each time you successfully attack it. Choose an aspect when you choose this improvement, and once you've applied the aspect to a target, it lasts until the end of your next turn. When you apply this aspect to someone, you or one of your allies can tag it once for free. **Cost +2.**

Powerful: The weapon is simply more damaging than others of its kind and gains Damage: +1. This improvement may be taken more than once.

Recharge and Reuse: Most energy-based explosives release their charge when detonated, but this doesn't damage the device itself. If recovered, the explosive can be fitted with a new energy charge and used again.

Remote Detonator: Once you've thrown the grenade or set the charge, you can use a small device to detonate it remotely, reducing the risk to yourself and others.

Specialized: Some explosives are really good against armor, while others are extremely effective against synthetic targets, such as robots. When you choose this improvement, the explosive gains Damage: +2 or Accuracy: +2 under specific circumstances or against specific targets. The GM is the final arbiter of what circumstances or targets are too general or too specific; in general, you should get the benefit of the specialization at least a couple of times per session, but probably not much more than that. This improvement may be taken more than once, but not for the same circumstance.

Tamper-Proof: Usually used on charges, this improvement makes it very difficult to disarm the explosive. Complexity: +3. This improvement may be taken more than once.

Personal Defense

The galaxy is a dangerous place, full of people and creatures with dangerous weapons that want to shoot you, stab you, burn you, or blow you up. In order to protect yourself from such hostiles, it can be useful to wear body armor and to use personal energy shields. You can use one, both, or neither of these options, in any combination, but you can only wear one suit of armor, and you can only benefit from one personal energy shield; you can't stack layers of personal defense.

Armor and shields have a numerical rating, just like weapon damage. This result is directly subtracted from any stress inflicted on the character by an attack. When struck, only the highest level of protection is applied. If you have Armor: 4 and Shields: 2 and you're struck for 6 stress, apply the armor value and take 2 stress.

Armor

Armor is by far the more common of the two, primarily because most modern armor can be incorporated into environmental suits, allowing the wearer to protect himself against enemy gunfire and hostile environments with a single piece of gear. Armor is typically very strong against physical attacks, such as swords, fists, and bullets, but tends to be a bit weaker against things like fire, plasma, and lasers. A basic armored vest has an Average (+1) cost and confers Armor: 1.

Defense	Armor	Improvements	Cost
Ballistic Cloth	1	Aspect: Hard to Detect	Fair (+2)
Synthetic Mesh	2	Hardened, Aspect: Hard to Detect	Good (+3)
Synthetic Plate	2	Hardened	Fair (+2)
Commando Suit	2	Hardened, Camouflage, Enviro-Suit	Great (+4)
Battle Armor	3	Hardened (x2), Ray-Coating	Great (+4)
Power Armor	3	Hardened (x2), Ray-Coating, Powered	Superb (+5)

You can add improvements to your armor. Improvements increase the cost by 1 per improvement.

Aspect: You can add an aspect to armor. This aspect can be invoked and compelled just like any aspect. This improvement may be taken more than once.

Camouflage: Armor can be made to blend in with various environments—most modern armor utilizes a reprogrammable surface pigment system that allows for multiple camouflage patterns and colors. Camouflage armor gives you a +2 bonus to Stealth rolls.

Enviro-Suit: Armor with this improvement allows you to survive in hostile environments. It's equipped to mitigate the effects of extreme heat and cold, caustic or poisonous atmospheres, or even the vacuum of space. An enviro-suit gives you a +2 bonus to Survival and Endurance rolls made to resist the effects of hostile environments.

Hardened: The armor is harder to penetrate than normal and gains Armor: +1. This improvement may be taken more than once.

Powered: Powered armor is relatively rare, mostly because it's big, bulky, and obvious. It does, however, have advantages. The armor enhances the strength of its wearer, allowing him to perform feats of might that would otherwise likely be impossible. Powered armor grants you a +2 bonus to Might rolls.

Ray-Coating: This special, reflective coating was designed in response to the prevalence of laser weapons amongst assassins and snipers. It's designed to reflect as much of a laser's energy as possible, protecting the wearer from such weapons. Lasers suffer a Damage: −2 penalty against armor with ray-coating.

Shields

Shields are less common than armor, but they're also less cumbersome; it's also far easier to hide a shield's presence. Many politicians expecting an assassination attempt wear a shield, while their bodyguards often wear armor. Shields offer some protection against physical attacks, but they excel against energy-based weapons. A basic personal shield has an Average (+1) cost and confers Shields: 1.

As with armor, you can add improvements to your shield. Improvements increase the cost by 1 per improvement.

Aspect: You can add an aspect to a shield. This aspect can be invoked or compelled just like any aspect. This improvement may be taken more than once.

Shield Strength: The shield is harder to penetrate than normal and gains Shields: +1. This improvement may be taken more than once.

Stealth Field: Some shields are designed to be able to bend light around them, rendering the wearer effectively invisible to normal vision. However, enabling a stealth field is taxing on a shield, draining its power quickly. You can deplete your shield's charge in order to become effectively invisible, granting you a +4 bonus to Stealth checks—if the GM even rules that you need to make them—and causing enemies to suffer a −2 penalty to any attack rolls against you. This effect lasts for the rest of the scene. Recharging the depleted shield requires using an outlet in a building or on a ship for about an hour.

Defense	Armor	Improvements	Cost
Defense Screen	1	None	Average (+1)
Combat Screen	2	Shield Strength	Fair (+2)
Infiltrator's Screen	2	Shield Strength, Stealth Field	Good (+3)
Battle Screen	3	Shield Strength (x2)	Good (+3)

Personal Items

Shooting things and protecting yourself from being shot is all well and good, but it's only part of what you'll be doing in your **Bulldogs!** game. You need a variety of other gear to get various jobs done. From comm units to jet packs, having the right piece of gear for the situation can spell the difference between success and failure.

When you're designing a personal item, you start with a base item. Any item that you purchase without adding improvements or aspects has a cost of Mediocre (+0) and is assumed to allow you to use relevant skills with no modifiers or special effects. For your gear to have a mechanical effect, you have to customize it.

Also note that you shouldn't use this system to create gear that already has its own creation rules—so don't use this system to create weapons, armor, or shields (their rules exist in this chapter already), or to make vehicles (those rules are in the *Ships* chapter, page 140).

Once you've decided on a basic piece of equipment, start adding improvements to get the functionality you want. As with other types of gear, adding an improvement increases its cost by 1.

Alternate Usage: This item allows you to use one skill in place of another skill. A device might have sophisticated targeting systems, allowing you to use Systems rolls in place of Guns rolls; or it might amplify your telekinetic abilities, allowing you to use Psychic in place of Might. **Cost +2.**

Armed: This item has a weapon of some sort attached to it, whether it's a barricade with a mounted gun or an armband that houses a concealed blade. Create and purchase the attached weapon separately, using the normal rules for whatever weapon you're creating.

Armored: This item has built in Armor: 1.

Aspect: You can add an aspect to an item. This aspects can be invoked and compelled like any aspect. This improvement may be taken more than once.

Conscious: This item incorporates true artificial intelligence; it's capable of thinking and reasoning, as well as performing complex tasks within a limited scope. **Cost +2.** Choose one of the following benefits:

- Three skills at Average (+1)
- Two skills at Fair (+2)
- One skill at Good (+3)

Craftsmanship: This item is particularly well made; you get a +1 bonus to your skill roll when you use it. If the item can be used with multiple skills, this improvement only applies to one skill, chosen when you create the item. You can only take this improvement once for each affected skill.

Independent: This item incorporates basic automation technology that grants it a limited form of independence. Choose one skill that the item can perform on its own; that skill is rated at Fair (+2).

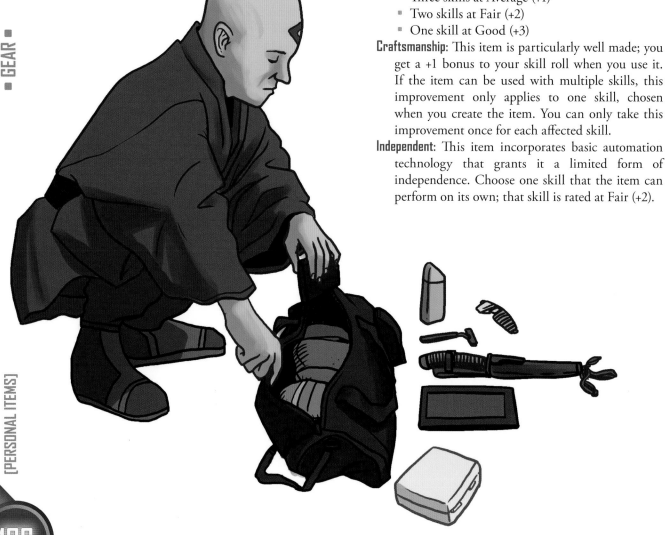

Item	Improvements	Cost
Navigation Computer		Mediocre (+0)
Engineer's Tool Box		Mediocre (+0)
Medkit		Mediocre (+0)
Lockpick Set		Mediocre (+0)
Encounter Suit		Mediocre (+0)
Advanced Flight and Navigation System	Conscious: Pilot Fair (+2), Systems Fair (+2)	Fair (+2)
Hi-Jack Infiltration Device	Independent: Systems Fair (+2), Upgrade (+2 Burglary to bypass security systems), Aspect: Right Tool for the Job	Good (+3)
Infocity Template Book	Alternate Usage (Systems in place of Academics), Upgrade (+2 Systems to research information)	Fair (+2)
Lock Spoofing Kit	Upgrade (+2 Burglary to bypass security systems)	Average (+1)
Medic's Field Kit	Craftsmanship (+1 to Medicine rolls), Upgrade (+2 Medicine on efforts to tend the wounded in the field)	Fair (+2)
Neurocomm	Alternate Usage (Psychic in place of Leadership), Upgrade (+2 Psychic to communicate with others using the neurocomm)	Good (+3)
Security Drone	Conscious: Guns Average (+1), Alertness Average (+1), Stealth Average (+1), Rugged, Armed	Great (+4)
Star Suit	Special Effect (controlled flight in low and zero-g), Aspect: Airborne Alacrity	Fair (+2)
Tech Binoculars	Upgrade (+2 Investigation to view long distant objects), Aspect: Tech HUD, Special Effect (light amplification)	Good (+3)
Zero-G Combat Suit	Special Effect (controlled flight in low and zero-g), Armored, Shielded	Good (+3)

Miniaturization: This item is much smaller than a normal item of its type. A miniaturized item is more portable and easier to conceal than a normal item of its type. Gain a +2 to Stealth, Deceit, or Sleight of Hand rolls to conceal the item.

Rugged: An item with this improvement is a bit tougher than a standard item, netting it two additional stress boxes over what it normally has—typically two. Note that these stress boxes are only taken into account when the item itself is being attacked. If it's an item you're wearing, this improvement doesn't grant you any protection.

Shielded: This item has a built in energy shield which gives it Shields: 1.

Special Effect: This is a sort of catch-all improvement for doing crazy things with your gear. If you're looking for an item that teleports you, or allows you to speak with the dead, or some other off-the-wall thing, this is the improvement for you. The benefit of this improvement is highly variable, depending on what you make your item do. Consequently, the cost of this improvement is also highly variable; work with your GM to come up with a reasonable price. Most things will have a cost of +1, but depending on the effect, the cost could go as high as +3 or +4. This improvement may be taken more than once.

Upgrade: This improvement grants a +2 bonus to efforts to do something fairly specific. For example, a computer terminal might have extensive databases on a specific planet, or a set of climbing gear might be designed specifically for low-gravity climbing. The GM is the final arbiter of what upgrades are too general or too specific; in general, you should get the benefit of the upgrade at least a couple of times per session, but probably not much more than that. This improvement may be taken more than once, but not for the same activity.

Making Things

You can create your own items from component materials if you're sufficiently inclined—and doing so can save you money! If you want to create an item from base materials, make an Engineering roll with a difficulty equal to the cost of the item in question. When you build something, it isn't free, though; you have to pay for the raw materials and tools required to build the device. The cost of the raw materials is equal to the item's cost –1. You must have access to a workshop of the appropriate type (see below) in order to build or improve an item.

In addition, it takes time to build your own gear. A simple item takes a few days to make, but more complex items can take longer—sometimes up to a year. The GM determines the amount of time required. You can, if you'd like, increase the amount of time it takes to make something by one increment on the time table (page 65, ***Doing Things*** chapter) in order to get a +1 bonus to the roll; you can do this as many times as you want—the bonus is cumulative, but it doesn't reduce workshop requirements or the cost. The reverse is also true; if you want to rush, you can take a –1 penalty to the roll for each increment by which you reduce the time.

If you fail your Engineering roll to create the item, two things happen. First, you increase the time increment that it takes to make the item by one as you go back over your work and fix your mistakes. Second, you reduce your Resources by 1 because you must buy more supplies to replace the ones you damaged when you botched the job. If you do both of those things, you can make another Engineering roll. If you can't do both of those things, you don't get to make another Engineering roll and you effectively waste the time and Resources that you spent on the item.

Example: Prbrawl decides to craft some tech binoculars. This item normally has a Good (+3) cost, so the materials to construct it will have a Fair (+2) cost. Prbrawl succeeds on his Resources roll, and he already has a workshop and a tool kit.

The difficulty for the Engineering roll is Good (+3)—equal to the cost of the final item. The GM says the binoculars will take a week to build. If Prbrawl wants to take some extra time and spend a couple of weeks building it, he can reduce the difficulty to Fair (+2). If he's in a rush and needs to do it in a few days, the difficulty goes up to Great (+4).

Improving Things

Improving an item works a lot like creating one from scratch, except that you're starting with the base item and, effectively, "creating" the improvements. To determine the cost of the improvements you're adding to your item, start with the base item's cost and add any improvements to that base item. Once the final cost with the new improvements is determined, you need a Resources roll with a difficulty equal to this cost –1 to make the improvements.

Each improvement takes between an afternoon and a week to add—determined by the GM—and this time is cumulative. All other rules for making items apply.

Workshops

You can purchase workshops—essentially collections of tools and supplies that you keep on hand in order to make creating things easier and cheaper. A workshop has two attributes:

- A workshop's **type** determines what kinds of items it applies to. A workshop can have multiple types, but each additional type increases cost by 1. You can choose from the following types:

  Arms: for creating guns and armor.
  Chemistry: for creating explosives, as well as any chemical-based items.
  Electronics: for creating shields, as well as any personal electronic devices.
  Handcraft: for creating archaic weapons, as well as other non-electronic items.
  Vehicular: for creating vehicles of all kinds.

- A workshop's **quality** determines how useful the workshop is in creating things. In order to use a workshop to create a particular item, the workshop's quality has to equal or exceed the item's cost. The cost of the workshop is equal to its quality.

Ships

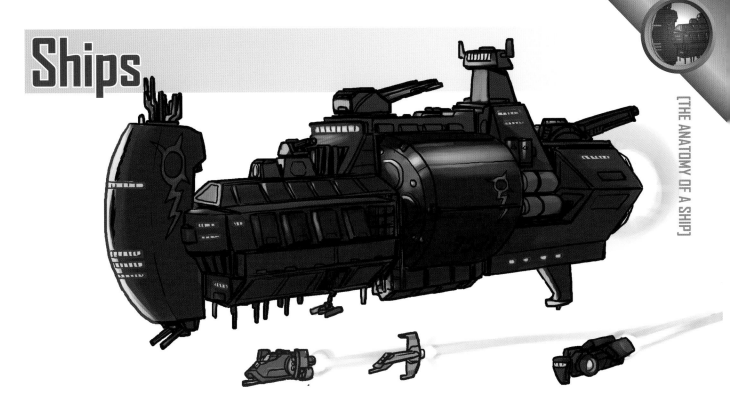

In **Bulldogs!**, ships are of the utmost importance; after all, how can you have a space opera without the ability to travel between planets and fly through the stars? Ships have a number of roles in the game—these are covered in more detail later—and ship combat is something that's likely to come up at least once during your time playing **Bulldogs!**

The Anatomy of a Ship

This section speaks in terms of ships because ships are what you're most likely to deal with on a regular basis. These rules can be used to create any vehicle, and all vehicles have the same attributes. So when we say "ship," think "whatever vehicle you happen to be dealing with."

Speed

All space-faring ships have a speed and, in this day and age, most are capable of hyperspace travel. There are some exceptions to these general guidelines; fighters, for example, rarely have hyperspace capability since they're usually attached to capital ships of some sort.

A ship's speed is expressed as a value, usually ranging from Mediocre (+0)—which is fairly slow—to Great (+4)—which is very fast—though speeds above or below these levels are certainly possible. Speed affects the difficulty of the roll when the pilot is trying to do something beyond moving the ship at a standard speed.

Maneuverability

Whether you're trying to navigate through an asteroid field or dodge an enemy ship's fire, maneuverability is the ship's overall agility. Maneuverability represents a combination of the responsiveness of the controls and the construction of the ship that can greatly increase—or decrease—your ability to perform such complex and dangerous actions.

Whenever you make a Pilot roll that requires quick reactions or agile movement, your ship's maneuverability value applies to your Pilot roll as either a bonus—such as for a quick fighter—or a penalty—such as for a slow, ponderous destroyer. This includes most defensive rolls; it's considerably harder to dodge enemy fire in a large freighter or pleasure cruiser than in a small, one-man fighter.

Armor and Shields

Some ships are equipped with shields—energy-based protection with the advantage of self-regeneration—while others must make do with simple hull plating. Shields are common on larger combat-worthy vessels—destroyers and frigates, for example—as well as some exploratory vessels and mercenary vessels. Fighters rarely have shields—a shield's energy requirements mean larger, more expensive fighters, which typically isn't a good trade-off. Freighters usually have fairly heavy hull plating—the better to withstand pirate attacks—and are rarely equipped with shields. In game terms, armor and hull plating are represented by the ship's own stress boxes—those with heavy hull plating simply have more stress boxes. Shields behave similarly to personal energy shields (page 135, **Gear** chapter), in that your ship's shields reduce damage.

Weapons

All military vessels carry at least some armaments, ranging from the relatively weak weaponry of a light fighter to the truly devastating weaponry of a heavy destroyer or mobile military space station. The weaponry on pirate or mercenary ships is wildly variable—some prefer to rely on boarding parties, while others try to completely disable an enemy (or victim) ship before sending anyone aboard. Some freighters are equipped with weapons, depending on the danger presented by the paths they tend to travel. Class D ships are always armed.

Other Considerations

There's a multitude of different ship models, and they vary in more than speed and armaments. Some have large cargo holds and little room for passengers, preferring to get by with only a basic crew; others have spacious passenger quarters, restaurant decks, tennis courts, and entertainment theaters. You can represent many of these differences with aspects placed on the ship. For the most part, these aspects will inform role-play, being more plot devices than mechanical considerations. Ship aspects can be invoked and compelled just like any aspect placed on any scene, and it's conceivable that any aspect—no matter how mundane—could be useful in some situation.

Other systems, like shipboard AI, a sensor jammer, or power-boosting technology are represented by improvements that you can add to your ship.

> Shipping out with TransGalaxy is a real hardship. The company is notoriously cheap with Class D ships, buying old junkers or other defective vehicles and making them barely spaceworthy. When constructing a ship for a Class D crew, the cost of the ship or any individual weapon can never be greater than Superb (+5).

Vehicle Creation

There are pre-made ships later in this chapter, but your group will probably want to design—or help the GM design—the ship that you're all aboard when the game starts.

It should be noted that, while this section mostly talks about creating ships, it's a system for *vehicle* creation—you can use this system to create any kind of vehicle, not just ships. Some improvements may not make sense for more terrestrial craft, and some improvements don't make a lot of sense for space-faring ships. Use what you need for the specific vehicle you're making and ignore the rest.

To make a vehicle, follow these steps:

1. Choose Vehicle Base Cost

First, choose a base cost for your vehicle. In addition to determining cost, this indicates the amount of stress the vehicle starts with and its starting maneuverability. Also listed in the table are examples of what vehicles fall under a particular base cost.

Base Cost	Stress	Maneuverability	Examples
Fair (+2)	2	Great (+4)	Hovercycle, gravsled, runabout
Good (+3)	4	Good (+3)	Groundcar, tank, shuttle, yacht, fighter
Great (+4)	6	Fair (+2)	Cutter, corvette, freighter
Superb (+5)	8	Average (+1)	Battleship, large freighter
Fantastic (+6)	10	Mediocre (+0)	Capital ship, carrier
Epic (+7)	14	Poor (-1)	Space station

Example: The group decides to build their ship, the *Black Watch*. The *Black Watch* is a small freighter, so its base cost is Great (+4). The stress of 6 and maneuverability of Fair (+2) are noted down on the ship record sheet.

2. Set Speed

All vehicles have a speed and are capable of movement; even orbital space stations can be repositioned or set to orbit, albeit slowly. Your vehicle's speed affects its cost—increasing cost for a higher speed, reducing it for lower speed. In addition, the faster something is, the harder it generally is to perform complex stunts with it, meaning that a higher speed reduces maneuverability.

Speed	Cost	Maneuverability Reduction
Poor (-1)	-2	0
Mediocre (+0)	-1	0
Average (+1)	0	0
Fair (+2)	+1	-1
Good (+3)	+2	-2
Great (+4)	+3	-3

Example: TransGalaxy is cheap, so they didn't to pay to increase the *Black Watch*'s speed. Average (+1) speed adds nothing to the ship's cost, so that's where it stays.

3. Add Shields (Optional)

Some vehicles, particularly combat-worthy spaceships, are equipped with shields designed to protect them from enemy fire, solar radiation, asteroids, and the like. The better your shields, the more they cost. Use these guidelines for adding shields to your ship:

- A basic shield gives a ship Shields: 1 and adds 1 to cost.
- For every additional point of shields, increase the cost of the ship by 1.

Example: Class D ships get shot at a lot, but the company won't spring for any shields. If the crew wants to add these later, they'll have to do it out of their own pocket.

4. Add Weapons (Optional)

Not all vehicles are equipped with weapons. Most commercial freighters have a crew ready to handle a boarding party, but don't have the armaments to repel an enemy ship. Many vehicles do have weapons, though, particularly those used by military and para-military organizations, as well as mercenaries, bounty hunters, and criminals. Weapons are purchased separately from the vehicle. The GM can limit the number of weapons on a vehicle based on size. Obviously, smaller vehicles can carry fewer weapons than larger ones. There are three types of weapons that can be added to a vehicle.

Energy weapons fire plasma, lasers, or some other unconventional form of energy. They're relatively small and cheap, but fairly ineffective against shields.

- Starting Damage: 2 (Damage: 1 vs. shields)
- Starting Accuracy: 1
- Starting Range: 3
- Base Cost Great (+4). Add 1 to the cost for each additional:
  - Damage: 1
  - Accuracy: 1
  - Range: 1

Mass drivers fire physical projectiles at high velocities; they're intended to bypass shields and puncture hull plating. They're powerful, but mass drivers take up a lot of space and are expensive to manufacture.

- Starting Damage: 2 (Damage: 3 vs. shields)
- Starting Accuracy: 0
- Starting Range: 2
- Base Cost Great (+4). Add 1 to the cost for each additional:
  - Damage: 1
  - Accuracy: 1
  - Range: 1

Ordnance consists of torpedoes, missiles, bombs, and other explosive and otherwise highly devastating weaponry. These take up a lot of space and are rarely found on smaller ships.

- Starting Damage: 6
- Starting Accuracy: 2
- Starting Range: 2
- Base Cost Fantastic (+6). Add 1 to the cost for each additional:
  - Damage: 1
  - Accuracy: 1
  - Range: 1
- Limited Ammunition: Because missiles and torpedoes are so large and volatile, you don't keep large quantities of them on your vehicle. You must *spend a fate point* to use ordnance; any member of the vehicle's crew may spend this fate point.

Once you determine the base cost of the weapon, you can add improvements; each increases the weapon cost by 1. Each weapon on a ship must be bought separately and doesn't add to the cost of the ship itself.

Autofire (energy or mass driver only): With a weapon capable of autofire, you can focus fire on a single enemy or attack multiple enemies in the same zone. You can either add Damage: +2 or you can attack one additional target within the same zone; however, it's a supplemental action and you suffer Accuracy: −1. Taking this improvement again increases the damage and the number of targets you can attack by one, but it also causes an additional Accuracy: −1 penalty; it doesn't add to the number of supplemental actions you need to take.

Indirect-Fire (ordnance only): Some ordnance systems have complex guidance subsystems, friend-or-foe seeking technology, or something similar that allows for indirect fire. When firing this weapon, you can ignore 1 point of borders.

Non-Lethal (energy or ordnance only): Some weapons are designed to disable enemy ships or stun soft targets rather than killing them outright. Any consequences or taken out effects must take this into account. **Cost +0.**

Persistent Effect: Whether it's an incendiary mass driver, an EMP beam, or some other effect that persists, this improvement allows you to apply an aspect to the target each time you successfully attack. The aspect is chosen when you choose this improvement. Once you've applied the aspect to a target, it lasts until the end of your next turn; you or one of your allies can tag the aspect once for free. **Cost +2.**

Example: Guns are something TransGalaxy will equip. The *Black Watch* is fitted with two sets. They get a big blast cannon—standard energy weapon with a Damage: 1 boost for a total cost of Superb (+5)—and a smaller laser turret—standard energy weapon, no boosts for a cost of Great (+4).

5. Add Improvements (Optional)

Just like when you're creating gear (page 136, *Gear* chapter), when you're designing a ship or other vehicle, you can add improvements to it once you've put together its basic attributes, weapons, and defense systems. Improvements on a vehicle represent various systems aboard the vehicle, and they cover a wide variety of functions. Adding an improvement increases the cost by 1 unless otherwise noted.

Agility: A vehicle with this improvement is more maneuverable than its size and speed indicate; it gains +1 Maneuverability. This improvement can be added multiple times.

Aspect: You can add an aspect to a ship. This aspectscan be invoked and compelled just like any aspect. This improvement can be added multiple times.

Heavy Hull Plating: Though it makes it somewhat bulkier, your vehicle is much more durable than other vehicles of its type, gaining an additional stress box. This improvement can be added multiple times.

Power Boost: Your ship can make a quick burst of speed. If one of the crew *spends a fate point,* the ship gains +1 to speed for one action.

Sensor Jammer: Your ship can become invisible to sensors for brief periods when any member of the crew *spends a fate point.* The Systems operator uses a maneuver action to engage the jammer, allowing the ship to mask itself from detection by passive sensors. When an opponent uses the Systems skill to try to detect the ship using active sensors, the Systems operator can oppose with a Systems roll of her own; success on the tech's part means that the ship remains hidden. Each additional time after the first that an opponent tries to detect the ship, *a fate point must be spent* by someone on the crew. If your vehicle is detected, the jammer is of no further use in the conflict.

Upgrade: This improvement grants a +2 bonus to efforts made to do something fairly specific. For example, a hovercycle might grant a +2 bonus while cornering, or a survey ship might grant a +2 bonus when using its sensors. The GM is the final arbiter of what upgrades are too general or too specific; in general, you should get the benefit of the upgrade at least a couple of times per session, but probably not much more than that. This improvement can be added multiple times, but it must be used for a different upgrade each time.

Example: During crew creation, the *Black Watch* got the aspect DECEPTIVELY FAST. The group decides to give that some additional mechanical backing and adds Power Boost to the ship, for a final cost of Superb (+5). The two weapons that TransGalaxy put on the ship had a final cost of Superb (+5) and Great (+4) respectively. These squeak in under the limit of TransGalaxy's Class D policy.

Ship Maintenance

Ships are expensive to operate. Fuel, life support, and various other fluids, lubricants, and assorted gunk must be constantly replaced and replenished to keep these machines from breaking down. The cost of operating a ship on a journey of a few months is equal to the cost of the ship. Shorter journeys reduce the maintenance cost by one step per time increment (page 65, ***Doing Things*** chapter). Many ships are just too expensive to maintain over a long journey, so shorter steps with refueling stops must be made.

Ship maintenance isn't required while a vessel is at dock. The ship generally shares the life support of the station or planet and is hooked up to power couplings and fueling cables at the station. Docking is rarely free, but it's significantly less expensive than operating a ship. Most docking stations charge a Fair (+2) cost per week for docking expenses, but isolated or popular docking berths may cost a bit more, and exceptionally large ships have to pay a higher price. There's generally no discount for staying less than a week.

> Class D Freight covers a ship's docking fees, as long as the vessel is making a delivery contracted by TransGalaxy. Basic maintenance—up to a Good (+3) cost—is also covered with no roll required. Any costs beyond this are the responsibility of the crew and a Resources roll must be made.

Example: The *Black Watch* is traveling on TransGalaxy business. The *Black Watch* has a cost of Superb (+5) and the trip will take a month, one time increment less than the standard maintenance period of a few months. That means if the crew flies direct, the maintenance cost will be Great (+4). TransGalaxy only covers maintenance costs up to Good (+3), so the crew will stop for refueling on the way, splitting the trip into two legs of a couple of weeks each. This reduces the maintenance cost to the amount TransGalaxy will pay, so the crew can skip the maintenance roll.

> Who makes the Resources roll for a ship? If you're working for TransGalaxy, the company usually covers expenses, with the strict restrictions detailed throughout this section. If a player character owns the ship, these rolls are generally that character's responsibility. The crew might want to set up a "ship fund" to handle expenses for repairs beyond what TransGalaxy or the owner will cover. A ship fund starts with a Resources of Mediocre (+0), but you can try to increase the fund by assigning Resources aspects to the ship itself and making a Resources test (page 125, ***Gear*** chapter). A member of the crew rolls the ship's Resources to try to cover the expenses that come up.

Failure to Pay for Maintenance

If your maintenance roll fails, you're in some trouble. You may still acquire the requisite maintenance by reducing your Resources score by one point. This means you liquidated assets, emptied your bank account, and permanently reduced your available cash in order to keep your ship running. If you don't want to reduce Resources based on the failed roll, then the GM can offer you one of the following options:

You need to gather the cash: If you wait a week and incur docking charges, you can make another maintenance roll. This can be a problem if you have a time-sensitive delivery or if your cargo could potentially spoil.

You get inferior maintenance: The ship now has a negative aspect that the GM can tag for free once per session. The ship gets one of these aspects for each shift by which your roll failed.

Example: The crew decide to risk it and take a one month journey in one go. They try to pay the maintenance fee of Great (+4) and fail the roll, getting only a Good (+3) result. They don't have time to wait around and try again, so GM decides they got bad maintenance. He adds the aspect LOW GRADE FUEL to the ship.

Travel Time and Maintenance

When you're preparing for a journey, the GM tells you how far away your destination is. Trips are measured in time, so the GM will say a planet is "a few days" away, or "a month" away, or, at most, "a few months" away. Pretty much any planet in the galaxy can be reached with a few months of travel time. Once you reach your destination, you need to make your maintenance roll.

Sometimes it's necessary to make a journey in a shorter amount of time than the GM says it'll take. You can attempt to travel more quickly using a Pilot roll to chart a faster route that skims closer to gravity wells and other hyperspace hazards. These routes are less efficient and put extra stress on the ship. For every time increment you reduce your trip by, the cost of maintenance increases by one step.

Example: The crew has a delivery to make, but the cargo is time sensitive. The trip usually takes one week, but they have to make it in a few days. Prbrawl succeeds on his Pilot roll, which means he can successfully plot and fly the course. The maintenance of a one week trip is normally Fair (+2), but taking the trip in a few days increases the cost of the wear and tear on the ship to Good (+3). Luckily, this is still within TransGalaxy parameters and they decide to rush the trip.

Ships in Play

Ships are a big part of the space opera genre and of the **Bulldogs!** game. This game spans an entire galaxy, after all, with multiple systems revolving around thousands of suns, comprised of hundreds of thousands of individual planets, many of them inhabited. Without a spaceworthy ship, you couldn't get from place to place. So, how do you get the most out of your traveling home base?

Your Ship as a Plot Device

From a purely utilitarian point of view, a ship is first and foremost a form of transport. Without a ship, you're limited to a single planet. Sure, lots of fun and exciting things can happen on a single planet, but those stories don't make for very good space opera adventures. A ship adds variety to your escapades, allowing you to hop from planet to planet and system to system as often as the plot demands it.

Of course, your adventure could be set entirely on a ship in transit. Perhaps a murder occurs on a long voyage, and it's up to your characters to find the culprit before the ship makes berth and the murderer can escape. Or perhaps a hostile alien life form has managed to stow away on the ship, and it's hunting passengers and crew down one by one. The occasional ship-board story adds variety—a dose of tension thanks to the isolating nature of being on a ship in the middle of space, far from outside aid.

The ship doesn't need to belong to your characters. You might be hitching a ride on someone else's ship because you're without your own at the moment for whatever reason. Maybe you're all stationed on a capital ship or cruiser of some sort; maybe you're hired as part of the crew for a smaller freighter, either temporarily or more permanently. Such scenarios can add a dose of intrigue to the story—not only do you have to deal with the situation at hand, but you're also in the dark about the true motives of the ship's owners; maybe you'll become embroiled—wittingly or not—in political machinations or power plays along the way.

Your Ship as a Home Base

Adventures typically deal with the unknown or the alien—these things are exciting and interesting, after all, and staples of the space opera genre. Sometimes, though, it's good to have a familiar place where you can regroup, resupply, and plan out your next move. When a ship becomes a home base, it can serve as a good counterpoint to the dangers of the adventures that your characters get involved in. Building drama is about alternating peaks and valleys—too much

excitement all at once and you risk diminishing its impact—so inserting episodes of down time between crescendos can be helpful.

Down time in a familiar place can also help you flesh out your world, particularly if your characters aren't the only characters that call the ship home. Consider filling out the ship's crew with non-player characters—maybe created by the whole group, instead of foisting it all the on the GM—to take over the unfilled or menial roles on the ship. Use time back at home base to build personalities and backgrounds for these characters, and use them as a lens through which you get a glimpse of the wider galaxy beyond your ship and the immediate adventure. This helps bring the universe to life, as well introducing seeds for future adventures. And here's the best part for GMs—when the players become attached to the ship and its occupants, you can put some or all of them in jeopardy to heighten the drama and invest the players more in the outcome. But don't overuse this technique—if the player characters' friends and home are constantly in danger, they're likely to avoid becoming too attached to them in the future.

Finally, a ship is a great place to store large objects or pieces of gear that are attached to one or more characters. If your character has a vehicle or a workshop or some similar large, unwieldy piece of equipment, a ship is a great place for it to stay when it's not in use. This way, it stays relatively—and plausibly—close; this means that you can use down time on the ship to utilize those crafting skills that aren't so useful if they're only available on a particular planet.

Your Ship as a Vehicle for Action

Sooner or later, it's pretty likely that your ship will encounter another ship. In a galaxy rife with conflict—mercenaries, pirates, power-hungry empires—the likelihood of this other ship being hostile is pretty high. That's where things get really exciting. After all, what's the point of having a fast ship if you never try to outrun someone else? Why have a ship bristling with guns if you don't blow something up with them?

In a more terrestrial action sequence—a gun fight in the streets, for example—it's fairly easy for everyone to be involved. If everyone's present for the fight, then everyone's got a stake in it, and everyone's likely to participate in one way or another. The same can be said for action sequences on a ship, to an extent—everyone on the ship is in jeopardy when the ship is, so everyone has some amount of automatic investment in the conflict. Ship conflicts, however, are a somewhat different animal because not everyone necessarily has an obvious role in the conflict. The pilot gets to out-maneuver the other ship's pilot, gunners get to shoot at other ships, and so forth, but what about everyone else?

The *Black Watch*

Cargo Loader

Main Airlock

Stairs Up

Barrels

Cargo Bay

Crates

Small Containers

Pallets

Lower Deck

Ladder   Ladder

Fusion Bottle

Engine Room

Engines

Bridge

Stairs Down

Eating Area

Galley

Head

Med Bay

Captain's Quarters

Bunk Room

Bunk Room

Bunk Room

Bunk Room

Bunk Room

Conference Room

Upper Deck

Ladder   Ladder

Catwalk

Some characters can find things to do fairly easily—a ship's engineer has to attend to the engine room, for example, and there are all sorts of ways to get her involved in the conflict and to have her actions have ramifications on everyone else. But what about passengers? What about a science officer? What about people who are great with face-to-face fights, but not so great with ship weaponry?

The trick for the GM is to construct these sequences so that everyone gets a chance to do something important. If a lot of people are waiting around while the people operating the ship do all the work, maybe it's time to introduce a boarding party. Maybe the ship takes heavy damage and the engineer has to enlist the help of passengers and other crew to help put out all the fires and make some hasty repairs. The specifics vary from conflict to conflict, but the basics remain the same—try to involve everyone, or you risk boring people. It's perfectly all right for the pilot to be the star of the scene, but other people should still be doing interesting and important things.

Map Your Ship

You group will spend a lot of time aboard the ship, so it's important to know the vessel's layout and rooms. After creating the ship in the character creation session, someone should make a quick sketch showing the various cabins and bays aboard the ship. This doesn't need to be an incredibly detailed drawing; just a rough sketch will do. Then, when boarding actions or conflict occurs aboard ship, you'll have a handy reference for the layout.

Most ships have the following areas:

- Cockpit
- Crew cabins
- Galley and mess
- Airlock
- Head and showers
- Cargo bays
- Engine room
- Space for engines and guns
- Gunnery stations

Ship Conflicts

When the ship's in danger, the pilot comes to the forefront. If others intend you harm, you have two basic options—fight or flight.

The quality of your ship makes a difference. In any of the conflict types detailed below, if a character makes a Pilot roll, the ship's speed *or* maneuverability—not both—is applied to the roll as a modifier. If a character uses the ship's weapons, the Artillery roll is modified by the accuracy of the weapon being used.

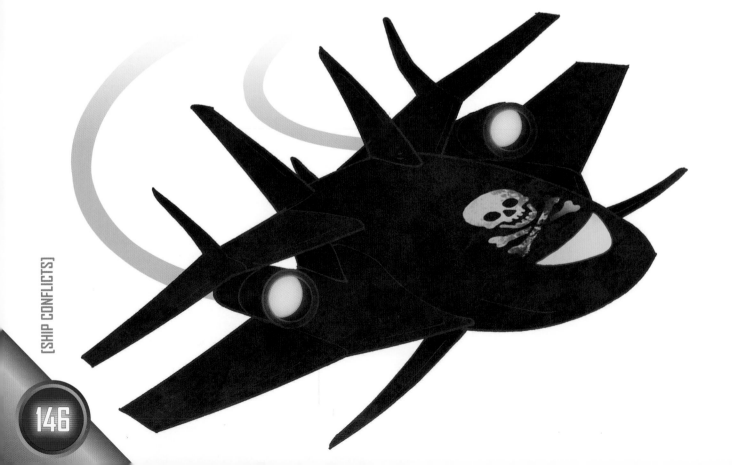

Chase Scenes

In some cases, the smartest choice is to take the better part of valor and try to outdistance your enemies. Maybe the enemies have you outnumbered or outgunned, or maybe you're on a strict time limit and you just can't spare the time it would take to defeat your foes toe-to-toe—or to deal with the repairs that you'd need to make afterward. When this happens, a chase scene begins.

Chase scenes are structured similarly to other conflicts, in that they're broken down into a number of exchanges. There are two basic roles in a chase scene— the lead ship (the one being chased) and the pursuer (the one—or ones—doing the chasing). If your scene has more than one lead ship, it's generally easier to handle this as multiple concurrent chase scenes.

Here's a breakdown of an exchange in a chase.

The players of the lead ship:

- Describe what the ship is doing.
- Set a difficulty.
- Roll against that difficulty.
- If the roll fails, determine stress taken.

The players of each pursuer:

- Roll against the difficulty set by the lead ship.
- If the roll fails, determine stress taken.
- If the roll succeeds, determine stress caused to the lead ship.

During each exchange, the players controlling the lead ship describe what they're doing and how they're attempting to lose their pursuers. This can range from simply pouring on as much speed as possible to trying to maneuver through an asteroid field. Once the action's described, the lead ship sets a difficulty for the action and makes a roll. This roll is usually a Pilot roll, though it could also be a Systems or even an Artillery roll if the lead ship is attempting to lose its pursuers by doing something other than flying fast and dodging. If the lead ship succeeds on the roll, everything goes as planned. If the roll fails, however, things go awry somehow. Maybe too much strain is put on the engines or the ship gets a little too close to an asteroid and sustains some damage. While the descriptions vary, the result is the same—the lead ship takes stress equal to the number of shifts by which the roll failed.

You might be asking yourself, "If there's such a nasty penalty for failure, why would I want to set the difficulty high in the first place?" There's a very simple reason—your pursuers have to make a roll against the exact same difficulty. If the pursuer fails the roll, the same effect is inflicted—stress equal to the number of shifts on the failure. However, if the pursuer manages to succeed, not only does his ship not take stress, he inflicts stress equal to his shifts on the lead vehicle, representing ground gained, shots fired, or other such things. Note that the skill rolled by the pursuer doesn't have to be the same as the skill rolled by the lead ship, though in most cases it will be. Eventually, one of the ships gets taken out, meaning that either the lead ship escapes or the pursuer catches up to the lead ship, perhaps disabling it or boarding it.

You can have a chase sequence with multiple pursuers. In this case, each pursuer makes a separate roll in response to the lead ship's roll. This is fine when there's one, two, or even three pursuing ships; however, if the lead ship is being chased through space by a swarm of fighters, it makes a bit more sense to use the minion rules to handle all the pursuers (page 78, ***Doing Things*** chapter). In this case, treat all of the pursuers as a single group of minions—or multiple groups, if you like that better—and roll once for the entire group. This way, with each successful roll for the lead ship and each failed roll for the pursuers, more ships are destroyed, disabled, or simply lost.

For the purposes of drama, it might be appropriate to make the last pursuing ship a little harder to shake— after all, he's not the last pilot for nothing! To do this, treat the last pursuer as a Good (+3) minion and also add one of the following benefits to up the ante a little:

- +3 stress boxes
- +1 to Pilot or System rolls
- Heavily Armed—any time the pursuer inflicts stress on the lead ship, increase that stress by 1

Example: The *Black Watch* is being chased down by a squadron of Templari fighters (don't ask). The GM decides that there are four fighters in the group and that they're Average (+1) minions. She also figures that, as fighters, they're fast and maneuverable; she sets their speed at Good (+3) and their maneuverability at Good (+3).

Piloting the *Black Watch*, Prbrawl first tries to simply outdistance the fighters, relying on his ship's speed to shake his pursuers. He sets the difficulty at Great (+4) and rolls his Pilot skill. Prbrawl's Pilot skill is Great (+4) and his ship's speed is Average (+1). He gets a Great (+4) result on the roll, just good enough to pull off his run! The GM then rolls for the Templari fighters, getting a result of Good (+3). The fighters take a box of stress from the shift, taking one of them out of the chase. Prbrawl has managed to lose one of the fighters thanks to his skillful piloting! There are still three left, though.

Prbrawl next tries to maneuver through some debris he sees floating nearby, hoping that the fighters will take the bait and not make it through. He sets the difficulty at Superb (+5) this time, figuring that he can afford to take some stress, but the fighters might not be able to. He makes another Pilot roll, this time coming up with a result of Fair (+2). That's three shifts in the negative, meaning that Prbrawl has to mark off his ship's third stress box; this could be bad! The fighters follow him in, and the GM rolls their Pilot skill, generating a Good (+3) result. They take two stress, meaning that two of the fighters manage to crash into debris, leaving only one left!

There's a single Templari fighter left, but this one's special. He's the best pilot of the group, and he'll be tough to shake. He's a Good (+3) minion, meaning that he's got three stress boxes and a Pilot skill of Good (+3); the GM decides to increase the fighter's Pilot skill to Great (+4), though. This guy's a real ace, so Prbrawl is going to have to do some fancy flying to get away from him.

Ship Combat

When running isn't an option—or when you just want to stop your enemies cold—having weapons mounted on your ship can be pretty helpful. In the broadest terms, ship combat is similar to standard, person-to-person combat. The same actions are available—attack, maneuver, full defense, block, movement, and an array of supplemental and free actions. The main difference when it comes to ship combat is that, in most cases, multiple people control different parts of a single combatant. The pilot flies the ship, the gunners attack other ships, and the engineer deals with the shields, damage control, and so forth. In a ship combat, the various participants on a ship are divided into a number of roles aboard that ship, and these roles determine how they interact with their allies and their enemies. The roles are:

Captain: the captain makes the decisions. This role doesn't allow for direct interaction with the ship or its systems; in general, the captain doesn't have access to the attack, full defense, or movement actions. Instead, the captain usually utilizes actions like maneuver and block and can use the Leadership skill to do so. Not every ship has—or needs—a captain; in many cases, the captain assumes one or more other roles in addition to captain.

Pilot: the pilot actually causes the ship to move through space. The pilot generally has access to the maneuver, full defense, and movement actions, although specific circumstances may present other options. It's possible for two people to assume this role on a single ship, though one of them is technically the co-pilot.

Gunner: any number of people can assume the gunner role, assuming there are sufficient guns. Some guns—such as missiles and forward-facing cannons—are usually controlled by the pilot, but many ships include cannon turrets that allow for independent firing. In general, gunners have access to the attack action, though it's possible for them to block and maneuver, as well.

Engineer: the engineer makes sure that the ship continues to work correctly. Engineers typically utilize the maneuver and block actions, as well as make on-the-fly temporary repair rolls during combat.

Systems Tech: while the engineer manages the mechanical aspects of the ship, the tech manages electronic systems such as communications, jamming systems, cyberwarfare, and the like. Techs typically make maneuver and block actions; even when the tech is attacking, the attack usually causes an effect rather than dealing stress, so it's better modeled as a maneuver than an attack.

Example: Captain Laf't decides it's time to turn around and fight this last Templari fighter, rather than trying to outrun him. He gets on the comm and tells everyone to man their battle stations. Prbrawl is the pilot, but he's also the ship's engineer, so he turns the helm over to his co-pilot Quinn. Brunda controls the ship's guns. The Templari fighter, being a much smaller ship, has only two crewmen aboard—the pilot (and captain) and a gunner (and tech).

Ship Actions

Each participant in the combat gets his or her own actions as normal—this means that a single ship with many people in various roles on it is capable of doing a lot of different things at once. This requires some degree of coordination among players. Luckily, instead of a specific initiative order for each individual participant, initiative is determined for each ship in the conflict using each pilot's Pilot skill, with either speed or maneuverability—whichever is lower—applied as a modifier. Characters on a single ship can discuss their actions and coordinate; a single turn includes everyone's actions on the ship.

Anyone with access to a ship-board weapon can **attack** another ship; this follows the normal rules for attacking, using the attacker's Artillery skill and the defending pilot's Pilot skill for defense. In a pinch, a pilot can use her Pilot skill for attack, ramming into the other ship; this, however, causes both ships to take stress as if they had both been hit by the attack. **Block** actions can be taken as the tech changes the facing of the shields, the gunners lay down suppressing fire, or the pilot takes evasive action.

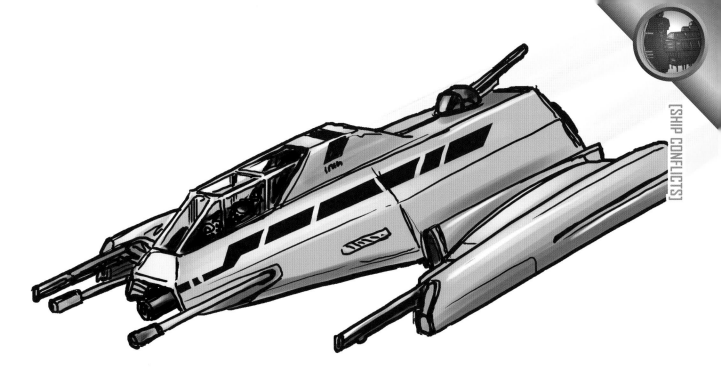

Example: Brunda takes aim at the enemy ship, preparing to fire. She wants to blast the enemy into oblivion, so she chooses to attack. She rolls her Artillery skill (with a +1 bonus from the weapon's Accuracy: 1), which the Templari defends against with his Pilot skill.

The pilot can also go on **full defense**, granting the ship a +2 bonus on reactions and defenses during that exchange. Note that, if the pilot takes the full defense action, gunners can't use the attack action—the ship's erratic and unpredictable movement makes it impossible for weapons to be used effectively. In addition, just as with standard combat, the pilot can **move** as a supplemental action; a move action can move the ship only a single zone. It's also possible to move at **full speed**—equivalent to a sprint action in standard combat—by making a Pilot roll with an Average (+1) difficulty modified by the ship's speed; the ship moves a number of zones equal to the shifts generated. Just as with the full defense action, this has consequences for the gunners—they take a penalty equal to the number of zones the ship moves in the exchange when they roll attacks to fire their weapons.

Example: The *Black Watch* has taken a bit of a beating already; Quinn decides that she'll focus on putting some distance between the ship and her enemy. She elects to take a full speed action. She gets on the comm to Prbrawl, telling him that she needs max engine power. The full speed action allows the *Black Watch* to move three zones, but Brunda will have to take a penalty to aim, reducing her Artillery roll by –3.

Nearly everyone in the conflict can make **maneuver** actions using a variety of skills. The pilot might use his Pilot skill to get into an advantageous position; the gunner might use Artillery to take out key parts of the enemy ship; the captain might use Alertness to determine what the enemy ship is about to do or a Leadership roll to bolster his crew's morale. Just as in standard combat, a maneuver places an aspect on the scene or on an enemy ship. It's possible to use a maneuver to place an aspect on your own ship, such as an engineer rerouting power to the ship's thrusters or its guns. When you place an aspect on your own ship, an ally on your ship can tag the aspect for free.

Example: Prbrawl, down in the engine room, is working on the engine to make sure that Quinn gets as much power to the thrusters as possible. He makes his Engineering roll and puts the aspect FULL SPEED AHEAD! on the *Black Watch*, meaning that Quinn can tag that aspect to eke a little more speed out of the ship when she rolls for her full speed action.

Splitting the Difference: Chases with Guns

A canny reader has probably already noticed that the rules for chase scenes are fairly simplified, while the ship combat rules are somewhat more robust. The chase rules are designed to be quick and exciting, boiling down an entire chase sequence into a few rolls of the dice. However, it's possible to merge the two systems, using them simultaneously; this has both drawbacks and advantages. On the down side, it adds more complexity to a chase scene and naturally causes it to take longer (in general, it feels more natural for a chase scene to be resolved quickly, though this isn't always the case). However, in return for this disadvantage, you garner a system that allows everyone aboard the ship to be involved in the conflict, and you wind up with something that's neither a chase nor a fight, but something in between. This in-between conflict—a chase with guns—can heighten the drama of the scene and get everyone invested in it, particularly if the stakes are high.

Combining the two systems is relatively easy. The player characters take on their respective roles as described under *Ship Combat* (page 148). The pilot's role, however, is slightly modified. In effect, the pilot gets two new actions—escape and pursue.

An escape action puts the pilot in the role of the lead ship, allowing him to set a difficulty and try to make it. This is handled identically to the lead ship's role under the chase rules. However, the rest of the crew now has the opportunity to help the pilot—making maneuvers to grant the pilot free use of aspects and blocking to prevent stress generated from a missed roll. If someone takes a blocking action—such as the engineer making sure the engine doesn't overheat, or the gunners shooting down asteroids before they hit the ship—the pilot can use the blocker's roll in place of a single Pilot roll during that exchange. This means that, should the blocking roll exceed the Pilot's target difficulty, the ship takes no stress even if the pilot fails his Pilot roll. However, this block doesn't help against the stress the pursuer inflicts if his roll is successful.

The pursue action, conversely, puts the pilot in the role of pursuer, trying to chase down the lead ship and stop it by any means necessary. In general, this works the same as described under the chase rules, with the same additions described for the lead ship above. However, depending on the lead ship's description of what's being attempted, someone other than the pilot might make the roll to catch up to the lead ship. Instead of flying quickly, for example, the gunner might simply try to blast the lead ship's thrusters into oblivion, or engage a grapple—in this case, a Systems roll modified by Artillery would be appropriate. It's possible for multiple people aboard the ship to make rolls to try to catch the lead ship, provided they all make sense. In such a case, only the highest applicable roll is used.

Example: After a bout of dogfighting, Captain Laf't suspects that the *Black Watch* is outmatched by this Templari pilot and his fighter. He decides to run again, but he orders everyone to stay at their battle stations and provide cover while Quinn attempts the escape. Quinn uses the escape action, setting the difficulty at Superb (+5); she's going to fly through the ring of a nearby planet, dodging chunks of rock and ice and hoping that the Templari can't follow them. Meanwhile, Prbrawl takes a maneuver to add a FULL POWER TO MOTILITY THRUSTERS aspect to the ship, and Brunda uses her Artillery skill to try to blast asteroids that get too close, adding an OBSTACLES BLASTED TO BITS aspect to the scene. When Quinn makes her Pilot roll, she can tag both aspects for a +4 to her roll.

Repairing Damage to Ships

All too often during the course of a mission, your ship gets damaged. Ships can be repaired with an Engineering roll, but repairs require spare parts, which cost money. During a fight, your engineer can make temporary repairs to the ship to keep it running until a more permanent solution can be found. This defers the monetary payment for the damage, but after the fight is over, your ship gets a TEMPORARY REPAIRS aspect that the GM can tag for free once during each subsequent fight until the repairs are made permanent.

Using Engineering to repair your ship in the middle of a fight requires a full action. Make a roll against a target of Mediocre (+0); if it succeeds, you may remove a checkmark from the ship's one-stress box. Every two shifts improve the effect by one; for example, with four shifts, you can remove a checkmark in the ship's three-stress box.

Success can also be used to stabilize a vessel that's taken a severe or lesser consequence that would appear to be catastrophic (e.g., a HULL BREACH aspect)—in game terms, this means the aspect can't be compelled during the course of the current conflict. A single ship can only be the target of one emergency Engineering action in an exchange.

To use Engineering to address a ship's long-term damage, spend a scene assessing and attempting to repair the damage; this Engineering roll directly addresses the ship's long-term consequences (page 71). If your roll is successful, you can make good the repairs. The time it takes to repair the ship's consequence may be reduced by one step on the time table (page 65, *Doing Things* chapter) for every two shifts by which the difficulty is exceeded. You can't make multiple Engineering checks—the first roll stands. The ship must be docked in order to make permanent repairs.

Class D Freight will cover repairs, but they're exceptionally stingy. If you have TransGalaxy pay for repairs on damage greater than mild, the ship always suffers from the inferior parts outcome. Add one aspect for a moderate repair and two for a severe repair. TransGalaxy wants you back out making deliveries as quickly as possible, so the time is always as listed.

A separate Resources roll must be made to obtain the proper parts; if the roll fails, you may either reduce your Resources accordingly, or allow the GM to impose one of the following outcomes for each shift by which you fail your roll:

You need to gather the cash: If you wait a week and incur docking charges, you can make another Resources roll. Additional problems may result if you have a time-sensitive delivery or if your cargo could potentially spoil.

You get inferior parts: The ship now has a negative aspect that the GM can tag for free once per session. The ship has one of these aspects per shift by which your roll failed. This can be remedied by making another Resources roll to obtain parts to replace the defects.

You get parts tooled for a different kind of ship: And you must modify them to fit your vessel. Add an additional time increment to the repairs.

Use the following table to determine the time and cost for repairs.

Damage	Difficulty	Time	Cost
Any Stress	Mediocre (+0)	A few days	Average (+1)
Mild	Average (+1)	A week	Fair (+2)
Moderate	Fair (+2)	A few weeks	Good (+3)
Severe	Great (+4)	A month	Superb (+5)

Example: The *Black Watch* took a couple of hits in their dogfight with the Templari. The ship has checkmarks in the three and four stress boxes and took a mild consequence. Luckily, the damage is slight enough that TransGalaxy will pay for the repairs. Prbrawl works on it after docking, aiming to repair the mild consequence first. He gets a Great (+4) result on his Engineering roll, getting three shifts over the difficulty of Average (+1) to repair a mild consequence. He uses the shifts to reduce the time required from a week to an afternoon. While the rest of the crew is handling the delivery, he clears the mild consequence from the ship.

Matters of Size (Optional)

The ladder in **Bulldogs!** has thirteen steps (page 16, *FATE Basics* chapter), from Abysmal (–4) to Legendary (+8). It may not have escaped your notice that, while this works fine when you're dealing with adversaries of roughly equivalent sizes, it makes little sense for a hand-held gun—no matter how powerful—to be able to deal significant damage to a capital ship, or even a small freighter for that matter. Similarly, no matter how bad a shot you are, or how inaccurate your weapon, you'll probably hit that capital ship (or freighter) with little difficulty.

Because of this conundrum, **Bulldogs!** has rules for **size** to represent the different capabilities of differently sized objects or combatants. There are three sizes in **Bulldogs!**—**person** size, **vehicle** size, and **ship** size. The person scale is reserved almost exclusively for small, roughly Arsubaran-sized creatures—which most player characters will be—and is the lowest of the scales. Virtually all person-to-person conflicts are assumed to be taking place in person size. Vehicle size—the middle size—encompasses land-based, sea-based, and some atmosphere-based vehicles; particularly large creatures may fit this category as well. Ship size includes any spacefaring vehicle. It should be noted that sizes aren't hard-coded to specific items or creatures, so you won't find scale listed as an attribute on anything in the book. Most of the time, size isn't important; it only becomes important when things of vastly different sizes come into direct conflict; in such cases it's up to the GM to determine what size which combatants are in.

If something is significantly bigger than you, it's easier to hit but harder to damage; if it's smaller than you, the reverse is true. Whenever you're attacking something of a size different from your own, you gain a +1 bonus on your attack roll per step of difference when the thing you're attacking is larger, or you take a –1 penalty per step when the thing you're attacking is smaller. However, if you hit, you take a –4 penalty to Damage per step on a larger target or a +2 bonus to Damage per step if the target is smaller. This means that it's possible to attack something, hit it, and deal no stress to it.

Example: Quinn gets attacked in the docking bay while the *Black Watch* sits nearby. Brunda heats up the laser turret and fires on the attackers. The attackers are person-sized and the *Black Watch* is ship-sized. Brunda has a –2 penalty to hit with the ship's guns, but she gains +4 to damage if she can hit them. If they're foolish enough to fire back, they gain a +2 to hit the ship, but suffer a –8 penalty to damage it.

Sample Vehicles

Here are some sample ships and vehicles created using the rules in this chapter. They can be bought by the players, used as settings for adventures, or used as antagonists as the need arises.

Vehicle	Speed	Maneuverability	Stress	Improvements	Cost
Hovercycle	Fair (+2)	Good (+3)	2	Power Boost	Great (+4)
Gravsled	Mediocre (+0)	Great (+4)	2	None	Average (+1)
Combat Cycle*	Average (+1)	Great (+4)	3	Heavy Hull Plating	Good (+3)
Groundcar	Average (+1)	Good (+3)	4	None	Good (+3)
Aircar	Average (+1)	Good (+3)	4	None	Good (+3)
Tank*	Average (+1)	Good (+3)	5	Heavy Hull Plating	Great (+4)
Starfighter*	Average (+1)	Good (+3)	4	Shields: 1, Agility	Superb (+5)
Gunship*	Average (+1)	Fair (+2)	7	Shields: 2, Heavy Hull Plating	Epic (+7)
Freighter	Average (+1)	Fair (+2)	6	None	Great (+4)
Cutter*	Fair (+2)	Average (+1)	7	Shields: 1, Heavy Hull Plating, Agility	Epic (+7)
Battleship*	Mediocre (+0)	Average (+1)	9	Shields: 2, Heavy Hull Plating, Aspect: BIG AND SCARY	Legendary (+8)
Orbital Space Station	Poor (−1)	Poor (−1)	14	None	Superb (+5)

* Vehicle typically armed. Purchase weapons separately.

Running the Game

Bulldogs! is a pretty straightforward system to play, but there are techniques that can help it run more smoothly. This section describes methods for running Bulldogs! that will help keep your game rolling along, and make a good game even better. Both GMs and players will benefit from reading through this material—a lot of the info is specifically for the GM, but if players are familiar with these tips, it makes things easier for the GM by taking some of the burden off her shoulders. And there's no downside to keeping your GM happy! Players can chime in and make suggestions based on these techniques.

Basic GM Techniques

The *FATE Basics* chapter (page 15) covers a lot of the rule issues for the game, but as a GM, there are some other things you need to know in order to effectively run Bulldogs! Here are a few more techniques to keep in mind when running the game.

Considering Success and Failure

Before you call for a die roll, it's critically important that you stop and do two things:

1. Imagine success
2. Imagine failure

It sounds simple, but it makes a critical difference. Success is usually the easy part; failure can be a bit trickier. You want to make sure that both outcomes are interesting—though interesting certainly doesn't need to mean positive. If you can't come up with a way to handle each outcome, you need to rethink the situation.

There are few things more frustrating to a player than making a skill roll and being told that it nets him no new knowledge, no suggested course of action, no new development for the story, and so on. So, whenever you call for a roll, be absolutely certain you understand what it entails. If one of the branches doesn't suggest a course of action, then calling for a roll is probably a bad idea.

Now, that said, not every roll has to have high stakes. Failure should always have some impact, but there are degrees of fallout, and minor setbacks may be overcome for a larger success. If there's a large issue on the table, try not to have it hinge entirely on one roll—spread it out across the scene. Just as a roll has significance, so does a scene, and the ramifications of a scene should be meaningful. If a single failed roll can derail the scene, it's likely to be disappointing all around.

Interesting repercussions keep players engaged and turn die rolls into something a little more meaningful than just hoping to get lucky. That fact should be your guide for setting difficulties. The goal is to make any roll satisfying, regardless of how it turns out.

With that in mind, as a general guideline, difficulties should be set low—although there are a few exceptions we'll cover later in this chapter. If you leave difficulties at the default of Mediocre (+0) then characters almost always succeed, but in most circumstances there's still a possibility of failure. This provides plenty of opportunities for the players to invoke their aspects to ensure success. With difficulties set low, shifts (page 65, *Doing Things* chapter) become critically important. The question isn't "Will they succeed?" Instead, it's "How (or by how much) will they succeed?" The number of shifts a character generates on a roll becomes the yardstick you can use to frame how something turns out.

You can increase difficulties from that, but always stop and think about why you want to do that. The answer should always be "because I want failure to be more likely"—hopefully because failure's cool, too. If you're tempted to make a roll so difficult that failure is almost inevitable, make sure you've got a solid reason for why that's the case and why you're calling for a roll.

The bottom line here is that every roll should be fun, whether it succeeds or fails.

Setting Declaration Difficulties

Some skills—mental skills like Academics come to mind—allow a player to make declarations. A declaration is typically a player-driven assertion that there's a particular aspect, determined by the player, on a particular target—an individual character, group, location, scene, or story. Broadly, declarations allow players to introduce facts into the setting and storyline. The difficulties for declarations should, honestly, be based on how interesting the proposed fact or aspect is. Ideas that would disrupt the game or are just unreasonable should simply be vetoed. These are the questions to ask yourself when determining difficulty for declarations:

1. Is the declaration interesting (or funny)?
2. Will the declaration have interesting consequences if it's acted on but is wrong?
3. Does the declaration propose a specific and interesting or heroic course of action?

Each "no" adds 2 to the base difficulty of Mediocre (+0). If the proposed fact is very amusing, proposes an interesting course of action, and has interesting consequences if wrong—three "yes" answers—a Mediocre (+0) difficulty is appropriate. By contrast, a boring fact with a dull course of action and no possible consequences has a difficulty of Fantastic (+6).

If your players don't quite have a grasp of how much they can do with declarations, you may want to lower the difficulties to suit—but you should let them know what makes a declaration more likely to succeed.

Setting Assessment Difficulties

Several skills may be used to make assessments, which is when a character tries to discover one or more hidden aspects about a particular target—an individual, group, location, or scene. If the target of an assessment is a person or a group, the difficulty of the assessment is usually an opposed skill roll. Static entities like locations or objects typically have difficulties based on their quality. If there's no obvious way to determine the assessment difficulty, consider the baseline difficulty to be Mediocre (+0).

At the GM's discretion, if a character gains spin (page 66, *Doing Things* chapter) on an assessment roll, he may gain insight into a more potent fact or one additional fact—potentially allowing good rolls to reveal two aspects.

Conflict Design

Bulldogs! is an action game. This means that, at some point in just about every session, there'll be some *action*! This section is designed to help GMs and players spice it up. Don't make combat boring!

Setting the Stage

When battle is joined, it's all too easy to set the stage in a way that doesn't create great action. A corridor, a docking ring, an open airfield—wide open areas with no cover and little maneuverability aren't interesting! Think about how a conflict scene in a movie is staged. There's almost always some sort of cover, obstacles, and other confounding circumstances to make the action more interesting and to reward innovative strategies. Rarely does a movie hero win a fight by just standing up to an opponent and exchanging blows. Instead, he uses the environment around him to help defend himself and get one up on his opponent. Setting the stage for combat in **Bulldogs!** should be the same.

Each conflict scene should have at least four or five physical features that do one of two things:

1. Provide cover or interesting opportunities for maneuvers, or
2. Provide current or potential hazards.

Features that do both at the same time are great! A conflict without these kinds of features soon becomes a boring slugfest.

Make a quick map for your players when combat begins. It doesn't need to be artistic or fancy. Dividing a sheet of regular paper into six or nine areas makes an easy map that gives the players an idea of the zones of conflict. Characters in the same box on the map are in the same zone, and each box adds a zone of distance. Sure, this is a crude and somewhat unscientific way of doing this, but it gives everyone a rough idea of the stage on which the conflict is taking place.

Next, add some features to the map. If the conflict's taking place on a loading dock, add in some crates, mark the location of the door and the ship. These provide areas where characters to hide, take cover, or maneuver around.

Now add in some hazards. It's a loading dock and the characters' ship is there, right? So add a fueling hose to the ship. If this gets hit, there'll be a volatile fuel spill and possibly an explosion. How about a steam pipe? Hot gases are run through the skin of the station as part of the power plant cooling system. This can create clouds of burning steam if opened or struck by gunfire. What sorts of materials were in those crates? Anything dangerous?

Write all of these features and hazards on notecards and make them scene aspects you and the players can invoke and compel. Encourage your players to make declarations about other features and hazards in the area.

Now you've got an exciting stage to set a conflict on. Let the bad guys start shooting!

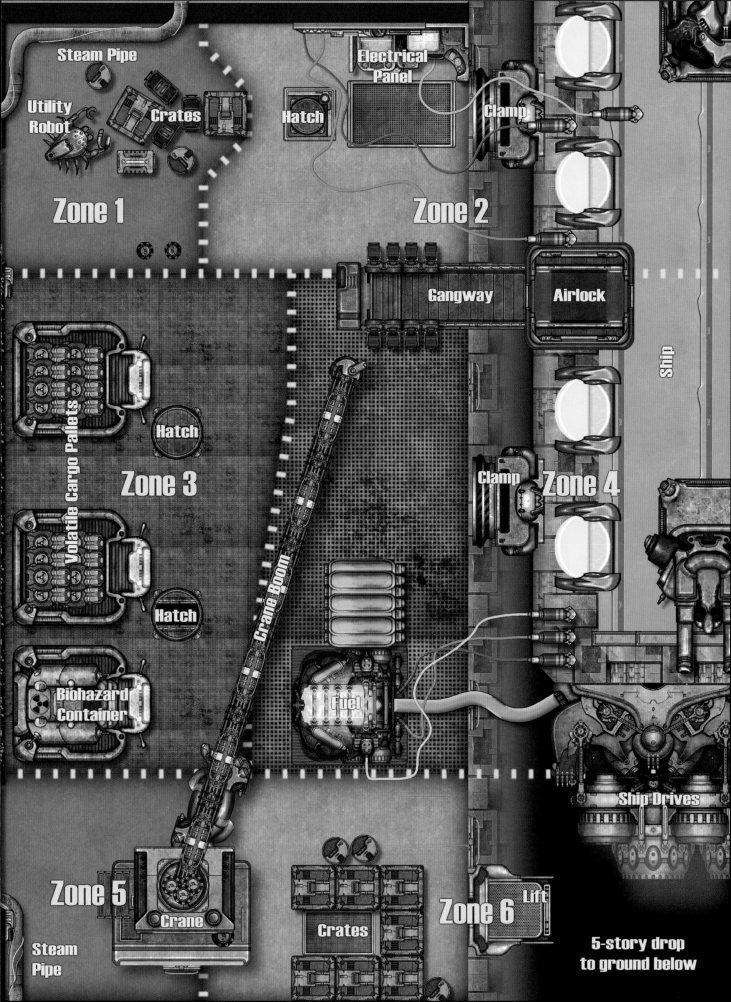

Social Conflicts

Not all conflict takes place in the physical realm. Characters get into all kinds of social scrapes as well. A lot of the same techniques apply to these conflicts as apply to the physical ones. Obviously, there's little need to sketch out zones and set a physical stage for such conflicts, but when setting up a social conflict, lay out the exact parameters of the challenge. Don't leave the player guessing what he should do—be clear about the objective and who or what stands in his way.

In social conflicts, vividly describing your non-player characters and fully characterizing them is essential—a social conflict with a two-dimensional cardboard cutout isn't interesting. Make sure the non-player characters have their own goals in the conflict—possibly something more complex than the defeat of the player's goals. Instead, the opponent may want a concession from the player character in exchange for doing what the player wants. Social enemies also lay traps, just not in the physical sense. Add in multiple characters in a social scene, all pursuing their own agenda, and then you've got some serious challenges. You can get some high-octane scenes out of people just talking, and these can be loads of fun.

If one of your players has a character who's an expert in this realm, it's essential to put some of these scenes in the game. If it's all fighting, all the time, the player with a social character will feel like he's been severely crippled. Give the villain a monologue before unleashing his minions, and the social character will have a chance to shine.

Ship Conflicts

Some of the characters will be very ship-oriented, like the pilot or engineer. It's important to include some ship-board action for these characters. **Bulldogs!** is a space opera game, so at least some of the time you ought to have space pirates or police cutters chasing and firing on the characters' ship. In any scenario—whether it's a ship conflict, a straight fight, or a social conflict—you'll most likely have one or two characters who aren't the best at that type of conflict. Just don't neglect any of the groups, and emphasize the types of conflict that the players are finding the most fun.

Using Minions

Minions in **Bulldogs!** are an excellent source of renewable, disposable adversaries. Singly, minions aren't much of a threat. In a small group, minions are equal to a low-ranked adversary. In a large group, they can be quite dangerous. As a GM, you can use minions to bring in a short quick attack and get the players' attention. Any combat skirmish that isn't meant to be serious can be minions only. When you're planning conflicts for a session, think about how the threats will escalate. Minions are great for a few quick early victories. This helps show off the player characters' competence and deadliness, and bigger villains can serve as bosses later on.

Minions are also great for helping beef up a villain character so he's better able to take on one or more of the player characters. Players often have the advantage of numbers, and their ability to use fate points really makes them a formidable threat to a villain. Having a squad of minions around to distract characters, throw up blocks, or just act as armor for the villain can increase the villain's threat considerably. Any pirate captain or mob boss worth his salt will have a decent sized squad of goons around to serve these functions.

Using Villains

No adventure is complete without some villainous enemies to spice things up. To effectively use villains in a scenario, you want to keep a couple of things in mind.

The villain is not your character. Villains, no matter how cool they are, exist to get schooled by the player characters. Don't get so attached to your villain that you go to extraordinary lengths to keep him alive or to let him succeed. Villains serve as opposition to players and should be defeatable. This isn't to say you can't have recurring villains. Recurring villains are wonderful, and they add a lot to a game. Just don't bend the rules to keep your villain alive because you like him. If the players have worked hard to trap and eliminate a villain, let them! Next session, however, his brother might have a beef.

Your players have all sketched out at least the beginning of a back story during character creation. Take a look at their past, especially their associates aspect. A lot of good villain ideas can be spawned here—you can almost always find something that one of the players set up that inspires a villain character. Having villains with a pre-existing tie to a player character creates a really effective adversary.

Use a tiered approach with villains when designing an adventure. The big boss should be the final encounter in a scenario. Sometimes, that means holding him in reserve through the initial conflicts, or at least making sure he has an escape route prepared when the player characters encounter him early in the adventure. Villains often have henchmen and minions that can provide early adversity. A couple of minion encounters, followed by a henchman, culminating in a big boss battle with more minions and henchmen is a great way to set up an adventure.

When the characters defeat a villain but he survives, you better believe he'll be back. Like we mentioned before, recurring villains are a great source of adversity. Players really start to get a hate on for someone who keeps coming at them, and you can build this to a really satisfying final showdown.

Keeping It Exciting

Bulldogs! is supposed to be an exciting game with lots of action. Don't skimp on the action for your players, and make sure there are credible threats during an adventure.

Scarce Resources

Keep the players hungry. If they have the Resources to do anything they want, there's little incentive to go adventuring. A great deal of the game play in **Bulldogs!** concerns the acquisition and retention of Resources. Expect players to be credit grubbers. This means rewarding the characters with a bit of cash when appropriate—if they've just made a big score, found some salvage, or captured a pirate ship. The best way to represent these sudden and brief infusions of cash is to give the group a Resources aspect. These make the characters feel flush, but they're one-use and leave the players wanting more.

Players will try to raise their Resources over time, and this is fine. Just remember that Resources can decline as well, and don't hesitate to make it drop if appropriate. If everyone ends up too rich, it can rob them of motivation. When the characters start accumulating a lot of Resources, enemies might start gunning for them, hoping to take some of it away. The more Resources the characters possess, the more powerful and potent their enemies become.

Put Them on the Clock

There's nothing like a clock for keeping your game's metronome regular. Whether you're running a pickup game or a longer series, you've already got one clock going—the length of real time for the session. You're already making sure you pack in enough events and interest in the bounds of that clock's timeframe; but here, we're talking about something else.

We're discussing the in-game clock—something the characters should always hear ticking away over their shoulder, hounding them. In-game time pressure is vital to encouraging a continuous atmosphere of action. Every situation that requires player action should come with some sort of time limit on it before dire consequences shall befall the dawdler.

As a GM, tune your ear to the sound of this clock and move quickly to renew it whenever it winds down. The tension in a dramatic scene should never fall slack; if it does—put them on the clock! Your players might need the occasional nudge to get going; they may be inclined to sit around and talk rather than take action—put them on the clock!

One method is setting up some dangerous aspects and informing the players that there's a countdown. Once a set number of exchanges has passed, the aspect activate sand then everyone needs to deal with it. Reactor core meltdowns, bombs, or all of the air leaking into space are great ways to ratchet up the tension.

Provide Plenty of Cues and Clues

You may think you've given the players all the clever hints and subtle cues necessary to solve the riddle and get to the heart of the matter…but they're sitting there looking unsure of what to do, or asking all the questions that *aren't* on target. The game is, in essence, paralyzed. What happened?

Unfortunately, it's likely you only have yourself to blame. If all those questions the players are asking are off-target, it's likely you didn't make the target big enough. If they're sitting around and unsure of what actions they can or should take, you probably didn't give them enough cues of what their options are.

We're not saying that you shouldn't leave the field open for players to pursue whatever agendas they want—after all, the characters are the big focus of the game. But when players stop having somewhere to go—and whether or not that's true from *your* perspective is irrelevant if it's effectively true from *theirs*—it's because you didn't show them what the possible destinations are. *Show them.*

This goes back to what we said just a little bit earlier. The targets you put into the story need to be big enough—big enough to be noticed and to suggest a course of action, and big enough to be hit from any number of directions.

Paralysis arises from a simple lack of the obvious. Don't be afraid of the obvious. Provide plenty of cues and clues and your players will keep moving forward.

Embrace Crazy Plans and Schemes

Players are more likely to take an action-oriented approach if they feel they won't be penalized for less-than-perfect plans. Be understanding of flaws and be willing to gloss over them in the interests of fun and entertainment.

Even if you see several holes in a plan, don't go taking advantage of those holes right off. Villains can have blind spots; they're not perfect either. Jeopardize the holes, certainly, to increase the drama, but don't go after them to the point of unraveling the plan. If it's even halfway decent—and especially if it involves explosions, firefights, and crazy risks—then it'll make for a solid, entertaining element of the story. Support their plan and be glad to be part of it!

Encourage Action over Contemplation

Bulldogs! is an action game and you should avoid letting things sit still and stagnate for long. The characters should never get too comfortable; danger and action are always lurking just around the corner to take them by surprise.

Dropping action into the middle of an otherwise contemplative scene can liven up the game, keeping things jumpy and in motion. Don't be shy about doing it. But *do* be shy about doing it when characters are interacting with each other excitedly. The idea here is to *encourage* action over contemplation—not to mandate it. A good social scene where everyone's chewing the scenery is fantastic—you don't want to nip that in the bud by any means. What you *do* want to prevent is the spiral from that point towards things which are less interesting. Stay sensitive to the nature and pace of the conversation, and when it starts slowing down, make sure that action awaits.

When the thinky or talky side of things comes up, make sure it's *valuable*. If the players have created characters who are eminent scholars and scientists, or people well-connected in the halls of power, they should get every chance to make use of those skills. But these sorts of examinations, discoveries, and conversations should be abbreviated where possible, and they should *always* lead to opportunities for action. They're the glue that connects two pieces of action—but if the action is missing, that glue is best kept in the bottle.

It boils down to this: When in doubt, fill out the second half of something thinky or talky with something dynamic, exciting, and potentially volatile—something shooty! Encourage action over contemplation.

When All Else Fails… Goons Attack!

Games inevitably stagnate at some point or another, no matter how much effort you put into heading off that undesirable eventuality. Leads get exhausted, players get frustrated with puzzles, and nobody comes up with a good, crazy plan to save the day. There's only one thing you can possibly do in such a situation.

Goons attack!

First of all, a good sudden explosive skirmish gives you time, as a GM, to think, and it gives everyone else something to do, what with all the blasters and cutlasses and hand grenades and fists and feet flying at their heads.

Secondly, the goons inevitably fall before the brilliance and proficiency of the heroes, and then they have someone to interrogate. By this point you've used the combat time to figure out where to send folks next.

Naturally, after a good Intimidate roll—okay, if you're at this point, really, any Intimidate roll—the captured goon in question offers just enough information to point the characters toward where to go and what to do next. And then a more talented villain nearby shoots him in the eye. But by that time, he's said enough and the game is back on a roll.

But beware! Use the power of the goon attack carefully. There *is* such a thing—though we know you may doubt it!—as *too many goons*. If you overuse this technique and your players get wise to it, these fights can start to feel like hollow or meaningless victories. Try the other things we've talked about first, but when all else fails… goons attack!

Slightly More Subtle Goons

Another trick to remember with goons—players get pretty used to threats to their characters. Nothing's more frustrating than having some gun toting thugs bust through the door, get creamed, and have the players go back to studying their navels.

To mix it up a bit, have the goons bust in *on someone else*! The players may be blasé about attacks on themselves, but if the goons attack their mechanic buddy at the dry dock, that's another story. Can they save the guy in time? And even if they can, why are goons after *him*?

Adventure Design

Conflicts are exciting, but if they don't take place within the context of a larger narrative, they aren't as interesting. A villain or conflict that's related directly to a character's history or goals is way more grabby than one that seems to happen randomly out of the blue. In the basic **Bulldogs!** setting, the player characters work as a delivery crew. TransGalaxy's Class D policy is guaranteed to put them in harm's way; but if all they're trying to do is overcome the immediate and impersonal opposition to their delivery jobs, things can get a bit flat. Mix in personal motivations and use the characters' aspects to keep the players deeply involved in what's going on.

Tying Events to Aspects

The great thing about **Bulldogs!** is that the players have already provided you with a whole bunch of hooks into their characters through their aspects. The other characters and motivations represented by these aspects give you, as a GM, a lot to work with, so don't neglect them! These aspects are notes for you about what the players are interested in and what parts of the characters can be tied into the adventure.

For every mission, try to tie in one or more aspects from at least two characters. The character creation process specifically creates aspects for you to use this way. The former associates aspect is an excellent hook, as are any aspects related to fundamental beliefs, either from alien species, homeworld, or other areas. When two or more characters have a direct hook into the other characters or the situation within an adventure, this helps involve the entire crew in what's going on. What may have been a regular delivery job suddenly becomes much more.

Personal Missions

Characters may work for TransGalaxy, but they're individuals with their own goals as well—and hopping around the galaxy all the time making deliveries might work real well with some of those goals. Encourage a character who has some side jobs or personal business to attend to. Everyone gets more involved if the mission has some personal investment, and this helps spice up the adventure grind as well. Players can do more than run jobs for TransGalaxy; this helps create some variety in the overall adventure roster.

Exposition and Knowledge Dumping

Sometimes you just need to give your group a lot of information, and the character with a high knowledge skill tends to be the conduit of that. When you need to drop a lot of information on your players, ask the character with the most knowledge if you can use him as a mouthpiece. Assuming the player agrees, you can share all appropriate background as information his character has gathered; you might want to give the player a fate point for temporarily commandeering his character.

Other Campaign Setups

The basic **Bulldogs!** setup is the TransGalaxy Class D Freight job. To make things easier and bit more coherent, this setup is used as a default for the game. This is by no means the only setup available, however. We expect—and hope!—that many groups will take a different premise as their starting off point. A few more examples are given below, along with some tips on how to handle initial setup and character design.

Free Traders

Free traders don't work for one of the massive Pangalactic Corporations, or even one of the smaller interstellar corporations. Although a free trader may be incorporated, they're usually small outfits with one or two ships, traveling from system to system taking up cargo that the bigger companies won't carry, often because the margin is too small. A free trading freighter has its work cut out for it. The big boys don't like competition, the profit is slim, and a lot of times you have to smuggle goods or carry things of dubious provenance in order to make ends meet.

In a free trader game, the crew either owns the ship collectively or run the ship for the owner. Owners often serve as the captain of these vessels, which are usually crewed with personal friends or relatives.

For a free trader game, build the ship and captain the same way. Just adjust the current berth questions (page 48, **Crew Creation** chapter) with those listed below:

Sign Up: why and how did you sign aboard this ship? Do you and the owner go way back? Did he poach you from a rival team? Are you a relative or in-law?
Job: same as Class D.
Shipmates: same as Class D.
Owner: just like Captain in Class D.

Free traders have a feel quite similar to Class D, but in some ways they're more desperate. No one is fixing the ship or paying docking fees, so the crew needs to make sure they're covering these expenses. On the other hand, a free trader crew tends to have a lot more autonomy, and no one's looking over your shoulder.

Explorers

Someone, at some point, has visited just about every corner of this galaxy. That doesn't mean records are easily available, nor does it mean that anyone has entered a system in the last 500 or 1000 years. There are things to be found, systems to map more fully, planets to prospect for resources. This is where explorers come in. They travel to these out-of-the-way planets and look for anything of value. Some explorers work for a large corporation; some do it freelance and sell the information they gather to the highest bidder.

During set up, determine who the crew and ship work for, and who owns the ship. Adjust the starting questions just like free trader.

Explorers deal a lot more with hostile environments, angry natives, or hidden pirate bases. Their threats are a bit different than a delivery campaign, but there should still be plenty of grist for the adventure mill. They're basically looking for it!

Mercenaries

There are no vast galactic wars, but there are plenty of smaller conflicts, especially in the Frontier Zone. Without a lot of citizens to call on in wartime, some governments and even corporations find guns for hire and bring them in for diplomacy by other means. A good living can be made in this trade—it just comes along with being shot at.

For setup, don't worry about the ship, unless your particular mercenary crew owns their own. Someone's leading this band, so you'll want to flesh out the commander, even if he isn't called a captain. For the current berth steps (page 48, **Crew Creation** chapter), use the following questions:

Sign Up: how did you become a mercenary? What made you want to be a private contractor of war? Are you looking for a quick score? Are you a violent person who wants a license to be violent?
Job: mercenaries split up some duties as well, but these are a little different than the typical shipboard duties. Are you a demolitions expert? Artillery and heavy weapons? Are you the one who sneaks into an enemy camp to take out the guards? What's your job in your mercenary team?
Comrades-in-Arms: the same as the usual shipmates option. Who are you working with?
Captain: who leads your band? Same questions as a Class D game.

Mercenary adventures are far more military in style, typically with mission-based adventures. Mercenaries are used a lot as strike teams or for small dangerous missions. No one really sheds a tear if a mercenary doesn't make it, so these missions are often more deadly than traditional military ones.

Espionage

The centuries-long cold war between the Saldrallans and Devalkamanchans has been a golden age of espionage. Spies, counterspies, double agents, and tricks of every measure have been implemented by both sides, and the ostensibly neutral territory of the Frontier Zone is thick with agents. To play a spy campaign, you'll want the entire group to be a team of spies, **Mission Impossible**-style. They go on covert missions for whatever government employs them in the hopes of countering the tactics of the enemy empire.

In espionage, lots of gear and equipment are provided by the host government, within reason. Money isn't the motivation in a game of this type—instead it's politics. Set up a ship, as usual, but you don't need to worry as much about problems with the ship. If there are weaknesses, they'll be slight. The leader of this group of spies should be determined and developed just like a captain. Leaders always have flaws, so make sure you follow the same order. After this, adjust the current berth (page 48, **Crew Creation** chapter) as follows:

Recruitment: how did you become a spy? What brought you into the world of espionage? Some crime committed against you by the enemy? A family member in someone's power? How did they get you to sign up?

Job: everyone on an espionage team has a specialty. Social skills are especially important in this type of game. Are you the disguise expert? The techie? The equipment expert?

Teamates: you rely on your team for your life in this game. Can you really trust them? Who do you trust implicitly? Who do you suspect of working with the enemy? Who is incompetent?

Captain: the leader of the team needs a close relationship with each of his people. Answer the Class D questions for this category.

Espionage works best in a mission-style game. The group has a regular mission objective, but the second objective is to perform their mission without getting caught or blowing their cover. This adds a great level of tension to a game.

Pirates

You're scurvy dogs plying the space-lanes for plunder! Freighters, beware; you and your crew are out to loot and rob your way across the galaxy. Not all pirate gangs are horrible bloodthirsty murderers—some spare the crews of the ships they seize—but no matter how they act, pirates are despised and hunted throughout the galaxy. The Frontier Zone offers a great place to plunder, as well as a great place to hide from the authorities.

A pirate's ship is hugely important, as is the captain of such a dangerous crew. Follow all of the same steps as Class D to create your character. The types of crew members on a Class D ship and on a pirate vessel are actually pretty similar.

A pirate game is based on opportunity. Pirates need to be motivated by the big score. They want to try to find the soft underbelly and attack.

Index

The Ladder

+8	Legendary
+7	Epic
+6	Fantastic
+5	Superb
+4	Great
+3	Good
+2	Fair
+1	Average
0	Mediocre
-1	Poor
-2	Terrible
-3	Awful
-4	Abysmal

Time Increments

Instant

A few moments

Half a minute

A minute

A few minutes

15 minutes

Half an hour

An hour

A few hours

An afternoon

A day

A few days

A week

A couple of weeks

A month

A few months

A season

Half a year

A year

A few years

A decade

A lifetime

Skills List

Academics	Mental
Alertness	Mental
Artillery	Physical
Athletics	Physical
Burglary	Physical
Contacting	Social
Deceit	Social
Empathy	Social
Endurance	Physical
Engineering	Mental
Fists	Physical
Gambling	Social
Guns	Physical
Intimidation	Social
Investigation	Mental
Leadership	Social
Medicine	Mental
Might	Physical
Pilot	Physical
Psychic	Mental
Rapport	Social
Resolve	Social
Sleight of Hand	Physical
Stealth	Physical
Survival	Mental
Systems	Mental
Trading	Social
Weapons	Physical

Skill Packages

Fresh Meat

These are the 20 skill point packages you can choose from:

Well-Rounded: 11 total skills: 3 at Good (+3), 3 at Fair (+2), 5 at Average (+1).

Strong Focus: 10 total skills: 1 at Great (+4), 2 at Good (+3), 3 at Fair (+2), 4 at Average (+1).

Extra Focused: 8 total skills: 2 at Great (+4), 2 at Good (+3), 2 at Fair (+2), 2 at Average (+1).

Trouble

These are the 25 skill point packages you can choose from:

Wide Ranging: 13 total skills: 4 at Good (+3), 4 at Fair (+2), 5 at Average (+1).

Focused: 14 total skills: 1 at Great (+4), 2 at Good (+3), 4 at Fair (+2), 7 at Average (+1).

Dual Focus: 12 total skills: 2 at Great (+4), 2 at Good (+3), 3 at Fair (+2), 5 at Average (+1).

Hard Boiled

These are the 30 skill point packages you can choose from:

Jack-of-All-Trades: 15 total skills: 5 at Good (+3), 5 at Fair (+2), 5 at Average (+1).

Well-Rounded: 14 total skills: 2 at Great (+4), 3 at Good (+3), 4 at Fair (+2), 5 at Average (+1).

Strong Focus: 12 total skills: 3 at Great (+4), 3 at Good (+3), 3 at Fair (+2), 3 at Average (+1).

Expert: 10 total skills: 2 at Superb (+5), 2 at Great (+4), 2 at Good (+3), 2 at Fair (+2), 2 at Average (+1).

Serious Badass

These are the 35 skill point packages you can choose from:

Jack-of-All-Trades: 19 total skills: 5 Good (+3), 6 Fair (+2), 8 Average (+1).

Well-Rounded: 17 total skills: 3 Great (+4), 3 Good (+3), 3 Fair (+2), 8 Average (+1).

Expert: 15 total skills: 1 Superb (+5), 2 Great (+4), 3 Good (+3), 4 Fair (+2), 5 Average (+1).

Acknowledged Master: 14 total skills: 2 Superb (+5), 2 Great (+4), 2 Good (+3), 3 Fair (+2), 5 Average (+1).

Endurance	Stress
Average-Fair	+1
Good-Great	+2
Superb-Fantastic	+3

Resolve	Stress
Average-Fair	+1
Good-Great	+2
Superb-Fantastic	+3

Trading	Starting Resources
Fair to Good	Fair (+2)
Great	Good (+3)
Superb	Great (+4)

Gambling	Starting Resources
Great	Fair (+2)
Superb	Good (+3)

# of Minions	Bonus
1	+0
2-3	+1
4-6	+2
7-9	+3
10+	+4

SHIP NAME

SCALE

SPEED

MANEUVERABILITY

MAINTENANCE COST

ASPECTS

CONCEPT

PROBLEM

STRENGTH

STRESS

☐☐☐☐☐ ☐☐☐☐☐ ☐☐☐☐☐

CONSEQUENCES   SHIELDS

MILD (-2)

MODERATE (-4)

SEVERE (-6)

IMPROVEMENTS

MAP

WEAPONS   IMPROVEMENTS

BULLDOGS!
SCI-FI THAT KICKS ASS

CHARACTER NAME
SPECIES
POWER LEVEL
BASE REFRESH   - SPENT REFRESH   = **CURRENT REFRESH** ◯

SKILL PTS   SKILL CAP

ASPECTS
HERITAGE

HERITAGE

HOMEWORLD

PERSONAL STRENGTH

PERSONAL WEAKNESS

FORMER ASSOCIATES

DESPERATE SITUATION

JOB

SHIPMATES

CAPTAIN

SHIP
CONCEPT

PROBLEM

STRENGTH

CAPTAIN
CONCEPT

TROUBLE

LEADERSHIP

STUNTS & SPECIES ABILITIES   COST

REFRESH SPENT ON STUNTS & ABILITIES ◯

STRESS   ARMOR/SHIELDS
☐☐☐   ☐☐☐   ☐☐☐

CONSEQUENCES   RESOURCES
MILD (-2)

MODERATE (-4)

SEVERE (-6)

SKILLS   RANK

GEAR   IMPROVEMENTS